Mining in Africa

Mining in Africa

Are Local Communities Better Off?

Punam Chuhan-Pole, Andrew L. Dabalen, and Bryan Christopher Land

in collaboration with Michael Lewin, Aly Sanoh, Gregory Smith, and Anja Tolonen

A copublication of the Agence Française de Développement and the World Bank

Africa Development Forum Series

The Africa Development Forum Series was created in 2009 to focus on issues of significant relevance to Sub-Saharan Africa's social and economic development. Its aim is both to record the state of the art on a specific topic and to contribute to ongoing local, regional, and global policy debates. It is designed specifically to provide practitioners, scholars, and students with the most up-to-date research results while highlighting the promise, challenges, and opportunities that exist on the continent.

The series is sponsored by the Agence Française de Développement and the World Bank. The manuscripts chosen for publication represent the highest quality in each institution and have been selected for their relevance to the development agenda. Working together with a shared sense of mission and interdisciplinary purpose, the two institutions are committed to a common search for new insights and new ways of analyzing the development realities of the Sub-Saharan Africa region.

Advisory Committee Members

Agence Française de Développement
Gaël Giraud, Executive Director, Research and Knowledge
Mihoub Mezouaghi, Deputy Director, Research and Knowledge
Guillaume de Saint Phalle, Head, Knowledge Management Division
Françoise Rivière, Head, Research Division

World Bank
Albert G. Zeufack, Chief Economist, Africa Region
Markus P. Goldstein, Lead Economist, Africa Region

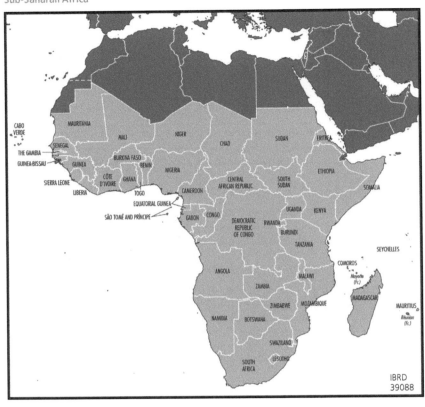

IBRD
39088

Titles in the Africa Development Forum Series

Africa's Infrastructure: A Time for Transformation (2010) edited by Vivien Foster and Cecilia Briceño-Garmendia

Gender Disparities in Africa's Labor Market (2010) edited by Jorge Saba Arbache, Alexandre Kolev, and Ewa Filipiak

Challenges for African Agriculture (2010) edited by Jean-Claude Deveze
Contemporary Migration to South Africa: A Regional Development Issue (2011) edited by Aurelia Segatti and Loren Landau

* *Light Manufacturing in Africa: Targeted Policies to Enhance Private Investment and Create Jobs*, «L'industrie légère en Afrique : Politiques ciblées pour susciter l'investissement privé et créer des emplois» (2012) by Hinh T. Dinh, Vincent Palmade, Vandana Chandra, and Frances Cossar

* *Informal Sector in Francophone Africa: Firm Size, Productivity, and Institutions*, «Le système d'approvisionnement en terres dans les villes d'Afrique de l'Ouest : L'exemple de Bamako» (2012) by Nancy Benjamin and Ahmadou Aly Mbaye

* *Financing Africa's Cities: The Imperative of Local Investment*, «Financer les villes d'Afrique : L'enjeu de l'investissement local» (2012) by Thierry Paulais

* *Structural Transformation and Rural Change Revisited: Challenges for Late Developing Countries in a Globalizing World*, «Transformations rurales et développement : Les défi s du changement structurel dans un monde globalisé» (2012) by Bruno Losch, Sandrine Fréguin-Gresh, and Eric Thomas White

The Political Economy of Decentralization in Sub-Saharan Africa: A New Implementation Model (2013) edited by Bernard Dafflon and Thierry Madiès

Empowering Women: Legal Rights and Economic Opportunities in Africa (2013) by Mary Hallward-Driemeier and Tazeen Hasan

Enterprising Women: Expanding Economic Opportunities in Africa (2013) by Mary Hallward-Driemeier

Urban Labor Markets in Sub-Saharan Africa (2013) edited by Philippe De Vreyer and François Roubaud

Securing Africa's Land for Shared Prosperity: A Program to Scale Up Reforms and Investments (2013) by Frank F. K. Byamugisha

* *Youth Employment in Sub-Saharan Africa*, «L'emploi des jeunes en Afrique subsaharienne» (2014) by Deon Filmer and Louis Fox

Tourism in Africa: Harnessing Tourism for Growth and Improved Livelihoods (2014) by Iain Christie, Eneida Fernandes, Hannah Messerli, and Louise Twining-Ward

* *Safety Nets in Africa: Effective Mechanisms to Reach the Poor and Most Vulnerable*, «Les fi lets sociaux en Afrique : Méthodes effi caces pour cibler les populations pauvres et vulnérables en Afrique» (2015) edited by Carlo del Ninno and Bradford Mills

* *Land Delivery Systems in West African Cities: The Example of Bamako, Mali*, «Le système d'approvisionnement en terres dans les villes d'Afrique de l'Ouest: L'exemple de Bamako» (2015) by Alain Durand-Lasserve, Maÿlis Durand-Lasserve, and Harris Selod

Enhancing the Climate Resilience of Africa's Infrastructure: The Power and Water Sectors (2015) edited by Raffaello Cervigni, Rikard Liden, James E. Neumann, and Kenneth M. Strzepek

* *Africa's Demographic Transition: Dividend or Disaster?* «La transition demographique de lAfrique» (2015) edited by David Canning, Sangeeta Raja, and Abdo S. Yazbeck

The Challenge of Fragility and Security in West Africa (2015) by Alexandre Marc, Neelam Verjee, and Stephen Mogaka

Highways to Success or Byways to Waste: Estimating the Economic Benefits of Roads in Africa (2015) by Ali A. Rubaba, Federico Barra, Claudia Berg, Richard Damania, John Nash, and Jason Russ

Confronting Drought in Africa's Drylands: Opportunities for Enhancing Resilience (2016) edited by Raffaello Cervigni and Michael Morris

* *Reaping Richer Returns: Public Spending Priorities for African Agriculture Productivity Growth* (2017) by Aparajita Goyal and John Nash

Mining in Africa: Are Local Communities Better Off? (2017) by Punam Chuhan-Pole, Andrew L. Dabalen, and Bryan Christopher Land

* Available in French

All books in the Africa Development Forum series are available for free at https://openknowledge.worldbank.org/handle/10986/2150

Contents

Foreword   *xvii*
Acknowledgments   *xix*
About the Authors   *xxi*
About the Contributors   *xxiii*
Abbreviations   *xxvii*

1 Overview   1
   Introduction   1
   A Framework to Measure How Local Communities Capture Benefits   6
   The Approach to Assessing the Local Effects of Mining   10
   Are Mining Communities Seeing Welfare Gains?   14
   Assessing the Role of Government   27
   Policy Priorities for Addressing the Local Impacts of Mining   29
   Notes   31
   References   31

2 Local Impacts of Resource Abundance: What Have We Learned?   33
   Introduction   33
   Theory and Evidence on the Impact of Resource Abundance
   at the Country Level   34
   Assessing the Local Impacts of Resource Abundance   39
   Conclusion   56
   Annex 2A: Schematic Model of Resource Endowment Changes   57
   Notes   58
   References   60

3   Insights from Three Country Case Studies   67
    Introduction   67
    Country Backgrounds: Gold Mining in the Case Study Countries   68
    Channel 1: Employment, Linkages, and Positive Spillovers   71
    Channel 2: Government Revenue   76
    Negative Externalities: The Costs Borne by Mining Areas   81
    Outcomes   82
    Conclusions   87
    Notes   87
    References   88

4   Socioeconomic Effects of Large-Scale Gold Mining:
    Evidence from Ghana, Mali, and Tanzania   91
    Introduction   91
    Gold Mining in Ghana, Mali, and Tanzania   93
    Empirical Methodology   96
    Evolution of Trends in Mining and Nonmining Areas   103
    Livelihoods and Occupations   105
    Household Accumulation of Assets   118
    Child Health   121
    Access to Infrastructure for Welfare Benefits   131
    Controlling for Mine-Induced Migration   133
    Summary of Results   137
    Annex 4A: Variable Definitions for Demographic and
    Health Surveys and Outcomes for Variables from Synthetic
    Control Analysis in Mali and Tanzania   139
    Notes   145
    References   145

5   Does Mining Reduce Agricultural Growth? Evidence from
    Large-Scale Gold Mining in Burkina Faso, Ghana, Mali,
    and Tanzania   147
    Introduction   147
    Remote Sensing and Economic Activity   148
    Data   151
    Growth Model and Results   154
    Conclusions   165

Annex 5A: District-Level Growth Pattern Results   166
Notes   171
References   171

Index   175

Boxes
1.1   Environmental and Health Issues in Gold Mining Areas   9
1.2   What Is a Mining Community?   12
1.3   How Remote Sensing Informs Agricultural Production   21
3.1   Artisanal and Small-Scale Mining   70
4.1   Small-Scale Mining Poses Challenges for Identifying
       Impacts of Large-Scale Mines   99
4.2   Effect of a Mine Opening on Household Access to
       Sanitation in Mali   125

Figures
1.1   GDP Growth by Country Groups, 2000–14   2
1.2   Mine Openings, 1870–2014   2
1.3   Human Development Index Scores in Selected African
       Countries, 2013   4
1.4   Channels through Which Natural Resource Abundance
       Affects Local Communities   5
1.5   How Market and Fiscal Mechanisms Affect Well-Being   7
1.6   Gold Production in Ghana, Mali, and Tanzania, 1980–2011 11
B1.2.1 Gold Mines in Mali and Spatial Buffers   13
1.7   Spatial Lag Model Illustrating the Geographic Distribution
       of Effects on Services Sector and Agricultural Employment
       for Women in Ghana, Mali, and Tanzania   17
1.8   Spatial Lag Model Illustrating Agriculture, Manual Labor,
       Mining, and Wage Earnings for Men in Ghana and Mali   18
1.9   Changes in Income, Wages, and Expenditures in Ghana   20
1.10   Night Lights and Normalized Difference Vegetation Index
       before and after a Mine Opening   22
1.11   Ownership of Assets from a Mine Opening in Ghana,
       Mali, and Tanzania   23
1.12   Household Access to Infrastructure with a Mine Opening
       in Ghana, Mali, and Tanzania   24

1.13   Child Health Outcomes from a Mine Opening in Ghana, Mali, and Tanzania   25

1.14   Access to Health Services for Children in Mining Districts in Ghana   26

1.15   Government Mining Revenues from Mining in Ghana, Mali, and Tanzania, 2001–13   28

2.1   Effects of a Fiscal Revenue Windfall   41

2.2   Effects of a Local Demand Shock   43

2.3   Negative Externalities of Environmental Pollution   46

2A.1   Changes in Resource Endowments   58

3.1   Gold Exports in Ghana, Mali, and Tanzania, 2000–13   69

3.2   Gold Exports as a Share of Total Exports in Ghana, Mali, and Tanzania, 2000–13   69

3.3   Mining Employment in Tanzania, 2005–13   72

3.4   Employment in Mining in Mali and Tanzania, 2005–13   73

3.5   Share of License Fees and Local Development Funds in Mali's Communes, 1994–2010   75

3.6   Government Mining Revenues in Ghana, Mali, and Tanzania, 2001–13   77

3.7   Government Mining Revenues as a Percentage of Total Revenue in Ghana, Mali, and Tanzania   77

3.8   Fiscal Burden in Mali   78

3.9   Source of Budget Revenues for Mining Communes and Neighboring Communes in Mali, 2011–13   81

3.10   Poverty Headcount in Mining and Other Areas in Mali   83

3.11   Population Growth Rate by Group of Communes and Mining Communes in Mali, 1998–2009   84

3.12   Registered Firms by Employment in Four Tanzanian Towns, 2001 and 2011   86

4.1   Gold Production in Ghana, Mali, and Tanzania, 1980–2011   98

4.2   Parallel Trends in Night Lights and Infant Mortality   104

4.3   Spatial Lag Model Illustrating Geographic Distribution of Effects on Services Sector and Agricultural Employment for Women in Ghana, Mali, and Tanzania   108

4.4   Spatial Lag Model Illustrating Migrants and Never-Movers, by Occupation in Services and Agriculture in Ghana, Mali, and Tanzania   109

4.5   Spatial Lag Model Illustrating Agriculture, Manual Labor, Mining, and Wage Earnings for Men in Ghana and Mali   111

4.6   Spatial Lag Model Illustrating Geographic Distribution of Effects on Household Radio Ownership in Ghana, Mali, and Tanzania   120

4.7   Spatial Lag Model Illustrating Geographic Distribution of Effects on Radio Ownership for Migrants and Nonmigrants in Ghana, Mali, and Tanzania   121

4.8   Child Health Statistics in Mining and Nonmining Areas in Ghana, Mali, and Tanzania   123

B4.2.1   Spatial Lag Model Illustrating Household Access to Toilets in Mali   125

B4.2.2   Spatial Lag Model Illustrating No Toilet or Pit Toilet among Migrants and Never-Movers in Mali   126

4.9   Diarrhea Incidence in Ghana for Children under Age 5, by Migration Status   129

4.10   Spatial Lag Model Illustrating Geographic Distribution of Effects on Electricity in Ghana, Mali, and Tanzania   132

4.11   Spatial Lag Model Illustrating Access to Electricity for Migrants and Never-Movers in Ghana, Mali, and Tanzania   133

4.12   Migration to Mining Areas in Ghana, Mali, and Tanzania   135

5.1   Actual and Predicted Log (GDP) Using Three Different Models in Burkina Faso, Ghana, Mali, and Tanzania, 2001–12   159

5.2   Night Lights and Normalized Difference Vegetation Index over a Mine's Lifetime   163

5A.1   GWR-Local R-Squared for Relationship between Dependent Variable Total Agricultural Production, by District and Independent Variable NDVI Intensity Sum, by District   166

5A.2   Log (global light sum), 2008–12   168

5A.3   Correlation between GDP and Household Expenditures per Capita Levels for Ghana, 1991/92 and 2005/06   170

5A.4   Correlation Between Night Light Intensity and Population at District Levels for Ghana, 2010   170

Maps

4.1   Large-Scale Gold Mines and Other Mines in Africa   92

4.2   Gold Mines and Gold Districts in Ghana   95

4.3   Gold Mines and Gold Districts in Mali   96

4.4   Gold Mines and Gold Districts in Tanzania   97

4.5   Gold Mines in Ghana and Spatial Buffers   101

5.1   Geographically Weighted Regression, by District in
Ghana, Mali, and Tanzania, 2007   156

5A.1   Spatial Analysis of Average Growth in Districts, Estimated
by Growth Model in Burkina Faso, Ghana, Mali, and Tanzania,
2001–12   169

Tables

2.1   Empirical Evidence of the Impact of Resource Abundance
on Local Growth   47

2.2   Empirical Evidence of the Impact of Resource Abundance
on Local Living Standards   48

2.3   Empirical Evidence of the Impact of Resource Abundance
on Corruption and Conflict   51

2.4   Empirical Evidence of the Impact of Mining-Related Pollution   53

3.1   Sectoral Spending, by Commune, of Mining Development
Funds in Mali, 1994–2010   76

3.2   Use of Infrastructure Services, by Group of Communes
in Mali, 1998 and 2009   85

3.3   Infrastructure Outcomes, by Group of Communes in Mali, 2013   85

4.1   Mines in Ghana, Mali, and Tanzania, 1990–2011   94

4.2   Household Survey Data for Ghana, Mali, and Tanzania   103

4.3   Summary Statistics from Demographic and Health
Surveys in Ghana, Mali, and Tanzania   105

4.4   Occupations of Men and Women in Proximity to
Mines in Ghana, Mali, and Tanzania   107

4.5   District-Level Effects on Occupation in Ghana's Gold
and Neighboring Districts   112

4.6   District-Level Effects on Employment in Gold Districts
in Mali and Tanzania   113

4.7   Changes in Income, Wages, and Expenditures in Ghana   116

4.8   Mapping Changes in Expenditure Composition in Ghana,
Using the Living Standards Survey   116

4.9   Wealth Outcomes for Variables from Synthetic Control
Analysis in Tanzania   117

4.10   Wealth Outcomes for Variables from Synthetic Control
        Analysis in Mali   118

4.11   Household Asset Accumulation in Ghana, Mali, and Tanzania   119

4.12   Household Asset Accumulation by Migration Status in Ghana,
        Mali, and Tanzania   119

4.13   Health Outcomes in Infancy and Children under Age 5 in
        Treatment Distance   124

4.14   District-Level Effects on Access to Health Services for
        Children in Ghana's Gold Districts   127

4.15   Health Outcomes for Variables from Synthetic Control
        Analysis in Tanzania   128

4.16   Health Outcomes for Variables from Synthetic Control
        Analysis in Mali   128

4.17   Child Health among Migrants and Never-Movers in
        Ghana and Mali   130

4.18   Household Access to Infrastructure in Ghana,
        Mali, and Tanzania   131

4A.1   Variable Definitions for Demographic and Health Surveys   139

4A.2   Outcomes for Variables from Synthetic Control Analysis, Mali   140

4A.3   Outcomes for Variables from Synthetic Control Analysis,
        Tanzania   143

5.1   Satellite-Year Pairs Used for Intercalibration Coefficients   153

5.2   Estimated Growth, Using Remote Sensing Data in Burkina Faso,
        Ghana, Mali, and Tanzania   160

5.3   Observed and Predicted Gross Domestic Product in Burkina
        Faso, Ghana, Mali, and Tanzania   161

5.4   Simple Difference Specification: Comparing before and
        after Mine Opening   164

5.5   Difference-in-Differences Specification   164

5A.1   GWR-Local R-Squared for Relationship between Dependent
        Variable Total Agricultural Production, by District and
        Independent Variable, Sum of NDVI Intensity by District   167

Foreword

Africa has experienced a boom in extractive commodities since about 2000. The substantial growth in exports of the region's abundant natural resources—ranging from hydrocarbons such as oil and natural gas to minerals such as gold, copper, and iron ore—significantly contributed to the remarkable turnaround in its economic growth trajectory. And Africa's resource-abundant countries have grown faster than other countries in the region. The global supercycle in commodity prices that began in 2000 boosted the production of extractives in Africa and increased investor interest in the region's natural resources. This led to an expansion in resource exploration and a surge in mine openings. During 2001–14, extractive industries comprised two-thirds of Africa's exports, contributing significantly to government finances with funds for capacity development and infrastructure building. Notwithstanding the recent sharp decline in commodity prices, the overall expansion of the extractives sector and the rise in commodity exports signal the importance of this sector as a contributor to financial resources for Africa in the years ahead.

Although the resource boom has underpinned growth in the region's commodity producers, it has been less successful in improving people's welfare. Overall, the conversion of growth into poverty reduction in Africa is much slower than in the rest of the developing world. People living in Africa's resource-rich countries are 3 percent less literate, have shorter life expectancy by 4.5 years, and have higher rates of malnutrition among women and children, compared to other countries in the region. This slow pace of poverty reduction is frequently attributed to economic growth that is led by natural resources, the so-called natural resource curse. That said, it is clear that the role of mining in economic development, and how to transform resource wealth into well-being, will remain important issues for Africa's economies. While researchers and policy makers focus on governance and macro-fiscal risks to identify areas for improvement, very little attention is being paid to the benefits gained by local communities living close to mining centers.

This study focuses on the fortunes of local communities. The authors consider how large-scale gold mining in three countries—Ghana, Mali, and Tanzania—affects local livelihoods and communities. Their analysis and results conclude that, on average, mining communities experience positive yet limited welfare benefits. Some benefits appear more frequently in localities close to a mine, but these benefits are not uniform across all mining communities. Mining and mineral processing can also produce well-known negative externalities—such as environmental degradation, health risks, pressure on other scarce natural resources, and social dislocations—which can affect local community welfare.

Developing effective policies to address these issues requires a deep investigation of not only how local mining communities are negatively affected by these externalities but also where and how they are gaining welfare benefits. This study provides a simple analytical framework to understand how resource booms can affect local livelihoods and communities. It delineates three broad channels—market, fiscal, environmental—through which local areas and regions may be affected. The authors apply this framework to large-scale gold mining in the three case study countries, employing robust econometric methods to evaluate local-level impacts. Drawing on these findings, they shine a light on the channels and transmission mechanisms that can be useful when studying other large-scale mining operations in Africa.

We hope that conducting similar analyses for other local mining communities, following the framework and methodology discussed in this study, will help to better inform public policy and corporate behavior on the welfare of communities in which resource extraction takes place. Addressing the natural resource extraction challenge in all of its dimensions can open potential channels for shared prosperity and improved equality, creating a better life for families and enhanced prospects for the countries in which they live.

Makhtar Diop
Vice President, Africa Region
The World Bank

Acknowledgments

This study was prepared by a core team led by Punam Chuhan-Pole, Andrew L. Dabalen, and Bryan Christopher Land, comprising Michael Lewin, Aly Sanoh, Gregory Smith, and Anja Tolonen. The principal authors and contributors to the various parts of the study include Fernando Aragón, Magnus Andersson, Ola Hall, Andreas Kotsadam, and Niklas Olén. Additional contributions were made by Nazli Aktakke, Meltem A. Aran, Joseph R. A. Ayee, Massaoly Coulibaly, Armstrong Dumisa Dlamini, Godbertha Kinyondo, Vijdan Korman, and Beyza Polat. Stuti Khemani, Ken Opalo, and Jamele Rigolini provided careful and insightful peer review comments. Several World Bank Group staff, including Kathleen Beegle, Megumi Kubota, William Maloney, Forhad Shilpi, and Sanjay Srivastava, provided comments at various stages of the study's development. The study was prepared under the general guidance of Francisco H. G. Ferreira, chief economist, Africa Region. Alastair McIndoe edited the study. Any errors or omissions are the responsibility of the team.

About the Authors

Punam Chuhan-Pole is Lead Economist in the World Bank's Office of the Chief Economist of the Africa Region. Her recent work includes launching a semi-annual World Bank publication—*Africa's Pulse*—which presents economic trends, prospects, and analyses of issues shaping Africa's future. Chuhan-Pole led a study examining development progress in Africa—*Yes Africa Can: Success Stories from a Dynamic Continent*, published by the World Bank in 2011. She is currently researching growth and poverty reduction in Africa and the management of mineral wealth for development. She has a PhD in economics from Georgetown University. She worked at the Federal Reserve Bank of New York before joining the World Bank.

Andrew L. Dabalen is Practice Manager in the World Bank's Poverty and Equity Global Practice. His work focuses on poverty and social impact analysis, inequality of opportunity, program evaluation, risk and vulnerability, labor markets, and conflict and welfare outcomes. He has worked in the World Bank's Africa Region and Europe and Central Asia Region, where he led or co-led country and regional analytic products. Dabalen has published scholarly articles and working papers on poverty measurement, conflict and welfare outcomes, and wage inequality. He has a master's degree in international development from the University of California, Davis, and a PhD in agricultural and resource economics from the University of California, Berkeley.

Bryan Christopher Land is Lead Mining Specialist at the World Bank and is developing research on the opportunities and challenges faced by resource-rich African countries. Prior to joining the World Bank, Land led the Commonwealth Secretariat's program on natural resource management; and before that, he worked at the extractive industry consulting firms IHS Energy and CRU International. He also spent three years at the Department of Minerals and Energy in Papua New Guinea. He has a bachelor's degree in economics from the London School of Economics, and master's degrees in international affairs from Columbia University and natural resources law from Dundee University.

Michael Lewin teaches economics at the Graduate School for Public and International Affairs at the University of Pittsburgh. A former senior economist at the World Bank, he has worked in all of its regions and was task manager for its country macroeconomic modeling program. A special area of interest is the economics of mineral exporting countries. His recent papers on Africa include "Botswana's Success: Good Governance, Good Policies, and Good Luck" in *Yes Africa Can: African Success Stories*, and "Harnessing Oil Windfalls for Growth in the Africa Region" in *Africa at a Turning Point?* published by the World Bank in 2008. He has taught at the Johns Hopkins School of Advanced International Studies and Middlebury College.

Aly Sanoh is an economist/statistician in the Poverty and Equity Global Practice of the World Bank. His work focuses on understanding the drivers of poverty and inequality reduction in the Sahel countries. He has held positions in the Office of the Chief Economist of the Africa Region, where he conducted macroeconomic and microeconomic analyses for *Africa's Pulse*. He holds a master's degree in energy and environmental policy from the University of Delaware and a PhD in sustainable development from Columbia University.

Gregory Smith is a Senior Economist with the World Bank, based in Zambia. He covers issues of macroeconomic and fiscal management and explores how growth can become more inclusive to tackle poverty and inequality challenges. He writes on eurobond issuance, sovereign wealth funds, debt management, and the fiscal management of natural resource revenues. He worked previously on Ghana, Mongolia, and Vietnam for the World Bank. He has also worked with finance ministries and central banks in Tanzania, Uganda, and Zimbabwe. He has a PhD in economics from Nottingham University.

Anja Tolonen is an Assistant Professor of economics at Barnard College, Columbia University, where she works on economic development. Her current work focuses on the local welfare effects of natural resource extraction in Africa, including employment, women's empowerment, health, and criminality. She teaches development economics and women in development economics at Barnard College. She is an affiliated faculty member at the Columbia Center for Development Economics and Policy and an external research member at the Oxford Center for the Analysis of Resource-Rich Economies. UNESCO has funded her research, and she has consultancy experience from the World Bank. She has a PhD from the University of Gothenburg and has been a visiting researcher at the University of Oxford and the University of California, Berkeley.

About the Contributors

Nazlı Aktakke is a Quantitative Research Analyst at Development Analytics. She works on multiple projects with research associates on various topics related to development. As the main data analyst, she worked on projects relating to Turkey to measure the effect of crises on labor force participation, evaluate the impact of a regional development program, analyze the impact of the country's health transformation program on maternal and child health outcomes, and conduct a mixed-methods analysis of supply and demand for child care. She has masters degrees in economics from Boğaziçi University, Istanbul, and Universidad Carlos III de Madrid; and a bachelor's degree in industrial engineering from Middle East Technical University, Ankara.

Magnus Andersson is Associate Professor of Economic Geography at Malmö University and an adviser on sustainable development for the United Nations Department of Economic and Social Affairs. His research focuses on socio-economic development in developing economies in Africa and East Asia, and draws primarily on data collected from household surveys and remote sensing data. His work has been published in academic journals and publications including *The Economist* and *Global Finance*. He has worked in the Department for Human Geography at Lund University and the European Institute for Japanese Studies at the Stockholm School of Economics. He has a PhD from Thammasat University and a master's degree from Lund University.

Fernando Aragón is Assistant Professor of Economics at Simon Fraser University, Canada. His research focuses on studying the role of natural resources in local economic development, and his work has been published in the *Economic Journal, Journal of Development Economics,* and *American Economic Journal: Economic Policy.* Before joining Simon Fraser University,

Aragón was a consultant for private and public organizations. He has a bachelor's degree from the Universidad del Pacifico, Peru, and a master's and PhD in economics from the London School of Economics.

Meltem Aran is a human development economist and founding director of Development Analytics, a social policy research center focusing on evidence-based social policy and program development in developing countries. Her research focuses on measuring women's empowerment, children's outcomes in low-opportunity settings, and the impact of inclusive social policies on children in developing countries. She is coauthor of *Life Chances in Turkey: Expanding Opportunities for the Next Generation*, published by the World Bank in 2010. She holds a dual bachelor's degree from Brown University in economics and international relations, a master's degree in international development from Harvard University, and a doctorate in economics from the University of Oxford.

Niklas Boke-Olén is a PhD candidate in geobiosphere science, at Lund University, specializing in physical geography and ecosystem analysis. He works on analyzing vegetation dynamics using methods and material connected to remote sensing, ecosystem modeling, and field measurements. His main research interest is savannah vegetation growth and its relation to net primary production and carbon storage. He holds a master's degree from Lund University.

Ola Hall is a geographer at Lund University's Department of Human and Economic Geography. He works on issues relating to the crop yield gap in Sub-Saharan Africa. His main areas of research include remote sensing, geographic information systems, and novel technologies for estimating and detecting crops and crop productivity. Before joining Lund University, he was with the Department of Geoinformatics at the Royal Institute of Technology, Sweden. He holds a PhD from Stockholm University.

Andreas Kotsadam is Senior Researcher at the Frisch Centre and the University of Oslo. His main research interests are family policies, comparative welfare state research, development economics, and inequality, often with a focus on gender. His main areas of research in development economics are gender-based violence, political participation, and the local impacts of natural resources. He has a PhD in economics from Gothenburg University.

Beyza Polat is an applied microeconomist with a primary interest in industrial organization and regional development. Her research focuses on the econometric evaluation of the effect of regional economic development policies on unemployment and firm behavior. She has a bachelor's degree in management and master's and doctoral degrees in economics from the London School of Economics, and she is a research affiliate at the Center for Economic Performance. She has taught undergraduate and graduate courses in microeconomics, econometrics, and mathematical economics at the London School of Economics. She is a research associate in development analytics and an assistant professor at Ozyegin University, Istanbul.

Abbreviations

DMSP-OLS	Defense Meteorological Satellite Program–Operational Linescan System
GDP	gross domestic product
km	kilometer
MODIS	moderate resolution imaging spectroradiometer
NDVI	Normalized Difference Vegetation Index

All dollar amounts are U.S. dollars, unless otherwise noted.

Chapter 1

Overview

Introduction

Economic activity in Africa saw a remarkable upswing beginning in the mid-1990s. Growth of gross domestic product (GDP) across the region averaged 4.5 percent a year in 1995–2014, nearly double the pace in the previous two decades. Progress has been broad-based, with both resource-rich and non-resource-rich countries seeing brisk expansion, a turnaround that fueled the narrative of a "rising Africa." Indeed, the region's growth performance since the early 2000s has matched that of the rest of the developing world. The spurt in economic activity also reversed the region's declining trend in average income per capita, although population growth kept gains for this measure at modest levels, averaging below 2 percent. Several factors—external and domestic—supported nearly two decades of sustained growth in Africa. The supercycle in commodity prices in the extractives sector that began in 2000 was notable on the external side, and this enabled the region's resource-rich countries to grow at an appreciably faster pace than non-resource-rich countries (figure 1.1).

Another consequence of sharply elevated commodity prices has been a boost in the production of extractives and increased investor interest in the region's abundant natural resources, ranging from hydrocarbons (oil and natural gas) to minerals (gold, diamonds, copper, and iron ore). Increased investor interest led to intensified resource exploration, a spate of new discoveries, and a surge in mine openings beginning in 2000 (figure 1.2). Devarajan and Fengler (2013) conclude that natural resource extraction is expected to be an important activity in all but five African countries in the coming years.

The heightened extractive activity has lifted the share of natural resources in Africa's exports. During 2001–14, extractive industries made up nearly two-thirds of exports from African countries—oil and gas alone accounting for close to 50 percent of total exports—a substantial rise from the 48 percent share in the previous 10-year period. Rising exports of natural resources contributed significantly to government finances, providing much-needed funds for building human and physical capital. Fiscal dependence on commodity-based revenues is now well over 50 percent in major commodity exporters. Overall, the

Figure 1.1 GDP Growth by Country Groups, 2000–14

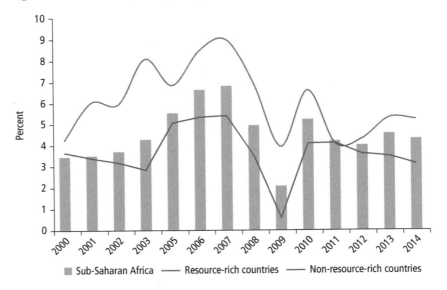

Figure 1.2 Mine Openings, 1870–2014

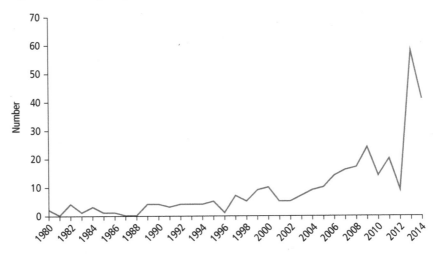

Source: World Bank 2015.

expansion of the extractives sector has enhanced its importance as a major source of income, raising hopes for sustainable growth in Africa. While the precipitous drop in commodity prices since June 2014 casts a pall on the region's prospects, natural resources are expected to continue contributing a significant share to exports and public revenues.

Although Africa's resource boom has underpinned growth in the region's commodity producers, questions remain on whether natural resource wealth has substantially improved living standards. Did this growth raise incomes and reduce poverty at a fast enough pace? And moving beyond income poverty, did nonincome dimensions of poverty such as education and health improve? Overall, the conversion of growth into poverty reduction is considered to be much lower in Africa than in the rest of the developing world. At −0.7, Africa's growth elasticity of poverty is one-third that of the rest of the developing world, excluding China (Christiaensen, Chuhan-Pole, and Sanoh 2013). This slow pace of poverty reduction is frequently attributed to natural-resource-led growth, the so-called natural resource curse. Examples abound of poor outcomes (on income poverty and social indicators) in African countries with abundant natural wealth. For example, in Zambia, a major copper producer, the incidence of poverty remained virtually unchanged, at 60 percent, during 2000–10, despite a doubling of economic output in this period.

Nonmonetary welfare indicators (controlling for per capita income) are also noticeably weaker in the region's resource-rich countries, such as Angola, Gabon, and Nigeria, pointing to the unmet potential of natural resource wealth (figure 1.3). The data show a penalty for living in a resource-rich country compared to a non-resource-rich country in Africa: literacy rates are 3.1 percentage points lower, life expectancy is 4.5 years shorter, malnutrition among women and children is more prevalent (by 3.7 and 2.1 percentage points, respectively), incidence of domestic violence is higher (by 9 percentage points), and voice and accountability measures are weaker (Beegle et al. 2016).

The inability of millions of people living in poverty to benefit from natural resource wealth is a disappointment that is all too familiar at the national level. But interest is growing in going beyond the national or aggregate impact to understand whether mining communities benefit from a resource boom and, if they do not, what could explain this. Despite long-standing interest in these issues in relation to Africa, studies have been slow in coming and research remains underdeveloped. One reason for this is that, in general, African countries do not collect detailed subnational economic data. Therefore, it is often difficult to assess how much of the growth that is reported is happening at the local level, or how large-scale mining is affecting local economic activity. But increasing the availability and application of

Figure 1.3 Human Development Index Scores in Selected African Countries, 2013

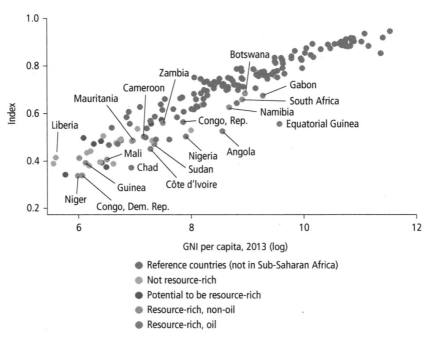

Sources: UNDP 2014; World Bank, World Development Indicators.
Note: Human Development Index scores range from a low of 0 to a high of 1. GNI = gross national income.

remote sensing data collected by satellite is making these measurements possible.

The study's focus on local impacts is motivated by the observation that, in general, the socioeconomic effects of large-scale mining are not well understood. But public opinion—to the extent there is one—on the impacts of mining on local communities is likely to be unfavorable. This is partly because, despite contributing substantially to countries' export revenue and, in many instances, GDP, the total employment numbers generated country-wide by mines are generally modest. In Mali, for instance, large-scale mining accounted for about 7 percent of GDP in 2013, but less than 1 percent of the population was employed by the industry (Sanoh and Coulibaly 2015). Adding to the negative perception of the industry is the concern that it causes negative environmental and health impacts for which local communities feel they are not adequately compensated. Moreover, the end of a mining boom may leave communities with little capacity for alternate livelihoods. Compounding these perceptions are the mining and oil companies that want government concessions. As a result, these companies tend to exaggerate the local and national benefits of their industries.

The objective of this study is to gain a better understanding of the socioeconomic impact of resource extraction on local communities in Africa. Specifically, the study explores the effect of mining on the composition of employment, wages, access to infrastructure (water, electricity), child health outcomes, and agricultural production in communities where resource extraction takes place. The study also examines the extent of resource revenues received by governments in mining areas, and assesses whether the size and composition of fiscal spending on these communities are affected by mining.

The study begins by laying out a simple framework of the potential channels through which extractive activity affects local livelihoods and communities. In many of them, the government, as the owner of subsurface resources on behalf of the people, is the conduit of the benefits to the rest of the economy, including to local communities. With this in mind, the study delineates three broad channels—market, fiscal, and environmental—through which local areas and regions may be affected (figure 1.4).

The study then applies this framework to a single extractive sector—large-scale gold mining—in three African countries: Ghana, Mali, and Tanzania. Gold was chosen because it is common in many countries and is found in areas that are fairly heavily populated, so the impacts on local communities will be clearer to identify. The aim of the research is to assess whether local communities benefit from mining or not. The focus is primarily on improvements in welfare, as measured by occupations for both women and men, asset accumulation, access to infrastructure, and children's health outcomes. This is because gains in these dimensions are key to higher earnings as well as to more stable, less vulnerable livelihoods.

The study adopts a two-pronged approach to evaluate the local-level effects of mining. First, through descriptive analysis, including the results of

Figure 1.4 Channels through Which Natural Resource Abundance Affects Local Communities

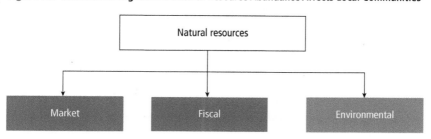

Source: Aragón, Chuhan-Pole, and Land 2015.

fieldwork, mining's impacts are examined in a country-specific context for each of the three countries. Second, a statistical analysis is used to test whether welfare improves with proximity to a mine. The empirical approach adopted treats industrial gold mining as a quasi-experiment in which the start or restart of a gold mine is the "treatment" or shock. Here, the object is to discern differences in the outcomes of local communities in mining and non-mining areas.

To increase the benefits of mining to local communities, the study identifies general areas in which government and private sector initiatives can lead to improved livelihoods and an improved future for men and women working for and near large-scale mining operations and for their families.

A Framework to Measure How Local Communities Capture Benefits

The avenues for extractive industries to affect local communities and regions are somewhat restricted in developing countries since the national government is the guardian of this wealth on their behalf (see chapter 2). Thus, the study identifies three broad channels—market, fiscal, and environmental—through which local areas and regions may potentially be affected by extractive activity (figure 1.4). These three channels can affect local welfare through several broad paths, and three in particular: employment, income, and links with other sectors; public spending; and negative externalities from production.

Working through the market channel, resource extraction can affect income, employment, and links with other sectors. Extractive industries employ local workers and purchase some goods and services locally and regionally. Thus, a boom in this sector should raise nominal wages and other incomes, increase nonmine employment opportunities, and generally improve local welfare and reduce poverty. Negative spillovers could, however, occur from this increased activity. Often, the start of an extractive industry, say, the opening of a mine, will attract workers from other districts. This could temper wage rises, put a strain on local services such as health and education, and raise the price of nontradable goods and services, such as housing, which could reduce the real incomes of some local residents. Figure 1.5 illustrates an analytical framework of market-based transmission channels and possible outcomes from exploiting a potential natural resource boom.

Positive spillovers from the extractive industry, in addition to the employment and wage effects already noted, could include improved productivity through worker training and education, which often spread beyond the mine or oil field. Also, improvements to public goods may occur through investment

Figure 1.5 How Market and Fiscal Mechanisms Affect Well-Being

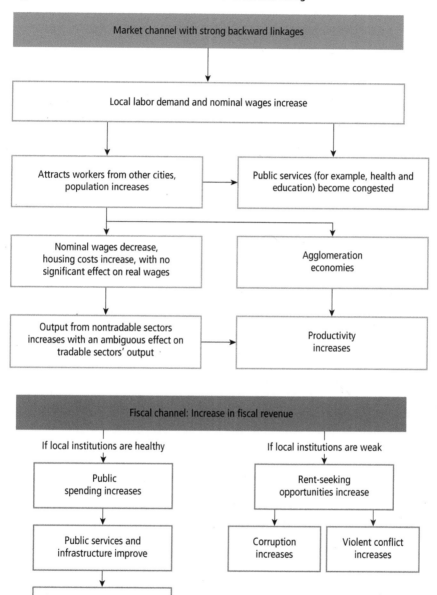

in roads, bridges, ports, and similar facilities, which are required by the extractive industry.

On public spending, governments have a major role to play in transforming resource wealth into sustained development. The value chain of natural resource management encompasses the organization of the sector and the award of contracts and licenses; regulation and oversight of operations; the collection of resource rents through taxes and royalties; the allocation of revenues and management of public investment; and sustainable development practices and policies (Barma et al. 2012). The benefits from a natural resource will depend to a large extent on whether the revenues received are put to good use. But if history is a guide, there is ample reason to be cautious. A fiscal revenue windfall eases hard budget constraints on local governments, and supports higher public spending. The fiscal arrangements between central and local governments at various levels will, therefore, determine how much of the benefits from mining find their way back to mining areas.

If the revenue windfall is used to improve the quantity or quality of local public goods and services, the potential is there to improve human welfare, such as health and education outcomes. Moreover, to the extent that public goods are productive inputs or create positive spillovers (as in the case of transportation infrastructure), a resource boom could also increase local income and growth. The positive effect of revenue windfalls is underpinned by several assumptions: namely, local politicians are responsive to the broad population, which requires well-functioning local institutions; a healthy degree of political competition; and local bureaucracies having the technical capacity to provide public goods and services. As such, the general competence, honesty, and overall implementation capacity of local-level government are vital for enhancing welfare and development. Where these conditions are lacking, the positive effect of revenue windfalls on the provision of public goods and local living conditions will not be realized. Hence, both nationally and locally, the quality of governance and the influence of resource revenues on governance will be major determinants of the welfare impacts of resource exploitation. Figure 1.4 shows some of the paths discussed in the literature through which a revenue windfall could impact local welfare.

Mining and mineral processing can generate several types of negative externalities. These include pollution, pressure on other scarce natural resources, and social dislocation, which can affect local community welfare.

Environmental pollution can adversely impact health, and this is a big concern, including in gold mining (see box 1.1). It can also lead to the loss of agricultural productivity (Aragón and Rud 2015) by directly affecting crop health and growth; by degrading the quality of key agricultural inputs, such as soil and water; and through the impact of air pollution on labor productivity.

BOX 1.1

Environmental and Health Issues in Gold Mining Areas

Like many other industries, gold mining (industrial and artisanal) is associated with environmental degradation and pollution, which have severe health implications.

Environmental degradation is manifested through effects on the land and land use, the spread of gold ore-related heavy metals such as arsenic and lead to nature, the discharge of cyanide to nature, and the spread of mercury from artisanal mining or air pollution. In Ghana, air pollution around industrial gold mines has been linked to increased cough incidence (Aragón and Rud 2013).

Similarly, pollution from heavy metals contamination from 800 mines in 44 developing countries has been shown to lead to an increase of 3 to 10 percentage points in the incidence of anemia among women and 5 percentage points in the incidence of stunting among children living in mining communities (von der Goltz and Barnwal 2014). Yet, controversies surround studies linking environmental degradation around mines to health outcomes because of the possibility that exposure to these pollutions may be linked to individual lifestyle, which result in biasing the outcomes (Tolonen 2014).

A Ghanaian environmental impact assessment in 2008 of 61 major mines and several smaller-scale operations sites found that mining areas have relatively higher concentrations of arsenic, particularly within the areas of old, large mines such as Obuasi, Bibiani, and Prestea. For example, in Obuasi's influence area, the mean arsenic concentration over one year of sampling was 25 millionths of a gram per liter, which is more than 50 times the World Health Organization's guideline for drinking water (European Union 2008). High concentrations of cyanide are infrequent in Ghana because most companies stick to stringent procedures.

Environmental and health issues for artisanal scale miners focus on the use of mercury to cheaply separate gold from other minerals. Mercury usage tends to always exceed the World Health Organization limit for public exposure of 1 millionth of a gram per square meter. In southwest Ghana, artisanal and small-scale gold miners have a significantly higher burden of mercury than other people living or working in mining areas (Kwaansa-Ansah et al. 2014). In Tanzania, a review of several studies points to major health and safety risks for mining communities (Sanjay et al. 2015). In the artisanal mining areas of Matundasi and Makongolosi, the mean mercury level in hair samples of miners is 2.7 times higher than the U.S. Environmental Protection Agency's reference limit of 4–5 millionths of a gram per liter. Approximately two-thirds of the hair samples exceeded this reference limit.

Another study in Tanzania looked at mercury levels in the breast milk of mothers living at artisanal and small-scale gold mining sites; it found that 22 of the 46 children from these mothers had a higher total mercury intake.

The loss of agricultural productivity can also have a negative impact on agricultural output, which, in turn, affects the incomes of farmers and rural populations. This externality is particularly relevant when extractive industries are located in populated rural areas, and where agriculture remains an important source of livelihood.

The Approach to Assessing the Local Effects of Mining

Sector Focus: Gold Mining in Sub-Saharan Africa

The mineral sector in Sub-Saharan Africa is large and diverse. This study selectively applies the framework of figure 1.4 to a single mineral: gold. The choice of gold for this study was predicated on the following factors:

- Gold mining is now an important industry in several countries in Sub-Saharan Africa, and is second only to crude oil as the region's top export earner. In 2013, several countries in the region—including Ghana, Mali, South Africa, and Tanzania—were among the world's top 20 gold-producing countries.
- Since the aim of the study is to assess the socioeconomic impact of mining on local communities, it is appropriate to select a sector that can have a potentially important local footprint. Because gold mining is onshore, unlike oil drilling, which is often offshore, it can be expected to have an impact on local populations.
- Conflict-affected countries were excluded from the study, to better capture the market channel through which extractive activity can affect local communities.

Three countries were selected for study: Ghana, Mali, and Tanzania. Gold mining operations in these countries have a number of common characteristics that make them suitable for this study. While industrial gold mining has a long history in Africa (especially in Ghana), gold production has sharply accelerated since the mid-1990s in each of these countries (figure 1.6), so that collectively they accounted for 35 percent of the region's gold production in 2015.

Gold exports are an important component of exports in all three countries— for Mali, the annual average was 69 percent of exports between 2000 and 2013; for Ghana, 38 percent over the same period; and for Tanzania, 31 percent. Although the value of gold exports is substantial, the contribution of gold mining to GDP is less dominant. In Mali, the poorest of the three countries, about 7 percent of GDP comes from mining and quarrying. In Ghana it is 5.5 percent, and it is 4.0 percent in Tanzania.

Figure 1.6 Gold Production in Ghana, Mali, and Tanzania, 1980–2011

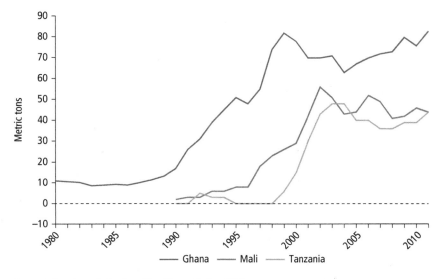

Source: Authors' compilation from MineAtlas and IntierraRMG.

Empirical Methodology for Measuring the Local Effects of Mining

The aim of the study is to assess whether local communities benefit from mining—specifically, industrial or large-scale gold mining—or not. To better understand how the benefits from the minerals sector are captured by local communities, this study measures the size of the impact of mining on local welfare by exploiting the "before" and "after" type of analysis using the opening and closing of mines. The focus is on improvements in welfare, as measured by four broad dimensions:

- *Occupations for men and woman.* Whether employment opportunities expand and incomes rise, and the impact on agricultural and nonagricultural activity.

- *Asset accumulation.* If there is a discernible increase in family asset accumulation (for example, a radio, bicycle, car, or toilet) with proximity to a mine, then one could conclude that the mine, at least in this respect, is welfare enhancing.

- *Access to infrastructure.* The key variables here are access to electricity and water, which are indicative of the provision of services by local governments.

- *Child health outcomes.* The analysis tries to determine whether there are improvements in key indicators of child health. Specifically, infant mortality and fever, cough persistence, and diarrhea in children under age five.

The analysis uses both descriptive analysis and robust econometric methods to evaluate local-level impacts. First, through case studies including the results of fieldwork, the impacts of mining are examined in a country-specific context for Ghana, Mali, and Tanzania (chapter 3). Second, a statistical analysis, combining mine-specific information and a rich dataset collected from various sources, is used to rigorously test whether the indicators of welfare improve with proximity to a mine (chapter 4).

The empirical approach builds on the earlier studies that used quasi-experimental events to estimate the impact of localized shocks on economic outcomes (Card and Krueger 1994). The identification strategy in these approaches is based on comparing outcomes in local units of observation (districts, municipalities, regions, and so on) affected by a particular event or intervention to units where such events or interventions are absent. The analytical approach adopted in this study views industrial gold mining as a quasi-experiment in which the vicinity of a mine can be thought of as the "treatment" area and areas outside of this as "nontreatment" areas. Because the areas chosen represent relatively recent gold mine starts (or restarts), it is also possible to compare outcomes "before treatment" and "after treatment"—the treatment, of course, being the start or existence of a mine. A difference-in-differences estimation strategy is used to test whether indicators of welfare improve with proximity to a mine, where proximity is defined in several ways (see box 1.2)

BOX 1.2

What Is a Mining Community?

Two broad measures of vicinity to a mine—that is, the treatment area—are used in the analysis: distance from a mine, and the administrative district where a mine is located.

Distance. How far the mine's influence extends is an empirical exercise. The analysis includes households within 100 kilometers of a mine location, with the baseline treatment distance being 20 kilometers from a mine (figure B1.2.1). To allow for nonlinear effects with distance, the analysis also employs a spatial lag model, in which the area around a mine is divided into small concentric distances (or bins), such as 0–10 km, 10–20 km, 20–30 km, and so on, up to within 100 km of a mine.

District. Arguably, mining can have additional impacts beyond the neighborhood of the mine if mining royalties and revenues are spent on populations living in districts

(continued next page)

Box 1.2 (continued)

Figure B1.2.1 Gold Mines in Mali and Spatial Buffers

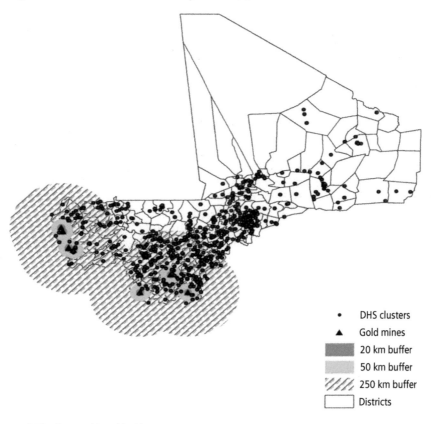

- •   DHS clusters
- ▲   Gold mines
-     20 km buffer
-     50 km buffer
-     250 km buffer
-     Districts

Note: DHS = demographic and health surveys.

where the mine is located. Injections of additional expenditures into the district could increase spending on welfare-enhancing services, such as schooling and health care. Thus, a second level of analysis is done with the treatment area as the district in which the mine is located. "District" refers to political or administrative units that have spending authority. Districts themselves are fairly arbitrary, and looking for impacts in only the districts that have a mine could miss the potential spillovers that result from mining. So spillover effects across districts are also considered, and the analysis compares outcomes in mining districts, neighboring districts, and nonmining districts. Outcomes in mining districts are also compared with those of a synthetic control group—a group which has no mines but has characteristics as similar as possible to those with mining districts.

Are Mining Communities Seeing Welfare Gains?

The results suggest that mining communities on average experience positive but limited welfare benefits. Although the evidence leans toward improvements in welfare with proximity to a mine, this is not uniformly true across all the dimensions of well-being that are studied. There is little indication, however, of deteriorating outcomes with proximity to a mine. Moreover, most of the positive welfare effects are experienced through the market channel.

This analysis finds that large-scale mining can support a structural transition in the economy of a local community. The results for employment and occupation suggest a move from farm labor to nonfarm occupations. These are robust, especially for countries where gold mining started earlier, such as Ghana and Mali. The shift is especially evident for women, who are tracked by better data. Nonfarm employment opportunities, especially in sales and services, were substantially higher for women living closer to mines than those living farther away. Similarly, their employment in agriculture declined, while the probability of working throughout the year rises for women living closer to mines and those who live in mining districts. Thus, although mining is capital-intensive and its direct labor effects are quite small, some indications point to transformative indirect effects. Where wage data are available, such as Ghana, results indicate that wages for those in mining are higher.

Unlike the common perception that large-scale mines are economic "enclaves" that provide little economic benefit to local economies, the findings from an analysis using remote sensing data show that economic growth increases in the period surrounding the start of a mine. Over time, however, areas near mines are not significantly better off than areas farther away. The analysis also suggests that despite the risks mines pose to agricultural productivity—through environmental pollution or structural shifts in the labor market, for example—there is no evidence of a decrease in agricultural production, as measured by the Normalized Difference Vegetation Index. The results point to better access to assets and to infrastructure. The evidence of an increased share of household expenditures on housing and energy is considered a strong indicator of rising access to electricity and asset accumulation.

The health of children in local mining communities often improves with increased wages, electricity, and in some cases clean water, although child health outcomes between mining and nonmining areas have mixed results. Infant mortality decreases faster and is statistically significant in mining communities and districts in Ghana and Mali, but it is not statistically significant in Tanzania. Stunting (ratio of height to age) decreases for children who live close to mines in Mali, and the estimated effect is negative but insignificant for wasting. In Ghana and Tanzania, these outcomes appear worse for mining areas, although the results are not always statistically significant. The incidence of cough declines in both Ghana and Mali, but not in Tanzania. Similarly, the incidence of diarrheal disease decreases in Mali but is positive and insignificant in Ghana. Migration patterns may explain some of the differences in child health outcomes across countries. For example, the increased incidence of diarrheal disease in Ghana appears to be driven by poor outcomes among migrants who live near mines.[1]

Signs of Economic Transformation: Occupation, Income, and Linkages

The mining industry in Sub-Saharan Africa is generally associated with weak direct employment generation compared with its contributions to GDP and export revenue at a national level. Yet mining has the potential for large local impacts that can begin to bring about structural transformation in local economies.

One key channel for transmitting benefits to a local community is through direct employment by the mining companies. However, gold mining is capital-intensive, and the country case studies show the linkages are likely to be modest. Only about 7,000 people were directly employed in gold mining in Tanzania in 2013, and the figures were similarly low for Ghana (about 17,100 in 2014) and Mali (averaging 3,635 during 2008–13). In many countries in the region, mining companies employ mostly nationals rather than expatriates, although managerial jobs often go disproportionately to foreigners. Sanoh and Coulibaly (2015) report a ratio of 14 national workers to each expatriate in Mali's mining companies, and that on average 78 percent of mining jobs are located in the three communes (local government entities) of Gouandiaka, Sadiola, and Sitakily. National labor survey data suggest that the mean income from mining is higher than the average income for all other sectors, and considerably so when compared to agriculture and industry.

The increase in employment, wages, and real income of local populations can bring about additional economic changes that can improve livelihoods. Yet, because of data limitations, it is difficult to estimate the wider local economic linkages to a mine. Although the description of large-scale mining as an enclave is not accurate (it does not, for one thing, mesh with the larger economy), it is also fair to say that the backward linkages are not large. For example, for South Africa, where better data are available, gold mining is estimated to have a multiplier of about 1.8; in other words, for every one mining job, an additional 1.8 jobs are created elsewhere through backward linkages and expenditure effects. Sanoh and Coulibaly (2015) report a ratio of 1.67 in Mali. However, these multiplier effects are limited, mostly because of a lack of local, cost-effective procurement opportunities but also partly because of the capital intensity of the mining industry.

The potential for more local procurement could increase as mining companies become better acquainted with local markets and suppliers, and if local entrepreneurs learn to take advantage of these emerging opportunities. This is happening in Tanzania, where efforts have been made to improve the potential for local procurement, including in services such as catering, vehicle repair, machine shop services, welding, metal work, electrical work, and plumbing. However, the proportions of inputs sourced locally remain low, as they are in Ghana and Mali.

One mechanism through which mining can have large impacts is agglomeration economies—gains in productivity unleashed with the clustering of economic activities around mines. The first sign of such a change would be the movement of labor and other factors away from traditional sectors to new sectors. For the three case study countries, that would mean a change in the structure of the local economy, from being dominated by "traditional" farming to a more balanced local economy.

In Ghana, Mali, and Tanzania, the influx of jobs, income, and infrastructure from large-scale mining appears to bring benefits, and research shows incipient signs of structural transformation. Both the individual- and district-level results find that employment in agriculture declined, while employment in nonfarm occupations—such as services, manufacturing, and mining—rose. These results are robust, especially for countries where gold mining started earlier, such as Ghana and Mali. Where wage data are available, as in Ghana, there is evidence that wages in mining areas are higher.

The nascent structural shift has also brought improvements in women's nonfarm employment opportunities. Employment in sales and services for women was substantially higher for women living closer to mines than those living farther away. In the same vein, their employment in agriculture declined, while the probability of working throughout the year rises for women closer to mines and those who live in mining districts.

Results from the spatial lag model using demographic and health survey data—which allow for nonlinear effects with distance—show that service sector employment for women is significantly higher close to active mines (figure 1.7). In fact, the effects are stronger 0–10 kilometers from a mine than at 10–20 kilometers. In Mali, the probability that a woman works in services and sales increases by 30 percentage points, and in Ghana by 17 percentage points, at the least distance. For Ghana and Mali, agricultural participation drops close to mines, at roughly 10 to 20 percentage points, respectively. Tanzania shows no evidence of a clear change either in services and sales or agricultural employment.

For Ghana, the results show there is an increase of 10 percentage points in the likelihood that a man living close to a mine works in mining (figure 1.8, panel c).[2] This contrasts with the findings for women, who are not benefiting

Figure 1.7 Spatial Lag Model Illustrating the Geographic Distribution of Effects on Services Sector and Agricultural Employment for Women in Ghana, Mali, and Tanzania

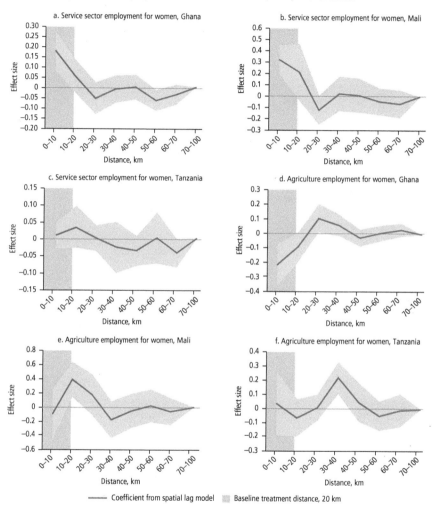

Source: Authors' estimates from survey data.
Note: Spatial lag model illustrating geographic distribution of effects on service and agricultural sector employment. Results are from demographic and health surveys. Shaded area along lines represents 95 percent confidence interval. km = kilometers

Figure 1.8 Spatial Lag Model Illustrating Agriculture, Manual Labor, Mining, and Wage Earnings for Men in Ghana and Mali

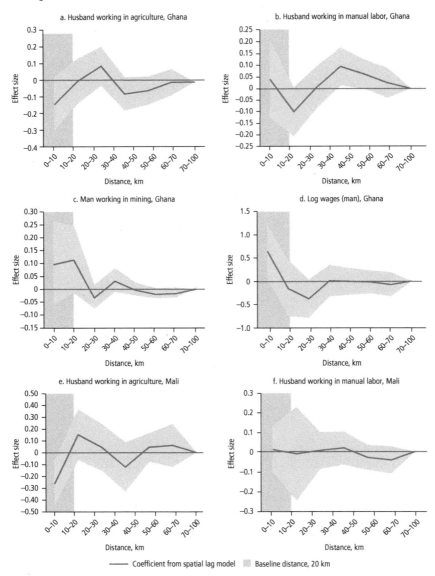

Source: Authors' estimates from survey data.
Note: Spatial lag model illustrating geographic distribution of effects on agriculture, manual labor, mining, and wage earnings for men. Results are from demographic and health surveys, except for those in panels c and d which are from the Ghana Living Standards Survey. Shaded area along lines represents 95 percent confidence interval. km = kilometers

(or are benefiting very little) from direct employment in mining.[3] Ghana Living Standards Survey data also show that men have (marginally) significantly higher wages. The demographic and health survey data for Ghana and Mali reveal that men are less likely to work in agriculture if they live within 10 kilometers of a mine (statistically significant in Mali). A pattern in the data indicates a propensity for distance-related occupational specialization: less engagement in farming activities from very close to a mine to slightly farther away (20–30 kilometers), especially in Ghana. The findings also show that men are not more likely to do manual labor in Ghana or in Mali.

District-level analysis, which compares outcomes between mining and nonmining districts for all three countries, confirms the finding that agricultural employment decreases in mining districts. For Ghana, the results indicate that, compared with nonmining districts, this decreases by 5.2 percentage points for men and 8.5 percentage points for women. In addition, the probability of a woman working all year increases by 5.4 percentage points, as does the probability of doing manual work. No such significant increases in employment in other sectors are discernible for men (the demographic and health surveys have no information on employment in mining for men).[4]

District-level analysis for Mali shows that, overall, agricultural employment decreases for men and women, although the results are not statistically significant. At the same time, there are significant increases in the likelihood of mining employment; men are almost 10 percentage points more likely to work as miners, and women are 2.3 percentage points more likely, compared with before a mine opening. Note, however, that these changes can also be due to increases in small-scale mining in these districts over the same period. For Tanzania, no recorded information on mining employment exists; but, as in Mali, we see a decrease in agricultural employment (8 percentage points for men and 11 percentage points for women), though these estimates are not statistically significant.

Wages for men and women are on the rise in Ghana, but those for men are not precisely estimated (figure 1.9). Household total wages are also on the rise, but household expenditures are decreasing. Because wage earnings are recorded for those who are in wage labor, what happens to total earnings in households without any wage labor is not clear.

Does Mining Reduce Agricultural Growth?

Agriculture is an important sector throughout Africa. Some 65 percent of workers in Sub-Saharan Africa are farmers, and agriculture accounts for 32 percent of the region's GDP. Most people in rural villages are farmers, and agriculture accounts for the largest share of economic activity in the countries studied in the analysis—Burkina Faso, Ghana, Mali, and Tanzania—on whether mining reduces agricultural growth. Because mines are land intensive, they open mostly

Figure 1.9 Changes in Income, Wages, and Expenditures in Ghana

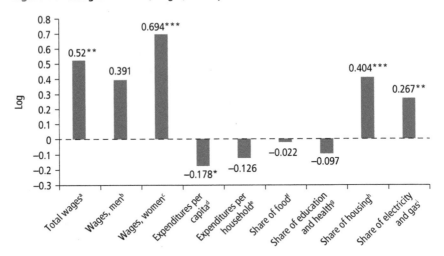

Source: Authors' estimates from Ghana Living Standards Survey data.
Note: pc = per capita.
a. Annual wages and salaries for individuals of all ages (nondeflated).
b. Annual wages and salaries for men of all ages (nondeflated).
c. Annual wages and salaries for women of all ages (nondeflated).
d. Real annual food and nonfood expenditures per capita (regionally deflated).
e. Total annual regionally adjusted household expenditures (local currency).
f–i. All expenditures and food share variables are used in natural logarithms.
All regressions control for household head, household size, district fixed effects, and year fixed effects.
All regressions control for year and district fixed effects, urban dummy, age, and years of education.
***p<0.01, **p<0.05, *p<0.1.

in rural areas, where land is relatively cheaper and where agricultural participation is often higher before a mine opens.

Mining can affect agricultural production in several ways. It can lead to a rise
in local wages, reduce profit margins in agriculture, and lead to the exit of many
families from farming—something akin to a localized Dutch disease. Negative
environmental spillovers such as pollution or local health problems can dampen
the productivity of the land and of farmers, reducing the viability of farming.
Conversely, mining can also create a miniboom in the local economy through
higher employment and wages, which can lead to an increase in local area
aggregate demand, including for regional crops.

To understand how large-scale mining impacts local economic activity, this
study uses georeferenced data collected by satellite to estimate changes in agricultural and nonagricultural production in mining and nonmining localities in
Burkina Faso, Ghana, Mali, and Tanzania (box 1.3).

How Remote Sensing Informs Agricultural Production

Night lights data gathered by satellite can depict human settlement and development, and are sensitive enough to detect streetlights and even the lights of vessels at sea. One of the central uses of the night lights data set is as a measure of and proxy for economic activity. However, night lights, while certainly informative of human activity, do not exhaust economic activity in all places. For instance, in countries that are mostly rural and where the mainstay of the economy is agriculture, an overreliance on night lights might miss a big fraction of economic activity.

Remote sensing technology that captures the type of light reflected by vegetation can be used for estimating the production of agricultural commodities. This study investigates the spatial relationship between mining and local agricultural development by using the Normalized Difference Vegetation Index. This is used as a proxy for agricultural production to learn whether the opening of a mine has spillover effects on agriculture. To estimate the level and composition of agricultural and nonagricultural production at the local level, the study selected a radius around 32 large-scale gold mining areas in Burkina Faso, Ghana, Mali, and Tanzania.

Unlike the common perception that large-scale mines are economic enclaves that provide little economic benefit to local economies, the findings using remote sensing data show that economic growth increases in the period surrounding the start of a mine. The night lights data show strong increases in night lights in mining communities within 10 kilometers of a mine in the years immediately before a mine opening.

Further, the data indicate that in the years following a mine's opening, the nearby areas (within 10 kilometers) have significantly higher levels of economic activity (figure 1.10, panel a). However, over time, the areas near the mines are not significantly better off than areas farther away. This may partially indicate that with time, the economic benefits from mining spread over a larger area from a mine's center point.

The results also suggest that the opening of a large-scale mine may not decrease local farming, in contrast to recent studies showing that mining increases urbanization rates or leads to decreased local farming. Using the Normalized Difference Vegetation Index, the findings show that areas close to mines have higher levels of greenness (figure 1.10, panel b). This could be indicative of mining areas being more rural in general, but this study found little change in the index with the onset of mining. Despite the risks that mines pose to agricultural productivity (for example, through environmental pollution or structural shifts in the labor market), there is no evidence of a decrease in greenness, which is the measure of agricultural production.

Figure 1.10 Night Lights and Normalized Difference Vegetation Index before and after a Mine Opening

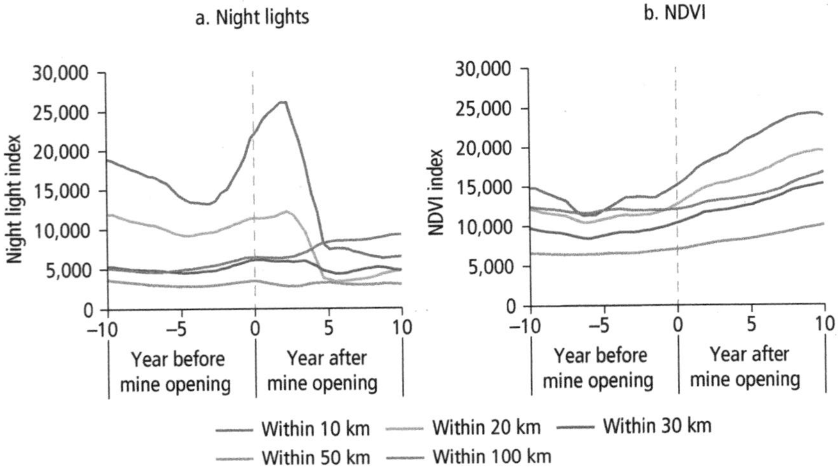

a. Night lights

b. NDVI

Source: Authors' estimates from survey data.
Note: Nonparametric (local polynomial smooth) measures of night lights and the NDVI close to mines. Years since mine opening on the x-axis counts the number of years from mine opening, with before the opening on the left of 0, and years after mine opening to the right of 0. Night lights and the index are measured as averages across limited geographic areas, varying from within 10 km from the mine center point, to 20 km, 30 km, 50 km, and 100 km. NDVI = Normalized Difference Vegetation Index.

Welfare Improvements: Asset Accumulation, Access to Infrastructure Services, and Child Health Outcomes

Asset Accumulation

The analysis finds some variation in how the opening of a mine close to a community affects the probability of a household owning or having access to assets such as improved flooring, radios, and cars. The results for the three case study countries show that households in Mali are 30 percentage points more likely to have floors made of cement, tile, wood, or materials other than earth, sand, or dung, and 5 percentage points more likely to own a car (but 11 percentage points less likely to own a bicycle) (figure 1.11). Households in Ghana are 14 percentage points more likely to own a radio. In some cases, there are differences for migrants and never-movers in the same communities. For example, in Mali, the positive effects on household assets seem to be driven by migrant households. In Tanzania, decomposition by migrant status shows that radio ownership in fact increased among non-migrant households. In Ghana, however, radio ownership increases for both migrant and nonmigrant women.

Figure 1.11 Ownership of Assets from a Mine Opening in Ghana, Mali, and Tanzania

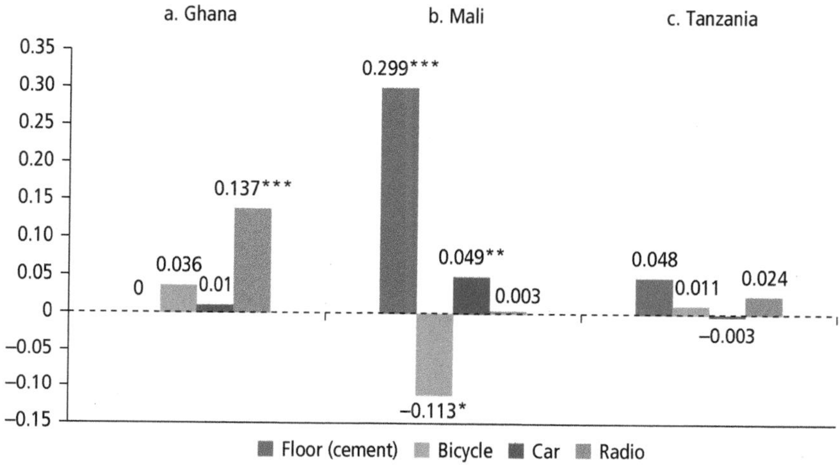

Source: Authors' estimates from survey data.
Note: Reported coefficients are the coefficients of the interaction variable for being close to a mine that was active in the survey year. Unreported coefficients include coefficients of the treatment dummy, year dummy, and the control variables. Error terms are clustered at the sample cluster level. All outcome variables are indicator variables that take a value of 1 or 0. Floor (cement) captures flooring made of cement, tile, wood, or other materials other than earth, sand, or dung. Bicycle, car, and radio capture whether the household has these assets.
***$p<0.01$, **$p<0.05$, *$p<0.1$.

Access to Infrastructure Services

Does the opening of a mine close to a community affect the probability of households having better access to some types of infrastructure services? Overall, the results on access are weak. The study finds that households close to a mine are generally more likely to have access to a private toilet in the three case study countries. For example, households in mining communities in Tanzania are 24 percentage points less likely to share a toilet facility with other households (figure 1.12). There are differences for migrants and never-movers in the same communities. Thus, migrants in Ghana are seemingly less well off than never-movers and have less access to electricity. In Mali, the relationship is reversed, with migrants having better access to electricity. District-level analysis shows very small insignificant effects on access to electricity in mining districts in all three case study countries, and on access to sanitation in Mali and Tanzania. Ghana shows a large positive, yet insignificant, effect on access to water in mining districts.

Figure 1.12 Household Access to Infrastructure with a Mine Opening in Ghana, Mali, and Tanzania

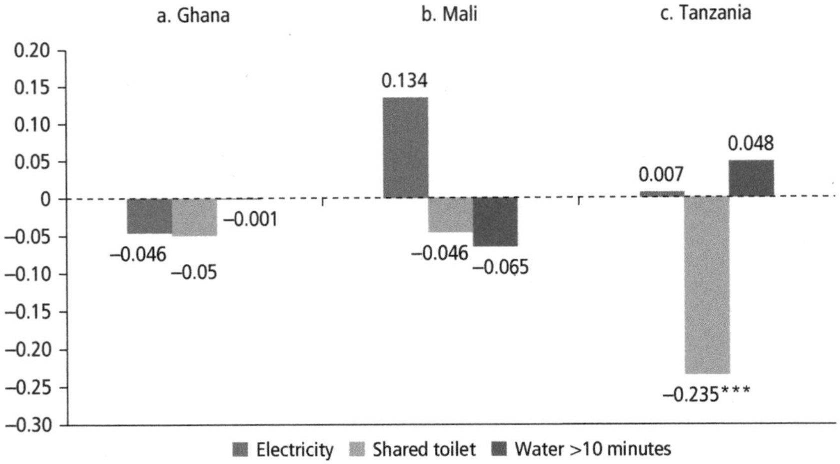

a. Ghana   b. Mali   c. Tanzania

■ Electricity ■ Shared toilet ■ Water >10 minutes

Source: Authors' estimates from survey data.
Note: Reported coefficients are the coefficients of the interaction variable for being close to a mine that was active in the survey year. Unreported coefficients include coefficients of the treatment dummy, year dummy, and the control variables. Error terms are clustered at the sample cluster level. All outcome variables are indicator variables that take a value of 1 or 0. Shared toilet is whether the household shares toilet facilities with other households rather than having a private toilet facility. Water >10 minutes indicates whether it takes more than 10 minutes from the home to fetch drinking water. Electricity is whether the household has connection.
***p<0.01.

Child Health Outcomes

Large-scale gold mining can affect children's health in different ways. For example, in households close to mines, it could positively affect outcomes through an improvement in household income and negatively through environmental degradation. Therefore, a priori, how a mine affects child health remains theoretically ambiguous.

In Mali, the study finds positive effects from a mine opening on access to health care and health outcomes (figure 1.13). Pregnant mothers receive many more prenatal health visits; infant mortality decreases by 5.3 percentage points (although it is not estimated with statistical significance); and stunting decreases by 27 percentage points, which is equivalent to a 45 percent decrease in the prevalence from the pre-mine average rate of stunting. The estimated effect is negative but statistically insignificant for wasting, but negative and statistically significant for being underweight, which is a composite measure of acute and chronic malnourishment.

Figure 1.13 Child Health Outcomes from a Mine Opening in Ghana, Mali, and Tanzania

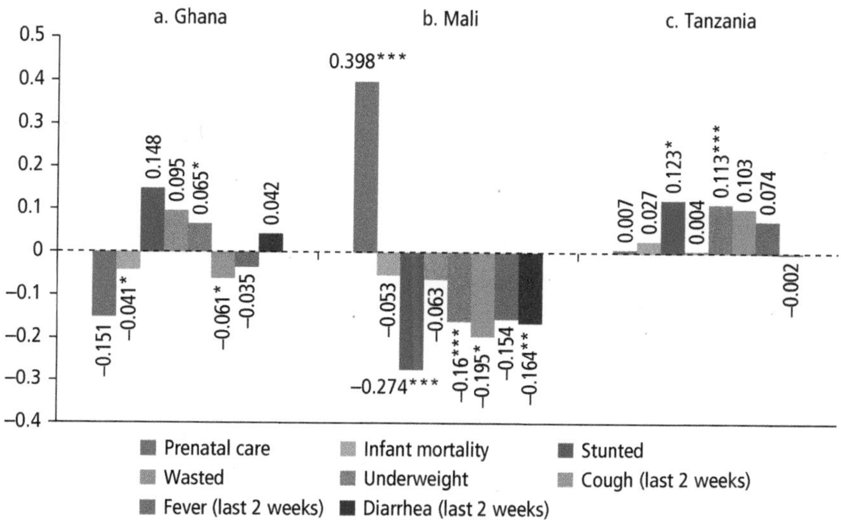

Source: Authors' estimates from survey data.
Note: Reported coefficients are the coefficients of the interaction variable for being close to a mine that was active in the survey year. Unreported coefficients include coefficients of the treatment dummy, year dummy, and the control variables. Error terms are clustered at the sample cluster level. See annex table 4A.1 in chapter 4 for variable definitions.
*$p<0.1$, **$p<0.05$, ***$p<0.01$.

The results also show the prevalence of cough, fever, and diarrhea decrease in Mali, although this is not statistically significant for fever. The significant drop in diarrheal incidence of children in Mali's mining communities is a welcome development since diarrhea remains a serious threat to children in developing countries, even though it is easy to cure and prevent. Opening or improving access to safe water and sanitation are ways in which Mali's mines can reduce diarrheal incidence.

Unlike Mali, the effects on child health are ambiguous in Ghana and Tanzania. The likelihood that a child is stunted increases by 12.3 percentage points in Tanzania, and being underweight increases in mining communities in Ghana and Tanzania. However, some positive effects of mine openings are evident. Ghana has seen a large decline in infant mortality and a decrease in cough prevalence. The effect of a mine on diarrheal incidence is positive but statistically insignificant in Ghana. When this outcome is disaggregated by groups, it reveals that migrants experience higher rates of diarrhea and never-movers lower rates.

It is not clear why child health outcomes at the local level differ across the three countries. Stunting, which is a measure of long-term nutritional deficiency, may decline for children living closer to mines because their families may have higher incomes, which can be used to buy more nutritious food for their children. By contrast, wasting is a short-term measure of nutritional deficiency and can be strongly explained by access to health services.

Migration patterns may also explain some of the differences in child health outcomes. For instance, Mali, which shows the most positive changes, is also the country with the lowest level of migration around the time of mine opening, and migrants in mining areas in Mali seem less vulnerable than in Ghana or Tanzania. Tanzania, which shows weak evidence for structural transformation and few gains in child health, appears to have the largest increase in migration flows after a mine opens.

Some positive effects on access to health services for children are discernible in Ghana's gold mining districts. District-level analysis for five measures of child health care and access shows that mothers in gold mining districts have 0.759 more prenatal visits per child, and are 12.5 percentage points more likely to be attended to by a trained midwife (figure 1.14). Moreover, infant mortality is

Figure 1.14 Access to Health Services for Children in Mining Districts in Ghana

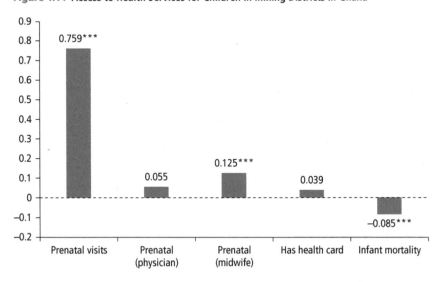

Source: Authors' estimates from survey data.
Note: Reported coefficients are the coefficients of the interaction variable for districts with active mines in the survey year. Robust standard errors are clustered at the district level.

8.5 percentage points lower in active mining communities. District-level results for Mali and Tanzania also show improvements in children's nutrition in mining and neighboring districts compared with control districts (using a synthetic control method), although not as dramatic as in Ghana.

Assessing the Role of Government

In many countries in Africa, most benefits from extractives will clearly be fiscal and national, because the government is the conduit of the benefits to the rest of the economy, including to local communities. The empirical evidence shows that the size of resource-related intergovernmental transfers to local communities has so far been modest. As such, there is considerable potential to improve welfare at the local level through larger transfers that can support investment in much-needed infrastructure and the development of human capital.

Government revenues increased considerably in each of the three case study countries from 2001 to 2013, although levels reportedly dropped in 2014 following a decline in international gold prices (figure 1.15). During 2005–13, gold mining provided Mali's government with $362 million a year (annual average), Ghana's with $300 million, and Tanzania's with $137 million. This revenue windfall could have been used to build health clinics and schools, enhance the quality of local services, and potentially improve human welfare for the country's poor. By creating positive spillovers, as in the case of transportation infrastructure, a resource boom could also increase local income and growth.

The fiscal arrangements between the central and local governments at various levels are important in determining how many of the benefits from mining find their way back to mining areas. Fiscal arrangements varied across the three case study countries. Mali has the highest degree of fiscal decentralization and, therefore, local authorities there received the largest proportion of the revenues compared to the other two countries. Ghana is in the middle, but its decentralization efforts are fairly new, so it may be premature to evaluate them. Tanzania has a centralized system, with all revenues collected and controlled by the central government, and transfers from the central budget fund 90 percent of local government. The funds are allocated according to criteria and priorities unrelated to the location of mines or the source of the funds.

The positive effect of revenue windfalls is underpinned by several assumptions. Key among them are that local politicians are responsive to the preferences of the broad population, local institutions function well, and local bureaucracies have the technical capacity to provide these public goods and services. As discussed in the section in this chapter on a framework to measure

Figure 1.15 Government Mining Revenues from Mining in Ghana, Mali, and Tanzania, 2001–13

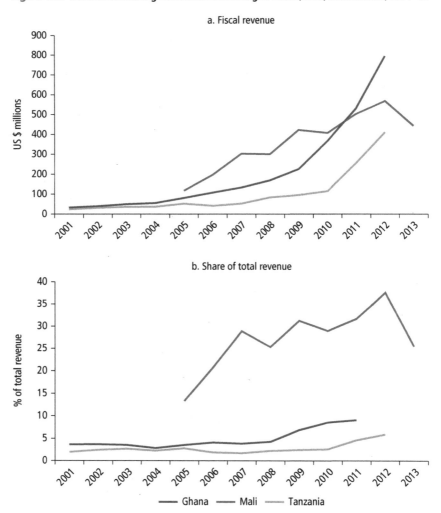

a. Fiscal revenue

b. Share of total revenue

— Ghana — Mali — Tanzania

Source: Authors' estimates from administrative data.
Note: Different starting points for the three countries are due to data availability.

how local communities capture benefits, an absence of these mediating factors may undermine the positive effect of the natural resource extraction revenues. The quality of governance—at national and local levels—and the influence on it of resource revenues are important determinants of the welfare impacts of resource exploitation. However, these are not assessed here.

Mining companies have made arrangements with many countries to provide funds directly to governments for supporting infrastructure and other projects to benefit families living near mines. Direct investment in community development has traditionally been labeled corporate social responsibility, and, in the case of mining companies, typical projects supported include building secondary schools, clinics, and water infrastructure. For example, Newmont Ghana Gold has supported Ghana's Ahafo region through a partnership in the health sector by building housing for resident nurses and three community health compounds in local villages, and by equipping 60 local health volunteers with bicycles and medical equipment.

Similar to almost all foreign aid and government interventions, particularly where implementation capacity is limited, these types of projects have had mixed success across the board and have generally taken a long time to implement. Even so, a growing trend is discernible in the three case study countries for more sustainable projects that offer alternative livelihoods to mining, such as brickmaking and fisheries, in communities around mines. This reflects the widespread recognition that positive impacts from mining on local communities have so far come in below expectations, and that interest is rising in helping these communities diversify their economic activities and so prosper after a mine closes.

Multinational mining firms still rarely improve infrastructure, although it does happen. While this study does not separately assess the impact of corporate responsibility efforts, the benefits are likely to be captured in the overall impact of mining on jobs, health outcomes, and the like.

As discussed earlier, all types of mining can pollute and cause environmental damage, which is injurious to health, unless carefully managed. But even when carefully managed, there are still substantial risks to local communities. Mercury is typically used in artisanal and small-scale mining, although it is not used in large-scale gold mining. Cyanide, which is highly toxic, is used in large mines, although its use is typically better controlled. Another possibly important pollution externality is the loss of agricultural productivity from degraded water and soil. Because of the negative externalities from mining, it is important to properly measure the social costs of this mining, and have a regulatory framework that addresses the environmental challenges of mining and compensates communities affected by these externalities.

Policy Priorities for Addressing the Local Impacts of Mining

The empirical analysis reveals little evidence that local mining communities suffer a resource curse because of resource abundance. If anything, these communities experience on average positive, albeit limited, welfare benefits in the near term. Most of these positive effects are experienced through the market channel.

One question is whether the market effects can be enhanced. There is always a temptation to increase backward linkages using local content laws, which implies replacing some imported inputs with costlier domestic ones. As with all protection, resources are pulled into activities in which they do not have a comparative advantage. Alternatively, local entrepreneurs could develop these inputs to become more productive as they acquire new technology and skills or learn by doing. Other positive spillovers from these linkages, such as increased managerial skills and experience, could also raise the productivity of other sectors. For these reasons, adopting local content laws has become widespread in Africa, and ubiquitous in the oil and natural gas sector.

But there are problems associated with local content laws. For one thing, many are too vague to be workable. In the end, governments may be well advised to focus on developing the conditions for improved procurement rather than mandating them. This could entail improving business conditions, such as better power and transportation infrastructure, access to finance, and regulatory reforms to spur competition to better stimulate linkages between the opening of a large-scale mine and the economy of mining communities as well as those located nearby.

Broadly, it is clear that most benefits from extractives in an African context are likely to be fiscal and national. But the empirical evidence shows that the size of resource-related intergovernmental transfers to local communities has so far been modest. Even so, considerable potential exists to improve welfare at the local level through larger transfers that can support investment in much-needed infrastructure and the development of human capital. By improving worker productivity, the public sector can help strengthen the impact of market forces unleashed by extractive activities. It will also help diversify the local economy, which will be important in sustaining growth after a large-scale mining boom ends.

Both nationally and locally, the quality of governance and its influence on how resource revenues are used will be key determinants of the welfare impacts of natural resources. Enhancing the capacity of local jurisdictions—that is, both bureaucrats and policy makers—to deliver public spending programs needs to be high on the policy agenda. More research is needed to understand the main technical and political constraints facing local governments, their effect on the ability of communities to benefit from revenue windfalls, and the best policies to alleviate them.

All change in an economy brings both costs and benefits, and gainers and losers. So it is with gold mining. There is little evidence of economic decline from gold mining at the local level in the three case study countries, but negative externalities such as pollution can affect communities close to gold mines.

The impacts in some cases are evident over a long time, and even after a mining boom is over. While the national benefits most likely outweigh these costs, the negative externalities need to be fully understood, minimized, and managed.

Realizing a brighter vision for Africa's future will require a clearer understanding of how to benefit from its endowment of natural resources. Meeting the natural resource extraction challenge in all of its dimensions (governance, economic, and social), as well as understanding the forces that created the challenge, can open channels toward better outcomes and prospects for local communities.

Notes

1. Migrant communities may be economically and politically weaker and have less access to health services and infrastructure.
2. Data are available on mining employment from the Ghana Living Standards Survey data set.
3. Chuhan-Pole et al. (2015) find that, using Ghana Living Standards Survey data, women are 7.4 to 10.4 percentage points more likely to work in services or sales if they live close to a mine, and 2.5 to 2.6 percentage points more likely to work in mining.
4. However, the insignificant point estimates indicate that men might be shifting toward service sector employment and manual work.

References

Aragón, Fernando M., and Juan Pablo Rud. 2013. "Natural Resources and Local Communities: Evidence from a Peruvian Gold Mine." *American Economic Journal: Economic Policy* 5 (2): 1–25.

———. 2015. "Polluting Industries and Agricultural Productivity: Evidence from Mining in Ghana." *Economic Journal.* doi.10.1111/ecoj.12244.

Aragón, Fernando M., Punam Chuhan-Pole, and Bryan Christopher Land. 2015. "The Local Economic Impacts of Resource Abundance: What Have We Learned?" Policy Research Working Paper 7263, World Bank, Washington, DC.

Barma, Naazneen H., Kai Kaiser, Tuan Minh Le, and Lorena Viñuela. 2012. *Rent to Riches? The Political Economy of Natural Resource-Led Development.* Washington, DC: World Bank.

Beegle, Kathleen, Luc Christiaensen, Andrew Dabalen, and Isis Gaddi. 2016. *Poverty in a Rising Africa.* Washington, DC: World Bank.

Card, David, and Alan B. Krueger. 1994. "Minimum Wages and Employment: A Case Study of the Fast-Food Industry in New Jersey and Pennsylvania." *American Economic Review* 84 (4): 772–93.

Christiaensen, Luc, Punam Chuhan-Pole, and Aly Sanoh. 2013. "Africa's Growth, Poverty and Inequality Nexus: Fostering Shared Prosperity." Unpublished. https://editorialexpress.com/cgi-bin/conference/download.cgi?db_name=CSAE2014&paper_id=381.

Chuhan-Pole, P., A. Dabalen, A. Kotsadam, A. Sanoh, and A. Tolonen. 2015. "The Local Socioeconomic Effects of Gold Mining: Evidence from Ghana." Policy Research Working Paper 7250, World Bank, Washington, DC.

Devarajan, Shantayanan, and Wolfgang Fengler. 2013. "Africa's Economic Boom: Why the Pessimists and Optimists Are Both Right." *Foreign Affairs*. May/June.

European Union. 2008. *Mining Sector Support Programme: Environmental Impact Assessment*, vol. 1. European Union.

Ghosh Banerjee, S., Zayra Romo, Gary McMahon, and others. 2015. *The Power of the Mine: A Transformative Opportunity for Sub-Saharan Africa*. Washington, DC: World Bank.

Sanjay et al. 2015. Socio-economic and Health Implications of Mercury Use in Artisanal and Small-scale Gold Mining. Unpublished manuscript.

Sanoh, A., and M. Coulibaly. 2015. "The Socioeconomic Impact of Large-Scale Gold Mining in Mali." Unpublished, World Bank, Washington, DC.

Tolonen, A. 2015. "Local Industrial Shocks, Female Empowerment and Infant Health: Evidence from Africa's Gold Mining Industry." Unpublished.

UNDP (United Nations Development Programme). 2014. *Human Development Report 2014*. New York: UNDP.

von der Goltz, Jan, and Prabhat Barnwal. 2014. "Mines: The Local Welfare Effects of Mineral Mining in Developing Countries." Department of Economics Discussion Paper Series, Columbia University, New York.

Chapter 2

Local Impacts of Resource Abundance: What Have We Learned?

Introduction

A well-developed academic literature examines the socioeconomic impacts of resource abundance, especially at the country level. The focus has been on whether natural resource abundance is bad for economic development—the natural resource curse. Aragón, Chuhan-Pole, and Land (2015) systematically review the evidence and theoretical arguments behind the resource curse, along with other impacts at the country level.[1] In this chapter, we develop a simple analytical framework to understand how resource booms affect local communities. The framework identifies four ways in which this can have a local economic impact—specialization in the resource sector and reallocation of inputs away from tradable sectors such as manufacturing; the market channel of increased demand for local labor, goods, and services; the fiscal channel of increased public spending on local services through the taxation of natural resource wealth; and negative production externalities such as environmental pollution.

This analysis highlights the importance of the market compared with fiscal mechanisms to create positive impacts, and shows that the channel through which resource rents reach a local community matters. This chapter also underscores the importance of local institutions for the effectiveness of the fiscal channel in creating beneficial impacts, because resource wealth creates rents—and often very large ones—that can be easily appropriated when institutions are weak.

Available empirical evidence on the impact of resource abundance on local growth, employment, and living standards is examined to better understand the importance of these different mechanisms. Similar to recent country-level findings, the evidence suggests that a local resource curse is not inevitable, and that in some cases extractive activity has lifted local growth. It also supports the importance of the channel through which resource rents are distributed. When these are distributed using public channels, a resource windfall does not seem to improve welfare. But when resource rents reach a local community through the market channel, some positive effects may occur. More research is needed to see whether developing local supply chain linkages is more effective in improving local living standards than sharing revenue windfalls with local governments when institutions are weak. Despite the paucity of empirical evidence, especially for developing countries, the emerging literature is opening new ways of looking at the relationship between natural resources and economic development.

Theory and Evidence on the Impact of Resource Abundance at the Country Level

The literature on the economic impact of natural resources in developing countries is largely dominated by the phenomenon that some resource-rich economies tend to perform worse than resource-poor ones; that is, they are afflicted by the resource curse.[2] Examples abound of poor outcomes in countries with abundant natural wealth. For instance, Nigeria's oil revenues increased almost tenfold between 1965 and 2000, but real income stagnated and poverty and inequality increased (van der Ploeg 2011). Similarly, Venezuela, a primary beneficiary of increases in oil prices in the 1970s, suffered a steep decline in output per capita of 28 percent from 1970 to 1990 (Lane and Tornell 1996). In Zambia, Africa's largest copper exporter, the incidence of poverty remained virtually unchanged, at 60 percent, during 2000–10, despite a doubling of economic output. There are exceptions to the resource curse—notably, Botswana, Chile, and Norway, all of which were successful in transforming their resource wealth into economic prosperity. Moreover, resource-abundant countries such as Canada, Sweden, and the United States, which are now high-income countries, were long ago able to diversify their economies and reduce their dependence on natural resources.

Analytical Underpinnings of the Negative Impact of Resource Abundance

Theoretical explanations for the resource curse can be grouped into three broad categories. First, a boom in extractive industries can crowd out other industries, such as manufacturing, that are more conducive to long-term economic growth—the Dutch disease argument. Second, dependence on primary sectors could leave an economy vulnerable to changes in commodity prices, which may be more volatile. And third, the windfall from natural resources can exacerbate rent seeking, corruption, and conflict in a society. These phenomena can lead to bad economic policies, the deterioration of institutions, and lower income and growth. We now look in more detail at the three categories of explanations for the resource curse.

Dutch disease. This provides one of the earliest explanations of the linkage between resource abundance and lower economic growth (Corden 1984; Corden and Neary 1982). Dutch disease models typically assume that an economy produces traded goods (manufacturing) and nontraded goods (services). In these models, a boom in natural resource exports represents an income windfall that increases aggregate demand and raises the price of nontraded goods relative to traded goods.[3] In the short run, this relative price movement, which is effectively an appreciation of the real exchange rate,[4] causes the output of the nontraded sector to expand, while the traded sector contracts and factors of production such as labor and capital reallocate from the traded sector to the nontraded sector. The effect on the wage-rent ratio depends on the labor intensity of the nontraded industry. In particular, if this industry were more labor intensive, the wage-rent ratio would increase.[5]

This market response to a revenue windfall is not by itself negative. To explain why resource booms can weigh down economic growth, one needs to assume that the traded sector, crowded out by extractive industries, is somehow more conducive to supporting growth. This would be the case if the traded sector benefits most from learning by doing and other positive externalities, such as human capital externalities (Krugman 1987; Matsuyama 1992; Sachs and Warner 1995; Torvik 2001). If the traded sector exhibits increasing returns to scale, as in big push models (Murphy, Shleifer, and Vishny 1989), then a shift of resources away from this sector could also be detrimental to growth.

Exposure to changes in commodity prices. A second argument for the negative effect of resource abundance on growth relies on the observed pattern of higher volatility and, until early 2000, the long-term decline of commodity prices. Thus, natural resource exporters may be exposed to higher terms-of-trade volatility. The uncertainty stemming from this could, in turn, reduce investment in physical or human capital.[6] If technological progress is assumed to be driven by learning by doing or human capital externalities, then the decline of investment associated with price volatility can constrain economic growth. In resource-exporting countries, fiscal revenue is often heavily dependent on resource revenue. For example, Angola, the Republic of Congo, and Equatorial Guinea rely on oil for about 75 percent of government revenues. Price volatility and associated boom/bust cycles can make it more difficult to implement prudent fiscal policies.

Rent seeking, corruption, and conflict. Political economy channels for explaining poor development outcomes in resource-rich countries is receiving increasing attention. This is because resource abundance, as noted earlier, creates rents that can be easily appropriated when institutions are weak. In the absence of strong institutions, resource rents may foster rent-seeking behavior, increase corruption, erode the quality of institutions, and, in extreme cases, even generate violent conflict.

Aragón, Chuhan-Pole, and Land (2015) identify at least five political economy channels in the literature through which resources can hinder economic
growth and welfare. First, resource abundance may increase rent seeking—for
example, the appropriation of resource rents via production taxes or other
transfers—and reduce net return to investments, which lead to lower growth
(Lane and Tornell 1996; Tornell and Lane 1999). Second, resource windfalls
can attract entrepreneurial skills away from productive activities to more
profitable but socially inefficient rent seeking (Mehlum, Moene, and Torvik
2006; Torvik 2001). Third, rent-grabbing possibilities can increase political
corruption (Brollo et al. 2013), and undermine the development of democratic
institutions (Ross 2001). With additional revenues, politicians can appropriate
rents, while increasing spending to appease voters. The increased opportunities for grabbing rents, in turn, attract other corrupt individuals to the political
arena, leading to a deterioration in the quality of politicians. The high reliance
of budgetary revenue on natural resources, as opposed to the taxation of citi-
zens, also weakens government incentives to build or strengthen institutions
of accountability. Fourth, resource booms can increase the returns to preda-
tion and promote rapacity over these resources, which can fuel violence and
civil conflict (Collier and Hoeffler 2005; Grossman 1999; Hirshleifer 1991).
Conflict can have adverse consequences for a country's capital stock and
investment, reversing development gains and weakening state capacity. But
resource booms do not necessarily increase violence. Dal Bó and Dal Bó
(2011) argue that resource booms could reduce violence if they raise the
opportunity cost of participating in violence—for example, by increasing the
returns from productive activity. And fifth, ethnic differences allow the formation of stable coalitions, which can facilitate resource-fueled conflict (Caselli
and Coleman 2013).

Country-Level Evidence of the Natural Resource Curse
Several studies systematically examine the empirical evidence on the resource
curse. Early analyses from a cross-section of countries found a negative association between resource abundance (measured as the relative size of primary
exports) and gross domestic product growth (Gylfason, Herbertsson, and Zoega
1999; Leite and Weidmann 1999; Sachs and Warner 1995, 2001; Sala-i-Martin
1997). Recent empirical studies (Lederman and Maloney 2007, 2008), however,
find that evidence of the natural resource curse is far from conclusive.

One concern regards the robustness of the results to alternative specifica-
tions and measures of resource abundance. A fundamental critique offered is
that the measure of resource abundance (usually the relative size of commodity
exports) is endogenous. For instance, other confounding factors, such as the
quality of institutions, may affect the growth and size of commodity exports. In
that case, the resource curse would just reflect the fact that countries with bad

institutions have lower growth and are less industrialized, and therefore are more dependent on primary sectors. For instance, Sala-i-Martin and Subramanian (2003) and Bulte, Damania, and Deacon (2005) find that when adding measures of institutions as additional controls, the relation between resource abundance and growth disappears. Brunnschweiler (2008) and Brunnschweiler and Bulte (2008) go a step further by arguing that the usual measures of resource abundance are actually a measure of resource dependence. They treat this variable as endogenous, and find that the negative relation between resource dependence and growth disappears.

One possibility emerging from the empirical literature is that the effects of resource abundance on growth may be heterogeneous, and could depend on the quality of institutions. For instance, the effect could be negative in a country with bad institutions, but positive where institutions are good (Robinson, Torvik, and Verdier 2006). Failing to account for this heterogeneity may lead to the wrong conclusion that the effect is insignificant.

Political Economy Explanations for the Resource Curse

The cross-country empirical evidence points to the relevance of institutions, though it offers mixed support for Dutch disease and terms-of-trade volatility as explanations for the resource curse. This suggests that rent seeking and worsening governance play an important role in explaining the resource curse.

Three sets of results point to the importance of institutions in understanding the natural resource curse. The first suggests that the resource curse may be associated with "point source" resources. These are resources such as oil, minerals, and plantation crops whose production is concentrated in a few geographic or economic areas. This concentration makes it easier for interest groups to control and capture rents. For instance, Isham et al. (2005) and Bulte, Damania, and Deacon (2005) find that point source resources are associated with weaker political institutions and lower growth. Boschini, Pettersson, and Roine (2007) extend this analysis by interacting the type of resource with the quality of institutions. They find the combination of abundance of point source resources with low-quality institutions is detrimental for economic growth.

The second set of results suggests that resource abundance is associated with an increase in corruption, deterioration of democracy, and armed conflict, especially in countries with weak democratic institutions. These results are consistent with the rent-seeking explanation of the resource curse. For instance, Ades and Di Tella (1999), using a cross-section of countries, find that natural resource wealth is negatively correlated with subjective measures of political corruption. Bhattacharyya and Hodler (2010), using panel data for countries, find that natural resource abundance is associated with perceived corruption only in countries with a history of nondemocratic rule. They interpret this as evidence that resource rents lead to corruption if the quality of democratic institutions is poor. Tsui (2011) uses panel data for countries and oil discoveries to show that oil discoveries reduce the quality of democratic institutions, but only in already-nondemocratic regimes. Oil does not seem to affect institutions in countries with established democracies. A large body of cross-country evidence points to a positive relation between resource abundance and violent conflict (Collier, Hoeffler, and Söderbom 2004; Fearon 2005; Fearon and Laitin 2003; Humphreys 2005; Lujala 2010; Ross 2004). This relation seems to be driven by point source resources, such as oil, diamonds, and narcotics. These results, however, may not be robust to including country fixed effects, which account for several time-invariant unobserved omitted variables. For example, Cotet and Tsui (2013), using panel data for countries and including country fixed effects, fail to find a significant effect of oil discoveries (large and small) on conflict. But nonlinearities in the relation between resource abundance and conflict might exist because, using a similar approach, Lei and Michaels (2011) find a positive relation between large oil discoveries and conflict.

The third set of results suggests that a negative relation between resource abundance and growth is present only in countries with bad institutions. In an influential paper, Mehlum, Moene, and Torvik (2006) show the evidence for the resource curse is essentially driven by countries with low-quality institutions; in countries with high-quality institutions, resource abundance does not affect growth. Similar results are obtained by Collier and Hoeffler (2009), who define poor-quality institutions as those lacking strong checks and balances; and Boschini, Pettersson, and Roine (2007), who find the resource curse is present only in countries with low-quality institutions and easily appropriable resources, such as precious minerals and diamonds.

Insights from the Country-Level Literature

Three conclusions emerge from the literature examining the impact of natural resource abundance at the national level. First, natural resources, by themselves, do not seem to be bad for economic growth. But they become a problem in the absence of good institutions. Second, the problem is bigger for some types of resources that are easily appropriated, such as oil, minerals, and diamonds. And third, deindustrialization and price volatility may also matter, but not as much as initially believed. We now discuss these conclusions in greater detail.

At the country level, the policy implications that flow from these insights relate to savings and investment of resource rents and macroeconomic measures to address commodity price volatility. The country-level empirical evidence, however, suggests that the main challenge is not to identify the right policies but to encourage the development of societies that are willing or able to adopt them. Hence, the main policy recommendation from this literature is that resource-rich countries should improve their institutions to make the best use of a resource boom and avoid its deleterious effects. This is consistent with several efforts to improve governance in resource-rich economies and to understand how to build durable and effective institutions. This recommendation is consistent with the vast literature in development economics that highlights the importance of institutions—especially the ones that improve property rights—for economic development (Acemoglu, Johnson, and Robinson 2005; Acemoglu, Robinson, and Woren 2012; Nunn 2009).

The use of country-level data has significantly advanced our knowledge about the impact of resource abundance. This literature, however, has several limitations. There are still relevant concerns over the causal interpretation of results, and the presence of omitted variables, reverse causality, and measurement errors are important empirical challenges. Scholars have tried to address them by including a richer set of covariates, exploiting panel data sets, and using instrumental variables. But these solutions still fall short relative to the experimental and quasi-experimental approaches currently used in applied economics.

The positive or negative impacts of resource abundance are unlikely to be uniformly distributed in a country. For instance, many negative spillovers, such as pollution and population displacement, have a local geographic scope, and the distribution of resource rents usually targets certain populations. Similarly, the impact of the demand by extractive industries for inputs may be felt more intensively in specific local markets. These local phenomena cannot be studied by looking at cross-country variations.

The main policy implication of all this—that countries need to improve institutions to benefit from a resource boom—may only offer limited practical policy insights. An unsolved question is what stakeholders—such as extractive firms, local communities, and funding agencies—can do short of fostering institutional reform to ameliorate the negative effects of resource abundance and enhance its potential benefits. Exploring the local impacts of resource abundance may shed some light on this question.

Assessing the Local Impacts of Resource Abundance

Attention is increasingly turning to analyzing the impact of resource windfalls on local communities where these resources are sourced. In contrast to the country-level literature, which focuses on the country as a unit of observation, the focus on subnational units such as states, counties, or municipalities has improved the empirical strategy for assessing the impact of resource booms by exploiting variations *within a country*. However, new empirical challenges need to be taken into account, in particular confounding changes in prices and population that may affect the interpretation of results.

Analytical Framework

The economic literature suggests at least four possible ways to analyze the local economic impact of natural resource booms. One is to analyze resource abundance as a change in local endowments, leading to specialization in primary sectors and corresponding changes in relative prices at the expense of other traded sectors, such as agriculture and manufacturing—in effect, a local Dutch disease. Another is to consider natural resources as a source of fiscal revenue for local communities, so that a resource boom translates into a fiscal revenue windfall. This fiscal channel is at the center of the country-level literature. A more novel approach relies on viewing resource booms as an increase in the demand for local goods and inputs; that is, a positive demand shock. There are also the impacts of resource abundance on local environmental and social conditions, such as pollution, which have started to receive empirical attention.

Resource Endowments and Specialization

If we treat local areas as small open economies, we can study the change in endowments within the framework of the standard Hecksher-Ohlin model of international trade. Specialization in the primary sector involves an increase in input prices such as wages, prompting a reallocation of inputs. In turn, this increases the cost and price of nontraded goods relative to traded goods. If traded sectors experience faster productivity gains, then specialization in natural resources would hinder long-term economic growth and local income, assuming the population is fixed. A schematic of this model is presented in annex figure 2A.1. Predictions from models incorporating this specialization mechanism can be tested empirically: a change in relative prices, with the price of nontraded goods rising relative to traded goods; a reduction in the local size of industries producing nationally traded goods—for example, measured by employment shares, share in wage bills, or share in local income; and a negative impact on local economic growth and income.

Local Fiscal Revenue Windfall

Natural resources can be considered a source of fiscal revenue for local communities; that is, a fiscal revenue windfall. This windfall eases the hard budget constraint of local governments and supports higher public spending. The revenue windfall could have both positive and negative effects on economic welfare. Figure 2.1 presents an analytical framework of the transmission channels and the impact on local outcomes. As long as the windfall is used to improve the quantity or quality of local public goods and services, such as roads, hospital, schools, and housing, the potential is there to improve welfare outcomes, such as in health and education.

Moreover, to the extent that public goods are productive inputs or create positive spillovers, as in the case of transportation infrastructure, a resource boom could also increase local income and growth. The positive effect of fiscal

Figure 2.1 Effects of a Fiscal Revenue Windfall

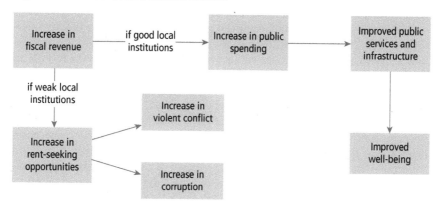

revenue windfalls is underpinned by several assumptions: local politicians are responsive to the broad population, which requires well-functioning local institutions and a healthy degree of political competition (Besley and Burgess 2002),[7] and local bureaucracies have the technical capacity to provide those public goods and services. Lack of responsiveness from local politicians to demands from the broad population, or lack of technical capacities among local bureaucrats, may undermine the positive effect of fiscal revenue windfalls on the provision of public goods and local living conditions.

At the local level, a vast literature suggests that clientelism and vote buying are important distortions. Clientelism refers to transfers made by a political elite to a narrow group of poor or disadvantaged voters to secure their votes and maintain political power. Evidence shows this targeted redistribution may cause a deterioration in the provision of public goods.[8] For instance, Khemani (2013) documents a negative relation between vote buying in the Philippines and the delivery of primary health services. A case study of local governments in rural Maharashtra shows that clientelism may lead to poor governance, even in a context of free and fair elections and active political competition (Anderson, Francois, and Kotwal 2015).[9]

The "rapacity" and "opportunity cost" effects, which are discussed in the country-level literature on conflict, may also explain a failure of resource windfalls to be converted into welfare gains at the local level. Booms associated with "point" resources such as oil and gold (as distinct from "dispersed" resources) may be more prone to generate a rapacity effect, since they mostly increase appropriable rents, but may have a relatively smaller impact on local wages.[10] The literature also indicates that an absence of adequate reallocation and compensation policies amid competition for scarce resources will have negative redistributional consequences and can lead to conflict.

The fiscal revenue windfall channel highlights the importance of local institutions, especially political institutions and fiscal decentralization arrangements. These institutions are the subject of increased attention in the local-level literature. The theoretical political economy literature has emphasized the importance of political institutions, such as electoral rules and the form of government (Lizzeri and Persico 2001; Persson 2002). Subnational evidence is consistent with these predictions. For instance, Besley and Case (2003) find that different political institutions between U.S. states—such as voter registration procedures, use of primaries, restrictions on campaign contributions, and supermajority requirements—affect the degree of political competition and representativeness of elected authorities. In turn, this translates into differences in spending and taxation. Pande (2003) finds that political reservation in India—where some seats in state legislatures are reserved to candidates from minority castes—affects the size of public transfers to some disadvantaged groups. Zhang et al. (2004) find that the use of elections to select local authorities in China (instead of appointment by the central government) was more conductive to a better allocation of public expenditures. Similarly, Besley and Coate (2003) find that elected utility regulators implement more proconsumer policies than appointed ones.

A second set of institutions includes fiscal decentralization arrangements. These are rules that define how fiscal revenue will be collected, distributed, and used at the subnational level. The literature on fiscal decentralization is discussed in more detail in a later section on the role of institutions at the local level.

Local Demand Shock
A resource boom can represent an increase in demand for local goods and inputs (Aragón and Rud 2013). A positive demand shock is plausible in contexts in which extractive industries use locally supplied inputs, such as labor or intermediate materials. Note that a similar effect could occur if the rents of extractive industries are transferred directly to the local population. Think of this as a direct dividend. Examples of this are the impact benefit agreements in Canada and the permanent fund dividend in Alaska. The extent of the economic linkages of extractive activities determines the size of the local demand shock. It should be noted, however, that strong backward linkages cannot be assumed in all contexts.

A useful framework for examining the general equilibrium effect of such localized demand shocks is provided by models of spatial equilibrium, which are increasingly used to analyze local housing and labor markets. One commonly used model is the Rosen-Roback framework, in which a country is made up of several cities or local economies, and every local economy produces a single internationally traded good using labor, land, and a local amenity. Labor is homogenous and in infinite supply, while land is in fixed supply and immobile. A resource boom would mostly benefit owners of immobile factors, and real wages are equalized across locations. Figure 2.2 shows a framework for understanding how this positive demand shock impacts local outcomes.

Extending this framework to incorporate an upward-sloping supply curve for both labor and land or housing (Greenstone, Hornbeck, and Moretti 2010; Moretti 2011) yields more nuanced effects for a local demand shock. A positive shock in local demand for labor would initially increase nominal wages. This, in turn, would attract workers from other cities, pushing down wages and increasing housing costs. The net effect, however, depends on the elasticity of

Figure 2.2 Effects of a Local Demand Shock

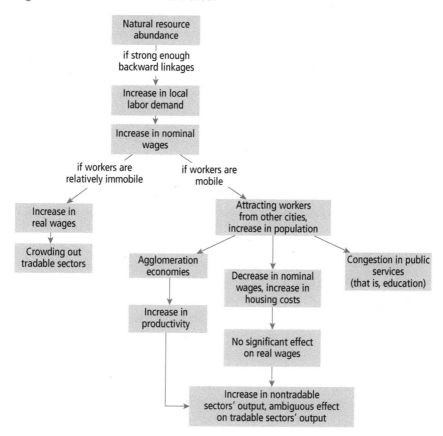

supply of both labor and housing. Thus, the demand shock can lead to an increase in real wages and the welfare of workers. Under certain conditions—for example, if workers in different industries are substitutable—wider positive spillovers are also possible.

Spatial equilibrium models suggest that local demand shocks attract workers and increase the local population. But this may well also increase congestion and create additional pressure on local services, such as education and health. Yet, population growth can also generate positive effects from agglomeration economies—gains in productivity associated with the clustering of economic activity. A growing body of evidence, mostly from the United States, suggests the size of agglomeration economies in manufacturing and high-tech industries is not trivial.[11] However, there is little evidence on the size of agglomeration economies generated by extractive industries. Agglomeration effects are explored by Fafchamps, Koelle, and Shilpi (2015) on the contribution of gold mining to proto-urbanization in Ghana, which draws on central place theory.

Spatial equilibrium models also suggest heterogeneous effects across tradable and nontradable sectors. In particular, Moretti (2011) predicts that demand shock will mostly benefit the nontradable sector, such as services. The effect on tradable sectors is ambiguous, and may be negative due to the increase in wages and land rents. But a beneficial effect may arise from increasing agglomeration economies associated with larger populations. It is therefore not clear whether a resource boom encourages or crowds out manufacturing, and therefore contrasts with the standard Dutch disease argument, which would predict deindustrialization.

Thus, a spatial-equilibrium-type framework for examining the effect of localized demand shocks predicts several impacts of a resource boom if there are strong backward linkages:

- Resource booms have a positive effect on nominal wages and labor outcomes, such as participation rate, number of hours worked, or employment rates.
- Resource booms can increase real wages and real incomes of local populations, and lower the incidence of poverty.
- Positive spillovers may occur in industries not directly linked to the extractive activity and surrounding localities.
- Resource booms may be associated with the migration of workers and an increase in the prices of nontraded goods, such as housing.

These predictions have important implications for empirical analysis. One is that migration induced by a resource boom may change the spatial distribution of a population's productivity. This could happen, for instance, if high-productivity workers benefit from the boom or face lower migration costs, or if low-productivity workers are displaced from resource-rich areas. The worry is that an increase in local real incomes would just reflect changes in the composition of populations and not real improvements in economic well-being. The importance of these compositional effects is case specific.[12]

While this framework predicts a possible positive impact of resource booms on real income, it is less clear what the effect would be on other measures of well-being, such as education and health. These outcomes could improve due to an income effect. Also, if the resource boom is biased toward high-skilled workers, it could increase the returns to education. But the increase in wages could also increase the opportunity cost of education and discourage educational attainment (Atkin 2012). A similar effect could occur if the extractive industry demands low-skilled workers, thus reducing the skill premium. An added consideration for health is that environmental pollution can reduce or offset the benefits from higher income.

However, the literature on country case studies amply highlights that extractive industries in less developed and remote settings are associated with limited local hiring, procurement, product sales, and distribution of profit, especially if large-scale and foreign owned. In the policy arena, the central pillar of the Africa Mining Vision of 2009 is the aspiration to move mining out of the enclave and into a more locally integrated form of socioeconomic development.

Negative Externalities

Mining and mineral processing are associated with several types of negative externalities affecting local community welfare. For instance, these activities often generate significant amounts of air pollutants, such as dust from blasting and earth-moving operations, fumes from smelters and refineries, and the engines of heavy machinery. If toxic emissions are quite large, they can deposit on the ground as acid rain, which contributes to environmental degradation (Menz and Seip 2004). Extractive activities also release industry-specific pollutants—such as cyanide, sulfuric acid, mercury, heavy metals, and acidic drainages (Dudka and Adriano 1997; Salomons 1995)—which also contribute to the negative, cumulative effects on the quality of soil and water sources. Similarly, small-scale and artisanal mining operations can pollute the air and water. The most notorious example is pollution from mercury used in gold amalgamation.

Environmental pollution can adversely impact health (Currie et al. 2013; Graff-Zivin and Neidell 2013) and, more broadly, labor supply and productivity (Graff-Zivin and Neidell 2012; Hanna and Oliva 2011). There is evidence that pollution adversely affects cognitive outcomes and educational attainment (Almond, Edlund, and Palme 2009; Lavy, Ebenstein, and Roth 2012) and increases school absenteeism (Currie et al. 2009; Gilliland et al. 2001; Park et al. 2002; Ransom and Pope 1992).

Loss of agricultural productivity is another important pollution externality (Aragón and Rud 2015), and recent literature has examined the mechanisms through which this takes place. One is by directly affecting crop health and growth (Heck et al. 1982; Miller 1988; Marshall, Ashmore, and Hinchcliffe 1997), which translates into lower yields. Another is by degrading the quality of key agricultural inputs, such as soil and water (EPA 2012; Menz and Seip 2004). For instance, deposition of air pollutants in the form of acid rain can lead to soil degradation. The increased acidity leaches nutrients from the soil, reduces the ability of plants to absorb remaining nutrients, and releases toxic metals such as aluminum. Air pollution can reduce labor productivity in general (Chang et al. 2014; Graff-Zivin and Neidell 2012). The loss of agricultural productivity can have a negative impact on agricultural output, which affects the incomes of farmers and rural populations. This externality is particularly relevant when extractive industries are located in the vicinity of rural areas where agriculture remains an important source of livelihood.

Figure 2.3 presents the framework for understanding the negative externalities of environmental pollution from mining. This framework has several implications for empirical analysis. It suggests that examining the effect of resource booms on nonincome measures of well-being, such as indicators of human health (mortality rate and incidence of illness), would be worthwhile. It points to other possible outcomes, such as worker productivity, labor supply, and agricultural output. It also emphasizes the loss of agricultural productivity, through which resource booms could negatively affect local incomes, especially in rural areas.

Figure 2.3 Negative Externalities of Environmental Pollution

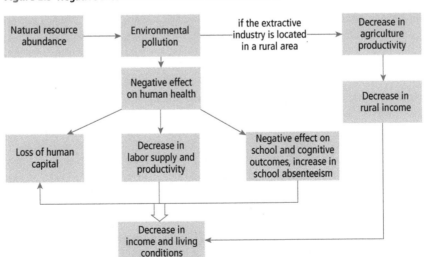

Empirical Evidence on Mining's Local Impacts

In contrast to the country-level literature, the empirical literature exploiting within-country variation is more recent and less developed. A growing number of studies are nevertheless expanding this literature, which is reviewed by Aragón, Chuhan-Pole, and Land (2015). Broadly, it focuses on the impact of resource abundance on growth, employment and local living standards, corruption and conflict, and pollution.

Impact on Growth

Using a cross-section of subnational data from the United States, several studies have replicated the growth regressions used in the cross-country literature (Douglas and Walker 2013; James and Aadland 2011; Papyrakis and Gerlagh 2007). Similarly, Zuo and Schieffer (2014) examine the impact of resource abundance on growth using data from Chinese provinces. For the most part, these studies detect a local resource curse (table 2.1). However, it is difficult to interpret these results in a causal way because they suffer from the same limitations of omitted variable bias, reverse causality, and measurement error as country-level resource curse empirics.

Impact on Employment and Local Living Standards

In a shift away from the cross-country growth regressions, several studies treat resource booms and busts in developed resource-rich countries (Australia, Canada, and the United States) as shocks to the local demand of labor and examined the resulting economic spillovers (table 2.2).[13] These studies show that booms in coal mining, oil, and natural gas generate positive employment spillovers—that is, an increase in jobs and nominal wages in other industries—in

Table 2.1 Empirical Evidence of the Impact of Resource Abundance on Local Growth

Paper	Explanatory variable	Outcome variable	Sign	Country, data level	Identification strategy
Douglas and Walker (2013)	Share of coal revenue in total county personal income		−	United States, county level	Cross-sectional OLS
James and Aadland (2011)	Share of earnings in resource-extraction industries		−	United States, county level	Cross-sectional OLS
Papyrakis and Gerlagh (2007)	Share of primary sector in local GDP	Income growth rate	−	United States, state level	Cross-sectional OLS
Zuo and Jack (2014)	Provincial annual energy production per capita, or provincial annual energy production, or ratio of regional energy production to GDP		−	China, province level	Fixed-effect panel model

Source: Aragón, Chuhan-Pole, and Land 2015.
Note: − = a negative relation; OLS = ordinary least squares.

Table 2.2 Empirical Evidence of the Impact of Resource Abundance on Local Living Standards

Paper	Explanatory variable	Outcome variable	Sign	Country, data Level	Identification strategy
Allcott and Keniston (2014)	Whether the county produces any oil or gas in any year after 1969	Income growth rate, wages	+	United States., county level	Difference-in-differences
		Manufacturing employment and output	+		
		Factor productivity	0		
Aragón and Rud (2014)	Gold mine production	Household income	+	Peru, household level	Difference-in-differences
	Mining transfer	Municipality revenues and expenditures	+		
		Household income	0		
Black et al. (2005)	Whether the county is the coal boom county	Employment and wages	+	United States, county level	Instrumental variables
Caselli and Michaels (2013)	Oil output	Local government revenues	+	Brazil, municipality level	Instrumental variables
		Local government spending	+		
		Local public service	0		
		Household income	0		
Fleming and Measham (2014)	Indicator of having a coal seam gas operation	Income growth, employment	+	Australia, individual level	Cross-sectional OLS
Jacobsen and Baker (2016)	Whether the county is the oil and gas boom county	Nominal income, wages, employment, and population	+	United States, county level	Fixed effect panel model
		Manufacturing employment	0		
Kotsadam and Tolonen (2014)	Mine openings	Service sector employment	+	Sub-Saharan Africa, individual level	Difference-in-differences
		Agriculture employment	−		
		Women: service sector employment	+		
		Men: skilled manual jobs employment	+		
	Mine closings	Women: agriculture employment	0		
		Men: agriculture employment	+		
Loayza et al. (2013)	Mining production	Household consumption, literacy	+	Peru, district level	Matching and propensity score
		Poverty rate	−		
		Consumption inequality	+		
Marchand (2012)	Indicator of getting 10% or more of their total earnings from the energy extraction sector	Employment and earnings	+	Canada, census subdivision level	Difference-in-differences

(continued next page)

Table 2.2 (continued)

Paper	Explanatory variable	Outcome variable	Sign	Country, data Level	Identification strategy
Michaels (2011)	Indicator of whether the county is located above an oil field or part of an oil field (or multiple oil fields) that contained at least 100 million barrels of oil before any oil was extracted	Employment share of mining	+	United States, county level	Fixed-effect panel model
		Employment share of agriculture	−		
		Employment share of manufacturing	0		
		Stock of educated workers	+		
		Nominal income	+		

Source: Aragón, Chuhan-Pole, and Land 2015.
Note: + = positive relation; − = negative relation; 0 = statistically insignificant; OLS = ordinary least squares.

the short term. But they provide less clarity on the crowding-out of local manufacturing, with some documenting a reduction in the relative size of manufacturing and others finding evidence of increased manufacturing activity. This points to resource booms generating possible agglomeration effects (increase in the size of local markets) that benefit local manufacturing. Another limitation of these studies is that they do not examine the effects on real income and other measures of well-being.

Whether the local effects of resource booms carry over to less developed countries is being addressed by a limited but growing literature. The analytical framework for local demand shocks suggests that the economic effects at the local level depend on several context-specific factors, such as the degree of economic linkages of extractive activities, which determine the size of the local demand shock, substitutability of labor among industries, and labor mobility.

Caselli and Michaels (2013) use municipality-level data to examine the local economic effect of oil-based fiscal windfalls in Brazil, and find that oil production is associated with an increase in oil royalties paid to local governments and in public spending. However, the impact on the provision of local public services is minimal. No significant improvement was found in housing quality or quantity, supply of educational or health inputs, or welfare receipts.[14] Oil production also had a negligible effect on household income and population size. These findings suggest that oil production has not been particularly beneficial for local populations because the extent of economic linkages between oil companies and local economies is limited in Brazil. Instead, circumstantial evidence suggests that oil revenues were used to fund patronage and extract rents, and were embezzled by officials. Using data from all municipalities (not only the recipients of oil royalties), Brollo et al. (2013) find that fiscal windfalls are indeed associated with an increase in political corruption.

Two studies have examined the impact of mining on local economies in Peru. Aragón and Rud (2013) analyze the importance of economic linkages in Yanacocha, a large gold mine in the Peruvian highlands. Using household-level microdata and a difference-in-differences approach, they find that backward linkages had a positive impact on real income and poverty reduction; and the benefits of the local demand shock extended to the local population not directly linked to mining, such as farmers and service workers. Similar to the findings of Caselli and Michaels (2013), Aragón and Rud find that the increased local revenue and public spending associated with a resource boom do not translate into higher household income. Using a rich data set at the district level, Loayza, Teran, and Rigolini (2013) find a positive relation between measures of living standards (such as poverty, consumption, and literacy) and mining production, but not with government transfers associated with mining tax revenue.[15] Findings from Brazil and Peru cast some doubt on the usefulness of revenue-sharing schemes as a policy instrument for local communities seeking to benefit from resource booms.

The more recent, though limited, literature on developing countries suggests that the presence of backward economic linkages from mining might play an important role in determining local economic outcomes.[16] But more research is needed to understand how revenue-sharing schemes can be an effective policy instrument for local communities seeking to benefit from resource booms.

In one of the few studies focusing on Africa, Kotsadam and Tolonen (2015) examine the effect of mining on local employment. They use a rich data set at the individual level for several Sub-Saharan African countries, and implement a difference-in-differences approach exploiting the opening and closure of mines. Their study finds that mine openings seem to create new employment opportunities outside agriculture and significant structural shifts. Interestingly, these effects are differentiated by gender. Women switch to service sectors, while men move to skilled manual jobs. Moreover, the participation rate of women decreases with mine openings, but it increases for men. These structural changes seem to persist after mine closures, at least for women. After a mine closure, men return to agricultural jobs, but women do not shift back to agricultural production; instead, they leave the labor force. The authors interpret these findings as evidence that mining works as a boom/bust economy at the local level in Africa, but with permanent (negative) effects on participation of women in the labor market.

Impact on Corruption and Conflict

A small but growing literature on within-country evidence linking resource booms to corruption and conflict is emerging (table 2.3). As discussed above, evidence from Brazil (Brollo et al. 2013; Caselli and Michaels 2013) suggests the fiscal revenue windfall associated with oil royalties has increased corruption

Table 2.3 Empirical Evidence of the Impact of Resource Abundance on Corruption and Conflict

Paper	Explanatory variable	Outcome variable	Sign	Country, data level	Identification strategy
Angrist and Kugler (2008)	Coca prices	Violent conflict	+	Colombia, individual level	Difference-in-differences
Brollo et al. (2013)	Oil royalty revenue	Political corruption	+	Brazil, municipality level	Regression discontinuity
		Quality of political candidates	–		
Dube and Vargas (2013)	Oil, coal, and gold prices	Conflict	+	Colombia, municipality level	Difference-in-differences
	International prices of agricultural products		–		
Monteiro and Ferraz (2010)	Oil royalty revenue	Incumbency advantage	+	Brazil, municipality level	Instrumental variables
		Public employment	+		
		Educational and health supply	0		
Vicente (2010)	Oil discovery announcements	Perceived vote buying and corruption on public services	+	Africa, individual level	Difference-in-differences

Source: Aragón, Chuhan-Pole, and Land 2015.
Note: + = positive relation; – = negative relation; 0 = statistically insignificant.

and rent seeking at the local level. A fiscal revenue windfall is also associated with changes in political outcomes. For example, Brollo et al. (2013) argue that an increase in revenues allows bad politicians to increase public spending, while diverting rents. This translates into higher reelection rates of incumbent politicians. Monteiro and Ferraz (2010) document a similar increase in incumbency advantage, but only in the short term.

Anticipation of a windfall could change political behavior even before resources are extracted. This could happen because anticipated rents (from future resource extraction) increase the value of political positions, and politicians immediately start competing for office to capture future rents. Vicente (2010) examines this in the context of São Tomé and Príncipe's announcement of oil discoveries, using microdata at the individual level with retrospective information on perceived corruption. The author finds that oil discovery announcements are associated with an increase in perceived vote buying and corruption across a range of public services, including customs, public procurement, state jobs, health care, and the police.

The empirical study of resource abundance vis-à-vis local conflict has focused on exploring two possible mechanisms, the opportunity cost and the rapacity effect, which have different implications for the effect of resource booms on conflict, depending on the type of resource being exploited. Resources that increase local wages, such as agricultural products, decrease conflict by affecting the opportunity cost of conflict. By contrast, resources that create appropriable rents, such as oil, diamonds, and minerals, may encourage conflict through a rapacity effect. Dube and Vargas (2013) provide convincing evidence of the importance of both opportunity and rapacity effects. Using municipality-level data from Colombia, they find that increases in oil, coal, and gold prices are associated with intensified conflict, while the opposite is true for increases in the international prices of agricultural products, such as coffee, banana, sugar, palm, and tobacco.

Impact on Pollution

A vast literature highlights the potential for mining and other extractive industries to pollute the environment. The negative effect of pollution on human health and, through that channel, on labor supply and labor productivity has also been documented in several studies (see the section on negative externalities). Despite these findings, empirical work directly examining the socioeconomic impacts of mining-related pollution is limited.

Recent work examining mining pollution points to localized impacts on health and education. Rau, Reyes, and Urzúa (2013) examine the impact on educational achievement of children living in proximity to a deposit of mineral waste with hazardous levels of lead and other heavy metals, in northern Chile.[17] These children were found to have higher concentrations of lead in their blood, and worse academic performance. The study estimates this translates into a significant loss of earnings in adulthood.[18] Von der Goltz and Barnwal (2014) examine the effect of mining on health outcomes using a rich micro-level data set from 44 countries and a difference-in-differences approach. They find suggestive evidence that mining is associated with an increase in stunting among women and anemia among children. The effects are localized in the vicinity of mines (that is, within 5 kilometers). Interestingly, these effects occur despite an increase in household wealth, spotlighting the trade-off between economic benefits and health costs that mining communities may face. These results are, however, not conclusive. In a related study, Tolonen (2016) finds that among African countries, the opening of gold mines significantly reduces infant mortality. This evidence suggests that, in some cases, the local economic benefits from mining may offset pernicious effects due to pollution.

The importance of a pollution externality (that is, loss of agricultural productivity) that may occur when potentially polluting industries are located in the vicinity of rural areas is well highlighted by Aragón and Rud (2015). Their study focuses on the effect of pollution on agriculture in the context of large-scale gold mining in Ghana. The authors find robust evidence that cumulative gold production (a measure of the stock of pollution) is associated with a significant reduction in agricultural productivity, with the effects concentrated closer to mines; that is, within a 20-kilometer radius and declining with distance.[19] This loss of productivity is associated with an increase in rural poverty. They rule out alternative explanations—such as mines competing for local inputs (and increasing input prices), or changes in the composition of the local population—that may occur in the presence of selective migration (table 2.4).

Insights on Impacts at the Local Level

Although the literature on the local impact of natural resource abundance is still emerging, it is already providing valuable insights. In line with the country-level literature, it suggests that a local resource curse is not inevitable; indeed, there are examples in which resource abundance has no detrimental effects. A provocative idea is that the channel through which resource rents reach a local economy might matter. When resource rents are distributed using public channels (such as a revenue windfall to local governments), resource booms do not seem to improve living standards, and may even foster negative side effects such as conflict, rent seeking, and corruption. But when these rents are distributed through market channels (such as an increase in demand for local workers), resource booms may bring some economic benefits to the local population, at least in the near term. The failure of fiscal channels can reflect preexisting institutional factors that limit the responsiveness of local politicians and facilitate rent seeking, as suggested by the country-level literature.

No conclusive evidence has emerged showing that resource booms lead to deindustrialization, despite the increase in the price of local inputs. In some

Table 2.4 Empirical Evidence of the Impact of Mining-Related Pollution

Paper	Explanatory variable	Outcome variable	Sign	Country, data level	Identification strategy
Aragón and Rud (2015)	Cumulative gold production	Agricultural productivity	−	Ghana, household level	Difference-in-differences
		Poverty	+		
		Respiratory diseases among children	+		
Rau et al. (2013)	Distance to the mineral waste site	Academic performance, earnings in adulthood	−	Chile, individual level	Two sample instrumental variables
von der Goltz and Barnwal (2014)	Indicator of whether the cluster is within 5 kilometers of the nearest mine	Stunting and anemia among children and young women	+	44 developing countries, individual level	Difference-in-differences

Source: Aragón, Chuhan-Pole, and Land 2015.
Note: + = positive relation; − = negative relation.

cases, resource booms are even associated with an increase in manufacturing activity. This finding is the opposite of what we would expect from the standard Dutch disease argument, and suggests that other effects, such as agglomeration economies, may be relevant.

The literature on the local impact of natural resource abundance highlights the importance of examining a broad range of outcomes, besides income and growth. Evidence linking resource booms to local demand shocks, employment shifts, and pollution suggests that natural abundance may also affect other measures of well-being, such as inequality, education, and health.

Input-Output Analysis

Analyses based on input-output and social accounting models are useful for economic planning and ex-ante impact evaluation. These tools construct mathematical models of an economy and then calculate the change on economic outcomes associated with changes in some variables, including spending or output. Depending on data availability, these models can be built to describe regional and local economies, and thus inform about impacts at the subnational level. Their predictions are informative about what the economic effect of a mining project could be. Some countries, including Canada and the United States, routinely use input-output models to assess the ex-ante economic impact of extractive industries. But a major limitation of these models is that they do not tell what the effect is, for reasons that are well known (the Lucas critique).

Role of Institutions at the Local Level

As noted above, a second set of local institutions for the effective use of fiscal revenues includes fiscal decentralization arrangements. These are rules that define how fiscal revenue will be collected, distributed, and used at the subnational level. Aragón, Chuhan-Pole, and Land (2015) find the literature points to a limited scope for the decentralization of mining-related taxes. The main sources of mining revenue, such as corporate tax and royalties, may be better managed by higher government tiers (national or regional) on grounds of efficiency, equity, and reduced administrative costs. Some tax tools, however, could be suitable to local governments, such as property taxes, surtaxes, and land-use fees. Importantly, this also points to the importance of intergovernmental transfers to match increased local needs and to compensate local populations.

In practice, intergovernmental transfers are important tools for redistributing mining revenue among local populations. Transfers consist of nonmatching unconditional transfers, nonmatching conditional transfers, and selective matching transfers (cost-sharing programs). From an analytical perspective, nonmatching transfers create an income effect, while matching transfers change the relative price of public goods, thus also creating a substitution effect.

Another way to classify transfers is based on their source of funding. Some transfers are paid for with funds from national budgets. Others are linked to a particular source of revenue or tax; this type of transfer, also called a revenue-sharing or tax-sharing scheme, is commonly used to distribute mining revenues. Revenue-sharing schemes usually define the sharing rate and allocation procedure by law and so are less subject to the uncertainties of annual budget negotiations. These schemes effectively give local recipients ownership over part of the stream of future fiscal revenue.

The main advantages of revenue-sharing schemes are their simplicity and transparency, but they also give incentives to local politicians to support mining activities. These schemes, have, however, four distinct disadvantages. First, if based only on certain taxes, they may bias national tax policy; in particular, they may discourage national fiscal efforts to collect those taxes. Second, if they share the revenue from origin-based production (as in the case of mining-related sharing schemes), they can break the linkage between revenue needs and revenue means at the local level. In other words, targeted localities may end up receiving too many resources. In turn, this can reduce the accountability of local politicians and their incentives to spend public funds efficiently. A similar phenomenon can occur if the sharing rate is applied uniformly, and thus revenue is unrelated to actual spending needs. Third, if revenue-sharing schemes depend on only a few taxes (such as mining firm taxes), then their funding is exposed to industry shocks, such as changes in commodity prices. This can increase the volatility of local fiscal revenue. And fourth, if tax collection is done locally and shared with the national government, then revenue-sharing schemes can create perverse incentives among local authorities to reduce fiscal efforts or underreport tax revenues.

There has been a lack of quantitative studies examining how different fiscal decentralization arrangements to distribute mining revenues can shape the effect of mining revenue windfalls. The current literature mostly focuses on examining how different degrees of decentralization affect income growth or corruption at the country or regional level.[20] These studies use measures of expenditure or revenue decentralization, such as the share of subnational governments in tax revenues or public spending. Although not aimed at understanding how decentralization of mining revenues affects local communities, the literature can be informative about the overall impact of fiscal decentralization.

Empirical work on the linkage between decentralization, corruption, and local capture in less developed economies shows that decentralization can facilitate capture of local governments and collusion between local officers and local elites. For instance, Galasso and Ravallion (2005) find the targeting performance of the Food for Education Program in Bangladesh is worse in communities where land inequality is greater; they interpret this as evidence of elite capture. In Ecuador, Araujo et al. (2008) found evidence that local capture of a social development fund was more likely in villages with greater inequality.

Jia and Nie (2015) show how decentralization has facilitated collusion between coal mines and industry regulators in China, and that this has poorer safety standards and an increased mortality rate for workers.

Conclusion

A review of the emerging research on the local impact of natural resource booms and sharing of resource rents is beginning to provide new insights on how the channels through which these shocks are transmitted matter. A number of empirical studies find that resource abundance may have negative effects, such as increasing corruption, causing a deterioration of local political processes, and even increasing conflict. This evidence is similar to the cross-country literature, but is far from conclusive.

The emerging research highlights the importance of studying other local phenomena, such as the general equilibrium effects of local demand shocks, migration, and environmental pollution. These factors may also affect welfare and make the impact of natural resources more nuanced. A well-developed literature is also discussing tools to distribute resource rents, and the principles that guide fiscal decentralization. Still, several limitations and unsolved questions merit further study.

A main limitation of the literature on the local impact of natural resource booms is that it is still emerging and, consequently, there is a paucity of robust empirical evidence on the effect of resource abundance on employment, local income, distribution of income, and poverty, especially in developing countries. The available evidence is sparse and focuses on a handful of countries—namely, Canada and the United States among developed countries and Brazil and Peru among developing countries. Research into other resource-rich contexts, particularly Sub-Saharan Africa, is needed to increase the external validity of these results and to better inform policy makers and practitioners.

A related issue is the limited number of quantitative studies exploring the effect of extractive industries on nonincome outcomes such as health, education, and pollution externalities. The few studies there are on this issue suggest that the impacts on health and agricultural productivity can be important and costly. Again, more research is needed to gain a more complete view of the scope and magnitude of these negative spillovers, and to better understand the mitigating actions.

Because the empirical literature on the local impacts of resource booms is still emerging, findings need to be interpreted carefully. For example, research highlights the importance of market compared to fiscal mechanisms to create positive local impacts. It suggests that in the context of already-weak institutions of governance, developing local supply chain linkages may be more effective in improving local living standards than sharing the revenue windfall with local governments. More empirical analysis is needed, however, to confirm these initial findings, and to evaluate the effectiveness of different policies in developing these local linkages.

The findings of the literature review suggest that more quantitative research is needed to examine the effect of resource abundance on political outcomes. The existing evidence, mostly from Latin America (Brazil and Peru), suggests that revenue windfalls from resource abundance may hinder political selection and increase corruption. There is a paucity of evidence, however, from other regions with different institutional contexts, such as Sub-Saharan Africa. Different institutional arrangements may attenuate or exacerbate these negative effects. Because the delivery of public services and programs is increasingly being shifted to local governments, focusing the analysis on local politicians, local governance issues and institutions of accountability is of paramount importance. Evidence examining the effect of resource abundance on less violent forms of conflict, such as riots and civil unrest, is also lacking.

Empirical evidence assessing the impact of different fiscal decentralization arrangements on the political economy is also scant. The existing evidence examines the effect of the overall degree of decentralization, but it does not inform on the importance of specific institutional arrangements, such as type of transfers, type of revenue-sharing schemes, or type of competences devolved. These features may affect the impact of resource revenues on local income, corruption, and local political responsiveness. Similarly, evidence is thin on which institutional factors contribute to the success or failure of fiscal decentralization. Understanding these questions is crucial to inform the design of fiscal decentralization.

A related issue is the role of technical capacities of local bureaucrats and public officials. Even if local governments have the political will to use revenue windfalls to promote local development, they may lack the technical capacity to formulate and implement necessary public programs and projects. Some studies using the case of Peru suggest that lack of capacity may be important and affect the spending ability of local governments (Aragón 2013; Aragón and Casas 2009). More research is needed to understand the main technical constraints faced by local governments, their effect on the ability of communities to benefit from a revenue windfall, and the best policies to alleviate them.

Annex 2A: Schematic Model of Resource Endowment Changes

Figure 2A.1 presents a schematic model of a change in resource endowments within the framework of the standard Heckscher-Ohlin model of international trade, and the resulting specialization in the resource sector and crowding-out of tradable sectors such as manufacturing.

Figure 2A.1 Changes in Resource Endowments

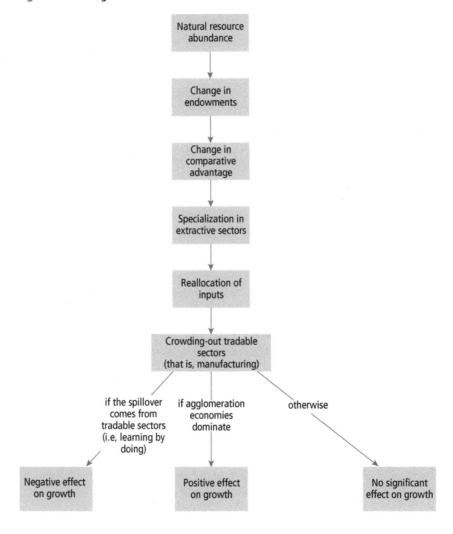

Notes

1. This chapter is a summary of Aragón, Chuhan-Pole, and Land (2015).
2. The literature on this is vast and has been reviewed extensively. For example, see Deacon (2011); Frankel (2011); Rosser (2006); Stevens (2003); and van der Ploeg (2011).

3. See van der Ploeg (2011, section 3.1) for a formal exposition.

4. This happens because the price of nontraded goods is set domestically, while the price of traded goods is set in international markets.

5. Note that in this context, short run and long run refer to whether capital is fixed or not. A more realistic model would assume that the extractive sector also employs labor and capital. In that case, in addition to the short-run changes in relative prices and crowding out of the traded sector (the spending effect), there would also be a reallocation of resources to the extractive sector, with negative effects on both traded and nontraded sectors.

6. Aghion et al. (2009) argue that with imperfect financial institutions, firms exposed to exchange rate fluctuations are more likely to hit liquidity constraints and be unable to invest. Gylfason, Herbertsson, and Zoega (1999) propose a model in which price volatility deters firms from moving toward high-skilled tradable sectors, which demand investments in human capital, and instead keep them producing commodities.

7. In the absence of good democratic checks and balances, the revenue windfall can fail to significantly improve the provision of public goods (Caselli and Michaels 2013) and lead instead to corruption and a worsening of political selection (Brollo et al. 2013).

8. For a comprehensive review of the literature, see Bardhan and Mookherjee (2012) and Vicente and Wantchekon (2009), and the references in these works.

9. In contexts with weaker democratic institutions, political capture may also be relevant. We discuss this literature in more detail in the section on the role of institutions at the local level.

10. However, booms associated with dispersed agricultural resources, such as coffee, bananas, and tobacco, may have a greater effect on local wages, and thus increase the opportunity cost for conflict participants (Dube and Vargas 2013).

11. See Moretti (2011, section 4.1) for a review of the evidence.

12. Some empirical strategies to address this concern include using individual panel data; focusing on subpopulations that reside in the locality before and after a resource boom; and examining observable population characteristics, such as measures of human capital, that may be indicative of the importance of compositional changes.

13. Black, McKinnish, and Sanders (2005) use county-level data from the coal-rich areas in Appalachia, United States, to examine the short-term economic impact of the coal boom of the 1970s and subsequent bust in the early 1980s. Marchand (2012) uses data from western Canada to examine the effects on local labor markets associated with the 1970s energy boom and bust. Fleming and Measham (2014) study the employment spillovers associated with the recent boom of coal seam gas in Australia. Michaels (2011) examines the long-term economic impact of oil discoveries in the southern United States using 1940–90 county-level data, and exploits geological variation in oil abundance. Allcott and Keniston (2014) extend Michaels's study to rural counties in the entire United States. Jacobsen and Parker (2014) extend Black, McKinnish, and Sanders's (2005) study to the western United States, focusing on oil and natural gas boomtowns created during the increase in energy prices in the 1970s. They also use county-level data, but observe a longer time span (1969–98), which allowed them to explore the effect of a bust after a longer period.

14. Using the same case but a different methodology, Monteiro and Ferraz (2010) document that oil windfalls are associated to reported increases in expenses and size of the public sector, but no improvement in public services to the local population.

15. Moreover, they find suggestive evidence that mining is associated with an increase in inequality. The authors highlight that this increase in inequality, among other factors, may explain the opposition of local communities to mining projects. A similar relationship among resource booms, income, and inequality was observed in Australia (Reeson, Measham, and Hosking 2012). Interestingly, this study suggests the relation between mining and inequality may have an inverted U-shape.

16. These economic linkages can also generate negative, unintended effects. For instance, Santos (2014) finds that the gold boom in Colombia increased child labor and reduced educational attainment.

17. This is a case of environmental negligence in northern Chile, in which hundreds of houses were built near a deposit of mineral waste.

18. The estimated figure is about $60,000 for the average affected individual.

19. Using satellite imagery, they also document an increase in the concentration of air pollutants near mines.

20. See Mookherjee (2015) for a more comprehensive review of the literature on the empirical relationship between decentralization, corruption, and government performance. Also see Fisman and Gatti (2000a, 2000b).

References

Acemoglu, Daron, James A. Robinson, and Dan Woren. 2012. *Why Nations Fail: The Origins of Power, Prosperity, and Poverty*, vol. 4. Santiago: SciELO.

Acemoglu, Daron, Simon Johnson, and James A. Robinson. 2005. "Institutions as a Fundamental Cause of Long-Run Growth." *Handbook of Economic Growth* 1 (Part A): 385–472.

Ades, Alberto, and Rafael Di Tella. 1999. "Rents, Competition, and Corruption." *American Economic Review* 89 (4): 982–93.

Aghion, Philippe, Philippe Bacchetta, Romain Ranciere, and Kenneth Rogoff. 2009. "Exchange Rate Volatility and Productivity Growth: The Role of Financial Development." *Journal of Monetary Economics* 56 (4): 494–513.

Allcott, Hunt, and Daniel Keniston. 2014. "Dutch Disease or Agglomeration? The Local Economic Effects of Natural Resource Booms in Modern America." Working Paper 20508, National Bureau of Economic Research, Cambridge, MA.

Almond, Douglas, Lena Edlund, and Mårten Palme. 2009. "Chernobyl's Subclinical Legacy: Prenatal Exposure to Radioactive Fallout and School Outcomes in Sweden." *Quarterly Journal of Economics* 124 (4): 1729–72.

Anderson, Siwan, Patrick Francois, and Ashok Kotwal. 2015. "Clientelism in Indian Villages." *American Economic Review* 105 (6): 1780–1816.

Angrist, Joshua D., and Adriana D. Kugler. 2008. "Rural Windfall or a New Resource Curse? Coca, Income, and Civil Conflict in Colombia." *Review of Economics and Statistics* 90 (2): 191–215.

Aragón, Fernando M. 2013. "Local Spending, Transfers and Costly Tax Collection." *National Tax Journal* 66 (2): 343–70.

Aragón, Fernando M., and Carlos Casas. 2009. "Technical Capacities and Local Spending in Peruvian Municipalities." *Perspectivas* 7 (1): 89–113.

Aragón, Fernando M., and Juan Pablo Rud. 2013. "Natural Resources and Local Communities: Evidence from a Peruvian Gold Mine." *American Economic Journal* 5 (2): 1–25.

———. 2015. "Polluting Industries and Agricultural Productivity: Evidence from Mining in Ghana." *Economic Journal* 26 (590).

Aragón, Fernando M., Punam Chuhan-Pole, and Bryan Christopher Land. 2015. "The Local Economic Impacts of Resource Abundance: What Have We Learned?" Policy Research Working Paper 7263, World Bank, Washington, DC.

Araujo, M. Caridad, Francisco H. G. Ferreira, Peter Lanjouw, and Berk Özler. 2008. "Local Inequality and Project Choice: Theory and Evidence from Ecuador." *Journal of Public Economics* 92 (5): 1022–46.

Atkin, David. 2012. "Endogenous Skill Acquisition and Export Manufacturing in Mexico." Technical Report, National Bureau of Economic Research, Cambridge, MA.

Bardhan, Pranab, and Dilip Mookherjee. 2012. "Political Clientelism and Capture: Theory and Evidence from West Bengal, India." WIDER Working Paper 2012/97, UNU-WIDER, Helsinki.

Besley, Timothy, and Anne Case. 2003. "Political Institutions and Policy Choices: Evidence from the United States." *Journal of Economic Literature* 41 (1): 7–73.

Besley, Timothy, and Robin Burgess. 2002. "The Political Economy of Government Responsiveness: Theory and Evidence from India." *Quarterly Journal of Economics* 117 (4): 1415–51.

Besley, Timothy, and Stephen Coate. 2003. "Centralized versus Decentralized Provision of Local Public Goods: A Political Economy Approach." *Journal of Public Economics* 87 (12): 2611–37.

Bhattacharyya, Sambit, and Roland Hodler. 2010. "Natural Resources, Democracy and Corruption." *European Economic Review* 54 (4): 608–21.

Black, Dan, Terra McKinnish, and Seth Sanders. 2005. "The Economic Impact of the Coal Boom and Bust." *Economic Journal* 115 (503): 449–76.

Boschini, Anne D., Jan Pettersson, and Jesper Roine. 2007. "Resource Curse or Not: A Question of Appropriability." *Scandinavian Journal of Economics* 109 (3): 593–617.

Brollo, Fernanda, Tommaso Nannicini, Roberto Perotti, and Guido Tabellini. 2013. "The Political Resource Curse." *American Economic Review* 103 (5): 1759–96.

Brunnschweiler, Christa N. 2008. "Cursing the Blessings? Natural Resource Abundance, Institutions, and Economic Growth." *World Development* 36 (3): 399–419.

Brunnschweiler, Christa N., and Erwin H. Bulte. 2008. "The Resource Curse Revisited and Revised: A Tale of Paradoxes and Red Herrings." *Journal of Environmental Economics and Management* 55 (3): 248–64.

Bulte, Erwin H., Richard Damania, and Robert T. Deacon. 2005. "Resource Intensity, Institutions, and Development." *World Development* 33 (7): 1029–44.

Caselli, Francesco, and Guy Michaels. 2013. "Do Oil Windfalls Improve Living Standards? Evidence from Brazil." *American Economic Journal: Applied Economics* 5 (1): 208–38.

Caselli, Francesco, and Wilbur John Coleman. 2013. "On the Theory of Ethnic Conflict." *Journal of the European Economic Association* 11 (issue supplement): 161–92.

Chang, Tom, Joshua Graff-Zivin, Tal Gross, and Matthew Neidell. 2014. "Particulate Pollution and the Productivity of Pear Packers." Technical Report, National Bureau of Economic Research, Cambridge, MA.

Collier, Paul, and Anke Hoeffler. 2005. "Resource Rents, Governance, and Conflict." *Journal of Conflict Resolution* 49 (August): 625–33.

———. 2009. "Testing the Neocon Agenda: Democracy in Resource-Rich Societies." *European Economic Review* 53 (3): 293–308.

Collier, Paul, Anke Hoeffler, and Måns Söderbom. 2004. "On the Duration of Civil War." *Journal of Peace Research* 41 (3): 253–73.

Corden, W. Max. 1984. "Booming Sector and Dutch Disease Economics: Survey and Consolidation." *Oxford Economic Papers*, New Series 36 (3) (November): 359–80.

Corden, W. Max, and J. Peter Neary. 1982. "Booming Sector and De-industrialisation in a Small Open Economy." *Economic Journal* 92 (368): 825–48.

Cotet, Anca M., and Kevin K. Tsui. 2013. "Oil and Conflict: What Does the Cross-Country Evidence Really Show?" *American Economic Journal* 5 (1): 49–80.

Currie, Janet, Eric A. Hanushek, E. Megan Kahn, Matthew Neidell, and Steven G. Rivkin. 2009. "Does Pollution Increase School Absences?" *Review of Economics and Statistics* 91 (4): 682–94.

Currie, Janett, Joshua Graff-Zivin, Jamie Mullins, and Matthew J. Neidell. 2013. "What Do We Know about Short and Long Term Effects of Early Life Exposure to Pollution?" Technical Report, National Bureau of Economic Research, Cambridge, MA.

Dal Bó, Ernesto, and Pedro Dal Bó. 2011. "Workers, Warriors, and Criminals: Social Conflict in General Equilibrium." *Journal of the European Economic Association* 9 (4): 646–77.

Deacon, Robert T. 2011. "The Political Economy of the Natural Resource Curse: A Survey of Theory and Evidence." *Foundations and Trends in Microeconomics* 7 (2): 111–208.

Douglas, Stratford, and Anne Walker. 2013. "Coal Mining and the Resource Curse in the Eastern United States." Social Science Research Netwwork. http://papers. ssrn.com /sol3/papers.cfm?abstract_id=2385560.

Dube, Oeindrila, and Juan F. Vargas. 2013. "Commodity Price Shocks and Civil Conflict: Evidence from Colombia." *Review of Economic Studies* 80 (4): 1384–1421.

Dudka, Stanislaw, and Domy C. Adriano. 1997. "Environmental Impacts of Metal Ore Mining and Processing: A Review." *Journal of Environmental Quality* 26 (3): 590–602.

EPA (Environmental Protection Agency), United States. 2012. "Acid Rain." http://www .epa.gov/acidrain/effects/forests.html.

Fearon, James D. 2005. "Primary Commodity Exports and Civil War." *Journal of Conflict Resolution* 49 (4): 483–507.

Fearon, James D., and David D. Laitin. 2003. "Ethnicity, Insurgency, and Civil War." *American Political Science Review* 97 (1): 75–90.

Fafchamps, Marcel, Michael Koelle, and Forhad Shilpi. 2015. "Gold Mining and Proto-Urbanization: Recent Evidence from Ghana." Policy Research Working Paper 7347, World Bank, Washington, DC.

Fisman, Raymond, and Roberta Gatti. 2002a. "Decentralization and Corruption: Evidence across Countries." *Journal of Public Economics* 83 (3): 325–45.

———. 2002b. "Decentralization and Corruption: Evidence from US Federal Transfer Programs." *Public Choice* 113 (1–2): 25–35.

Fleming, David A., and Thomas G. Measham. 2014. "Local Economic Impacts of an Unconventional Energy Boom: The Coal Seam Gas Industry in Australia." *Australian Journal of Agricultural and Resource Economics.* doi:10.1111/1467-8489.12043.

Frankel, Jeffrey A. 2011. "A Solution to Fiscal Procyclicality: The Structural Budget Institutions Pioneered by Chile." Technical Report, National Bureau of Economic Research, Cambridge, MA.

Gilliland, Frank D., Kiros Berhane, Edward B. Rappaport, Duncan C. Thomas, Edward Avol, W. James Gauderman, Stephanie J. London, et al. 2001. "The Effects of Ambient Air Pollution on School Absenteeism Due to Respiratory Illnesses." *Epidemiology* 12 (1): 43–54.

Galasso, Emanuela, and Martin Ravallion. 2005. "Decentralized Targeting of an Antipoverty Program." *Journal of Public Economics* 89 (4): 705–27.

Graff-Zivin, Joshua, and Matthew Neidell. 2012. "The Impact of Pollution on Worker Productivity." *American Economic Review* 102 (7): 3652–73.

———. 2013. "Environment, Health, and Human Capital." *Journal of Economic Literature* 51 (3): 689–730.

Greenstone, Michael, Richard Hornbeck, and Enrico Moretti. 2010. "Identifying Agglomeration Spillovers: Evidence from Winners and Losers of Large Plant Openings." *Journal of Political Economy* 118 (3): 536–98.

Grossman, Herschel I. 1999. "Kleptocracy and Revolutions." *Oxford Economic Papers* 51 (2): 267–83.

Gylfason, Thorvaldur, Tryggvi Thor Herbertsson, and Gylfi Zoega. 1999. "A Mixed Blessing." *Macroeconomic Dynamics* 3 (2): 204–225.

Hanna, Rema, and Paulina Oliva. 2011. "The Effect of Pollution on Labor Supply: Evidence from a Natural Experiment in Mexico City." Technical Report, National Bureau of Economic Research, Cambridge, MA.

Heck, Walter W., O. C. Taylor, Richard Adams, Gail Bingham, Joseph Miller, Eric Preston, and Leonard Weinstein. 1982. "Assessment of Crop Loss from Ozone." *Journal of the Air Pollution Control Association* 32 (4): 353–61.

Hirshleifer, Jack. 1991. "The Paradox of Power." *Economics and Politics* 3 (3): 177–200.

Humphreys, Macartan. 2005. "Natural Resources, Conflict, and Conflict Resolution Uncovering the Mechanisms." *Journal of Conflict Resolution* 49 (4): 508–37.

Isham, Jonathan, Michael Woolcock, Lant Pritchett, and Gwen Busby. 2005. "The Varieties of Resource Experience: Natural Resource Export Structures and the Political Economy of Economic Growth." *World Bank Economic Review* 19 (2): 141–74.

Jacobsen, and Parker. 2014. "The Economic Aftermath of Resource Booms: Evidence from Boomtowns in the American West." *Economic Journal* 126 (593): 1092–128.

James, Alex, and David Aadland. 2011. "The Curse of Natural Resources: An Empirical Investigation of U.S. Counties." *Resource and Energy Economics* 33 (2): 440–53.

Jia, Ruixue, and Huihua Nie. Forthcoming. "Decentralization, Collusion and Coalmine Deaths." *Review of Economics and Statistics.*

Khemani, Stuti. "Buying Votes vs. Supplying Public Services: Political Incentives to Under-Invest in Pro-Poor Policies." 2013. Policy Research Working Paper 6339, World Bank, Washington, DC.

Kotsadam, Andreas, and Anja Tolonen. 2015. "African Mining, Gender, and Local Employment." Policy Research Working Paper 7251, World Bank, Washington, DC.

Krugman, Paul. 1987. "The Narrow Moving Band, the Dutch Disease, and the Competitive Consequences of Mrs. Thatcher: Notes on Trade in the Presence of Dynamic Scale Economies." *Journal of Development Economics* 27 (1): 41–55.

Lane, Philip R., and Aaron Tornell. 1996. "Power, Growth, and the Voracity Effect." *Journal of Economic Growth* 1 (2): 213–41.

Lavy, Victor, Avraham Ebenstein, and Sefi Roth. 2012. "The Impact of Air Pollution on Cognitive Performance and Human Capital Formation." Unpublished.

Lederman, Daniel, and William F. Maloney. 2007. *Natural Resources, Neither Curse Nor Destiny.* Washington, DC: World Bank.

———. 2008. "Inrau Search of the Missing Resource Curse." *Economía* 9 (1): 1–56.

Lei, Yu-Hsiang, and Guy Michaels. 2011. "Do Giant Oilfield Discoveries Fuel Internal Armed Conflicts?" Technical Report 6934, Discussion Paper Series, Center for Economic and Policy Research, Washington, DC.

Leite, Carlos A., and Jens Weidmann. 1999. "Does Mother Nature Corrupt? Natural Resources, Corruption, and Economic Growth." Working Paper 99/85, International Monetary Fund, Washington, DC.

Lizzeri, Alessandro, and Nicola Persico. 2001. "The Provision of Public Goods under Alternative Electoral Incentives." *American Economic Review* 91 (1): 225–39.

Loayza, Norman, Alfredo Mier y Teran, and Jamele Rigolini. 2013. *Poverty, Inequality, and the Local Natural Resource Curse.* Washington, DC: World Bank.

Lujala, Päivi. 2010. "The Spoils of Nature: Armed Civil Conflict and Rebel Access to Natural Resources." *Journal of Peace Research* 47 (1): 15–28.

Marchand, Joseph. 2012. "Local Labor Market Impacts of Energy Boom-Bust-Boom in Western Canada." *Journal of Urban Economics* 71 (1): 165–174.

Marshall, Fiona, Mike Ashmore, and Fiona Hinchcliffe. 1997. *A Hidden Threat to Food Production: Air Pollution and Agriculture in the Developing World.* London: International Institute for Environment and Development.

Matsuyama, Kiminori. 1992. "Agricultural Productivity, Comparative Advantage, and Economic Growth." *Journal of Economic Theory* 58 (2): 317–34.

Mehlum, Halvor, Karl Moene, and Ragnar Torvik. 2006. "Institutions and the Resource Curse." *Economic Journal* 116 (508): 1–20.

Menz, Fredric C., and Hans M. Seip. 2004. "Acid Rain in Europe and the United States: An Update." *Environmental Science and Policy* 7 (4): 253–65.

Michaels, Guy. 2011. "The Long Term Consequences of Resource-Based Specialisation." *Economic Journal* 121 (551): 31–57.

Miller, Joseph E. 1988. "Effects on Photosynthesis, Carbon Allocation, and Plant Growth Associated with Air Pollutant Stress." In *Assessment of Crop Loss from Air Pollutants,* 287–314. New York: Springer.

Monteiro, Joana, and Claudio Ferraz. 2010. "Does Oil Make Leaders Unaccountable? Evidence from Brazil's Offshore Oil Boom." Pontifical Catholic University of Rio de Janeiro.

Mookherjee, Dilip. 2015. "Political Decentralization," *Annual Review of Economics* 7 (1): 231–49.

Moretti, Enrico. 2011. "Local Labor Markets." *Handbook of Labor Economics* 4: 1237–1313.

Murphy, Kevin M., Andrei Shleifer, and Robert W. Vishny. 1989. "Industrialization and the Big Push." *Journal of Political Economy* 97 (5): 1003–26.

Nunn, Nathan. 2009. "The Importance of History for Economic Development." *Annual Review of Economics* 1: 65–92.

Pande, Rohini. 2003. "Can Mandated Political Representation Increase Policy Influence for Disadvantaged Minorities? Theory and Evidence from India." *American Economic Review* 93 (4): 1132–51.

Papyrakis, Elissaios, and Reyer Gerlagh. 2007. "Resource Abundance and Economic Growth in the United States." *European Economic Review* 51 (4): 1011–39.

Park, Hyesook, Boeun Lee, Eun-Hee Ha, Jong-Tae Lee, Ho Kim, and Yun-Chul Hong. 2002. "Association of Air Pollution with School Absenteeism Due to Illness." *Archives of Pediatrics and Adolescent Medicine* 156 (12): 1235–39.

Persson, Torsten. 2002. "Do Political Institutions Shape Economic Policy?" *Econometrica* 70 (3): 883–905.

Ransom, Michael R., and C. Arden Pope. 1992. "Elementary School Absences and PM-10 Pollution in Utah Valley." *Environmental Research* 58 (1): 204–19.

Rau, Tomás, Loreto Reyes, and Sergio S. Urzúa. 2013. "The Long-Term Effects of Early Lead Exposure: Evidence from a Case of Environmental Negligence." Technical Report, National Bureau of Economic Research, Cambridge, MA.

Reeson, Andrew F., Thomas G. Measham, and Karin Hosking. 2012. "Mining Activity, Income Inequality and Gender in Regional Australia." *Australian Journal of Agricultural and Resource Economics* 56 (2): 302–13.

Robinson, James A., Ragnar Torvik, and Thierry Verdier. 2006. "Political Foundations of the Resource Curse." *Journal of Development Economics* 79 (2): 447–68.

Ross, Michael L. 2001. "Does Oil Hinder Democracy?" *World Politics* 53 (3): 325–61.

———. 2004. "What Do We Know about Natural Resources and Civil War?" *Journal of Peace Research* 41 (3): 337–56.

Rosser, Andrew. 2006. *The Political Economy of the Resource Curse: A Literature Survey.* Vol. 268. Brighton, UK: Institute of Development Studies.

Sachs, Jeffrey D., and Andrew M. Warner. 1995. "Natural Resource Abundance and Economic Growth." Technical Report, National Bureau of Economic Research, Cambridge, MA.

———. 2001. "The Curse of Natural Resources." *European Economic Review* 45 (4): 827–38.

Sala-i-Martin, Xavier. 1997. "I Just Ran Two Million Regressions." *American Economic Review* 87 (2): 178–183.

Sala-i-Martin, Xavier, and Arvind Subramanian. 2003. "Addressing the Natural Resource Curse: An Illustration from Nigeria." Technical Report, National Bureau of Economic Research, Cambridge, MA.

Salomons, W. 1995. "Environmental Impact of Metals Derived from Mining Activities: Processes, Predictions, Prevention." *Journal of Geochemical Exploration* 52 (1): 5–23.

Santos, Rafael José. 2014. "Not All That Glitters Is Gold: Gold Boom, Child Labor and Schooling in Colombia." Documentos CEDE 31, Universidad de los Andes, Colombia.

Stevens, Paul. 2003. "Resource Impact: Curse or Blessing? A Literature Survey." *Journal of Energy Literature* 9 (1): 1–42.

Tolonen, Anja. 2016. "Local Industrial Shocks and Infant Mortality: Evidence from Africa's Gold Mining Industry." Unpublished.

Tornell, Aaron, and Philip R. Lane. 1999. "The Voracity Effect." *American Economic Review* 89 (1): 22–46.

Torvik, Ragnar. 2001. "Learning by Doing and the Dutch Disease." *European Economic Review* 45 (2): 285–306.

Tsui, Kevin K. 2011. "More Oil, Less Democracy: Evidence from Worldwide Crude Oil Discoveries." *Economic Journal* 121 (551): 89–115.

van der Ploeg, Frederick. 2011. "Natural Resources: Curse or Blessing?" *Journal of Economic Literature* 49 (2): 366–420.

van der Ploeg, Frederick, and Steven Poelhekke. 2009. "Volatility and the Natural Resource Curse." *Oxford Economic Papers* 61 (4): 727–60.

Vicente, Pedro C. 2010. "Does Oil Corrupt? Evidence from a Natural Experiment in West Africa." *Journal of Development Economics* 92 (1): 28–38.

Vicente, Pedro C., and Leonard Wantchekon. 2009. "Clientelism and Vote Buying: Lessons from Field Experiments in African Elections." *Oxford Review of Economic Policy* 25 (2): 292–305.

von der Goltz, Jan, and Prabhat Barnwal. 2014. "Mines: The Local Welfare Effects of Mineral Mining in Developing Countries." Department of Economics Discussion Paper Series, Columbia University, New York.

Zhang, Tao, and Heng-fu Zou. 1998. "Fiscal Decentralization, Public Spending, and Economic Growth in China." *Journal of Public Economics* 67 (2): 221–40.

Zhang, Xiaobo, Shenggen Fan, Linxiu Zhang, and Jikun Huang. 2004. "Local Governance and Public Goods Provision in Rural China." *Journal of Public Economics* 88 (12): 2857–71.

Zuo, Na, and Jack Schieffer. 2014. "Are Resources a Curse? An Investigation of Chinese Provinces." Paper presented at the Southern Agricultural Economics Association Annual Meeting, Dallas, February 1–4.

Chapter 3

Insights from Three Country Case Studies

Introduction

Industrial gold mining is a natural choice for studying the socioeconomic impact of natural resources in Africa. As noted in chapter 1, Ghana, Mali, and Tanzania—the three case study countries—are not new gold producers, but the advent of large-scale industrial gold mining is recent and growing rapidly. Hence, it is possible to discern changes brought about by large-scale mining through "before and after" type studies, as well as by studying the outcomes and changes in mining areas as opposed to nonmining areas. That said, each of the three countries is a case in itself, so the studies constitute an integral part of the overall analysis by considering specific country contexts.[1] This chapter summarizes elements of the country case studies, noting similarities and contrasts.

The point of departure in each of them comes from the tension between the national or macroeconomic gains and local gains from minerals. This arises because in all three countries, subsurface minerals belong to the state, with the central government as guardian of the ownership rights; local host communities have no property rights to the minerals. For the country, the benefits flow from exports and fiscal revenue.[2] So for the mining areas, these benefits may appear remote and their impact minor or imperceptible.

Nevertheless, there are impacts, and these are felt through three mechanisms or channels: (1) market channel: employment, income, and other positive spillovers such as improved infrastructure, worker training, and management; (2) government revenue: since government is the main recipient of the benefits from the minerals, the channel by which revenues are distributed to subnational authorities and, particularly, mining ones, is a key determinant of the local impact; and (3) negative externalities: the revenue benefits are national but the environmental and other costs such as congestion and population displacement will be local. As noted in chapters 1 and 2, while the national cost-benefit analysis may have a positive balance, the mining areas themselves may not. The case studies therefore track the impact of mining through these channels to gain insights into the country-specific institutions, practices, and outcomes. This chapter examines the findings after giving a brief description of the role of large-scale mining in each of the countries.

Country Backgrounds: Gold Mining in the Case Study Countries

Large-scale gold mining and extractive industries in general are relatively capital-intensive. From a macro perspective, the returns to domestic factors of production, in particular labor, are quite small since foreign multinational companies own much of the capital. Thus, because mining is not a major employment generator, the national benefits from mining are mostly from government revenue and net exports.

The contribution of gold mining to gross domestic product (GDP) in each of the case study countries is modest. In Mali, the poorest of the three, about 7 percent of GDP is from mining and quarrying; in Ghana it is 5.5 percent (Bermudez-Lugo 2012); and in Tanzania 4 percent.[3] In all three countries, however, the value of gold exports is substantial (figure 3.1), and gold is an important component of exports. Gold averaged 69 percent of exports from 2000 and 2013 in Mali, 38 percent in Ghana, and 31 percent in Tanzania (figure 3.2). Mali is particularly sensitive to the price of gold because gold is such a large part of the country's exports. Indeed, Sanoh and Coulibaly (2015) note the perception that the price of gold is the key determinant of Mali's business cycles. Although this dependence is not as strong in Ghana and Tanzania, it is nevertheless significant. Not surprisingly, the price of gold is a key determinant of the terms of trade, which is always a crucial factor in the macroeconomic fluctuations of developing countries.

The contribution of gold mining to government revenue varies across the three countries. Revenue from gold mining constitutes 25 percent of central government income in Mali, 4.9 percent in Ghana, and barely 2.5 percent in Tanzania. The contribution of gold mining to fiscal revenues is discussed later in this chapter.

Recent trends show that large-scale mining has contributed to the surge in exports and government revenue from mining. Gold mining, however, is not new to the three countries, and has for the most part been done by artisanal and small-scale miners. Box 3.1 summarizes the background papers that explore this activity.

Figure 3.1 Gold Exports in Ghana, Mali, and Tanzania, 2000–13

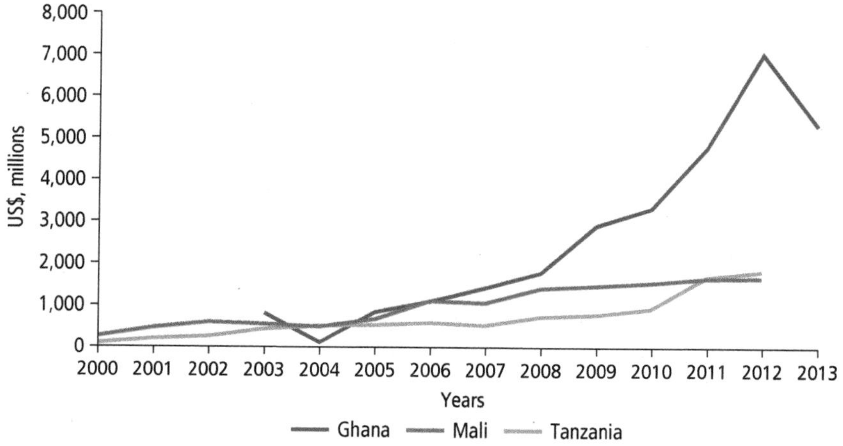

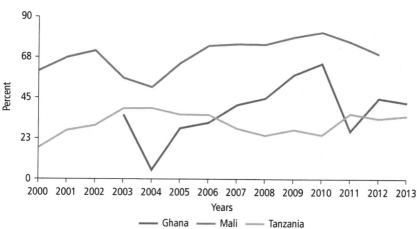

Source: World Integrated Trade Solution database.

Figure 3.2 Gold Exports as a Share of Total Exports in Ghana, Mali, and Tanzania, 2000–13

Source: World Integrated Trade Solution database.

BOX 3.1

Artisanal and Small-Scale Mining

Sometimes known as traditional or informal miners, artisanal and small-scale miners combine mining with activities such as agriculture and livestock breeding, or even with informal activities such as services and craftwork. The sector's size fluctuates with the gold price and other employment opportunities. The scale of artisanal and small-scale mining also varies considerably, from cooperative ventures to individual miners. Some operations are licensed, but others operate informally. For these reasons, it is also difficult to estimate the numbers involved in this activity at any given time.

For Ghana, the estimated number of artisanal and small-scale miners in 1998 was 200,000, and there are now thought to be as many as 1 million. The number is also difficult to estimate for Tanzania, though Smith and Kinyondo (2015) report 550,000. The authors also estimate Tanzania's output from artisanal and small-scale mining as being equivalent to that of a single large-scale mine. Their survey of a few informal mining sites in Tanzania showed that 50 percent of the artisanal and small-scale miners regarded this activity as their sole source of income, and about 25 percent of them had been active in the sector for five to 10 years. This suggests the activity is more stable than commonly thought.

For Mali, the exact number of artisanal mining sites is unknown, but was estimated by the government to be 350 in 2009. In addition, the number of communes reporting artisanal gold mining as an important economic activity has risen, from nine communes in 2006 to 17 in 2008 and 25 in 2013. Estimates of employment in the sector vary considerably—6,000, 200,000, and up to 1 million, according to different sources (Sanoh and Coulibaly 2015). However, the latest population census estimates the number of people involved in artisanal and small-scale gold mining at 25,000.

Because of its informality, the sector is notoriously difficult to tax and regulate. In Ghana, 300,000 workers are estimated to be involved in unlicensed (that is, illegal) mining; these are known as galamseys. Although the evidence is mostly anecdotal, the sector is thought to be riddled with lawlessness and hazardous working conditions. Accidents involving injury and death are frequent but often go unreported. Miners are also exposed to mercury and cyanide poisoning, and to environmental hazards including water pollution. In Mali, local authorities receive payment of duties and taxes in the allocation of permits or titles authorizing artisanal mining.

Despite the sector's importance, this study does not provide estimates of the impact of artisanal and small-scale mining because the household survey data used for the empirical part do not identify households that obtain their livelihood in the sector. Because of this, we cannot account for their contribution to these impacts or ways in which the opening of a large-scale mine affect artisanal and small-scale miners. This presents challenges to the exact identification of the impact of large-scale mining. However, we do encourage future work that will undertake data collection through surveys on artisanal and small-scale mining to underpin a systematic study of its impacts.

Channel 1: Employment, Linkages, and Positive Spillovers

Modern large-scale mining does not employ many workers. It has historically been capital-intensive, and this feature increased with technological progress. At the country level, this magnifies the extent of the windfalls through exports and central government revenue, but it may also lower the amount of value added paid to indigenous factors, mainly labor. Thus, extractive industries have been characterized as "enclaves," cut off from the domestic economy except through royalties and taxes. The benefits to the economy therefore depend crucially on how the central government uses the windfalls. And, as is well known, that is often not wisely in developing countries.

Partly in response to criticism that employment in mines is low, mining companies and chambers of mines argue that although globally small, the number employed is locally significant and can raise average incomes and expenditures in the vicinity of a mine. It is also argued that mines are linked to local industry through the use of inputs of other goods and services, and that employment is stimulated through these backward linkages. The country case studies examine these claims, complementing the empirical evidence given in chapter 4 on the employment and income effects of proximity to a mine. Analysts argue that industrial mining raises productivity in the area where it is operating by improving infrastructure for its own needs, and also through worker and management training. Mining companies sometimes invest directly through social responsibility endeavors, such as improving infrastructure, health, and education.

Employment

The country case studies report that mining companies employed mostly nationals rather than expatriates, although management jobs went disproportionately to foreigners. In Mali, Sanoh and Coulibaly (2015) report a ratio of 14 national workers to each expatriate, and that on average 78 percent of jobs are held by people working in mines located in three communes (local government entities): Gouandiaka, Sadiola, and Sitakily. Employees of mining firms in Mali earn $1,200 a month on average. National labor survey data suggest that the mean income from mining is higher than the average income for all other economic activities, and considerably so when compared with agriculture or industry.

In Tanzania, employees of large-scale mining firms are typically based at the mine site, but also internationally and in regional offices, including in Mwanza, the country's second-largest city, and Dar es Salaam, the commercial and administrative hub. The total number of mining jobs, as expected, is relatively small, particularly when compared to a workforce of 22.1 million (2012 census) and the 70,000 Tanzanians entering the labor force each year. Even so, employees of the large mining companies are typically well remunerated compared

Figure 3.3 Mining Employment in Tanzania, 2005–13

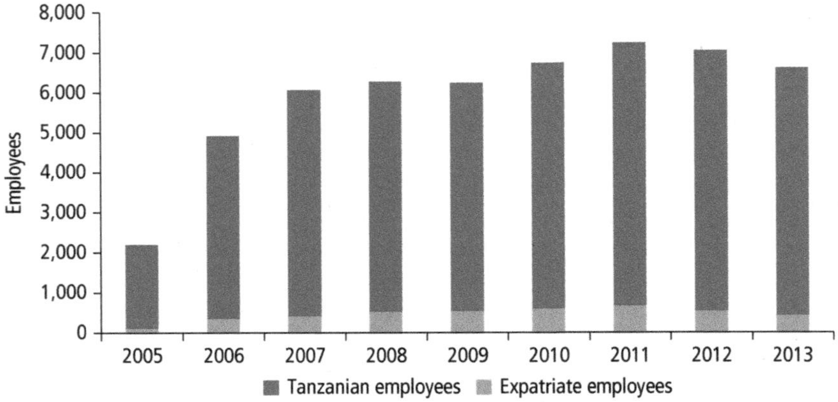

Sources: Ministry of Energy and Mining; Tanzania Chamber of Minerals and Energy; Tanzania Minerals Audit Agency

with national average income levels. The average monthly income from a manufacturing job is T Sh 103,407, compared to T Sh 76,277 in mining, T Sh 49,693 in construction, T Sh 31,301 in trade, and only T Sh 15,234 in agriculture, currently the largest source of livelihood for Tanzanians (ESRF 2009). Further, it is clear that most employees are Tanzanian and not foreign (figure 3.3), although the balance tilts toward foreign workers when only management positions are considered.

In Ghana, the total number of people employed in mining was 17,103 in 2014 (Government of Ghana 2014), of which only 289 were expatriates. In Tanzania, employment in mining increased from about 2,000 in 2005 to about 7,000 during 2010–13 (figure 3.4); and in Mali, the total number of workers directly employed in mining averaged 3,635 during 2008–13.

Linkages

It is difficult to estimate the linkages (or multipliers) because of data limitations. However, although the description of extractive industries as "enclaves" is not accurate, it is also fair to say that their backward linkages are not large. In South Africa, for example, where better data are available, gold mining is estimated to have a multiplier of about 1.8. In other words, for every one mining job created, 1.8 jobs are created elsewhere through backward linkages and expenditure effects. Sanoh and Coulibaly (2015) report that the multiplier is 1.67 in Mali.

Multiplier effects are limited, partly because of the capital intensity of the mining industry, but mostly because of the lack of local cost-effective

Figure 3.4 Employment in Mining in Mali and Tanzania, 2005–13

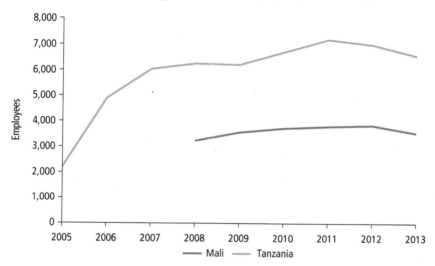

Source: Authors' estimates from administrative data.
Note: The different starting points for Tanzania and Mali are due to data availability. There are no data for Ghana.

procurement opportunities. This could change over time, as mining companies become better acquainted with local markets and suppliers, and as local entrepreneurs learn to take advantage of the new opportunities arising from the expansion of mining activity. In Tanzania, efforts have been made to improve the potential for local procurement, including in services such as catering, vehicle repair, machine shop services, welding, metal work, electrical work, and plumbing. However, the proportion of inputs sourced locally remains low, a situation mirrored in Ghana and Mali. Although there is always a temptation to increase the linkages through local content laws, governments may be better advised to focus on developing the conditions for improved procurement rather than mandating it. McMahon and Moreira (2014, 43) caution that "the failed experience of many import-substitution plans suggests that linkages cannot be forced upon the mining sector without enabling business conditions." Instead, they advocate a focus on improving business conditions, such as better power and transportation infrastructure, adequate human capital, access to finance, economies of scale, and outreach or technical assistance programs.

The country case studies and the empirical results confirm that mines do succeed in raising incomes for those living in their vicinity. The higher wages attract migrant workers, which can raise some prices such as rents and food, so that some local residents who may not be recipients of higher mine wages experience a loss of real income. The inflow of workers may also strain social services and crowd out some original residents.

Externalities

Direct development investment by mining firms has traditionally been labeled corporate social responsibility; typical projects include building secondary schools, clinics, and water infrastructure. For example, Newmont Ghana Gold supported Ghana's Ahafo region through a partnership in the health sector by building housing for resident nurses and three community health compounds in local villages, and equipping 60 local health volunteers with bicycles and medical equipment. However, a growing trend in the three case study countries is for more sustainable projects that offer alternative livelihoods to mining (for example, brickmaking and fisheries) in communities around the mines. This reflects greater interest in helping communities prosper after mine closures (World Bank 2002), and is evidence of widespread recognition of the disappointing development results of corporate social responsibility (Campbell 2012).

Corporate social responsibility projects have had mixed success and take a long time to implement. They face problems and challenges that are similar to those of almost all foreign aid and government interventions, particularly where implementation capacity is limited. The challenges include ensuring the investment has sufficient operational funding to provide an adequate level of the intended service. In Tanzania, for example, mining firms have often promised to build a school or classrooms, with the government pledging to fund equipment and the recurrent costs of providing education. But many of these complementary commitments are not legally binding, and are often not met in a timely manner or at all.

Infrastructure has sometimes been improved by multinational mining firms, but this is rare. It should be noted, however, that gold mining differs from bulk mineral mining, and infrastructure benefits in this sector are usually limited. Roads, for example, only have to be good enough to get inputs to mine sites, since mineral exports are typically flown out.

When linkages cannot be made to national electricity grids, large-scale mines develop their own exclusive power supplies. Other than road improvements, infrastructure benefits are usually associated with corporate social responsibility investments in the community, and therefore are not directly related to production needs. Ayee and Dumisa (2014) note that Ghana opinion surveys reveal unrealistically high expectations by the public from mining. These often focus on the provision of public goods and services, but local governments often lack the capacity to provide these benefits, even when additional revenues are present. Consequently, the public pressures mining companies to step in for the government; for example, by building schools, health facilities, and transportation infrastructure. Although this may sometimes be the best available option, Ayee and Dumisa (2014) point out that there are obvious risks to ceding responsibility for the provision of public goods to a foreign-based private corporation. Also, mines inevitably stop producing and close, which is always a blow to the local economy—and much more so when the departing company provided basic services.

In Mali, mining companies contribute substantially to local development funds that are not under the control of local authorities.[4] During 1994–2010, their contribution to these funds reached CFAF 20 billion. In addition, they contributed CFAF 7 billion in license fees. In general, the amount of license fees from each mine is lower than the amount of local development funds, except for the Yatéla, Loulou, and Morila mines, which represent 57 percent of the total license fees but only 17 percent of total local development funds. Sadiola commune is by far the biggest contributor, at 59 percent of license fees and 71 percent of local development funds, because the mine there has been operating for the longest (figure 3.5).

The sectoral distribution of development funds within mining communes depends largely on their needs and the complementarity with their budget spending. In Sadiola commune, 23 percent of its fund was spent on agriculture during 1994–2010; in Fourou, almost 83 percent went to education. In Sanso

Figure 3.5 Share of License Fees and Local Development Funds in Mali's Communes, 1994–2010

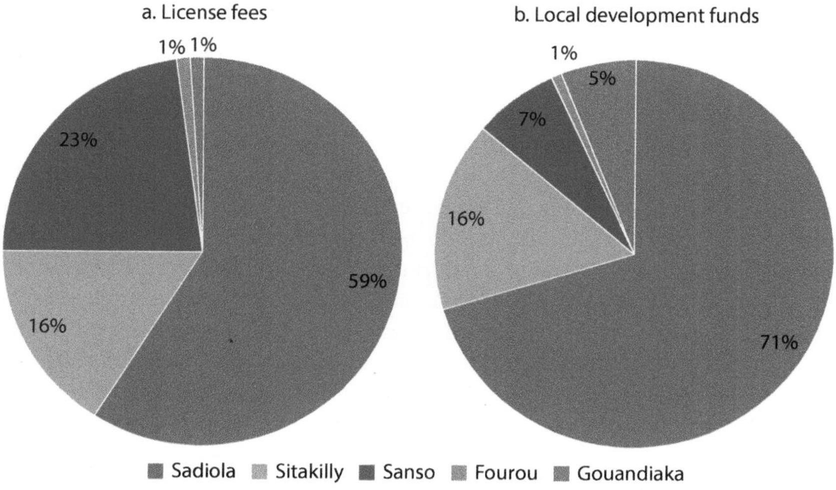

a. License fees

b. Local development funds

■ Sadiola ■ Sitakilly ■ Sanso ■ Fourou ■ Gouandiaka

Source: Sustainable Development Observatory 2011.

Table 3.1 Sectoral Spending, by Commune, of Mining Development Funds in Mali, 1994–2010
Percent

Sector	Sadiola	Sitakilly	Sanso	Fourou	Gouandiaka
Health	10.9	5.4	2.0	5.4	0.9
Education	13.9	4.6	26.9	82.7	33.4
Infrastructure	17.9	10.0	30.9	11.6	50.8
Agriculture	23.0	9.7	14.0	0.0	0.2
Other	34.4	70.4	26.3	0.3	14.7

Source: Sustainable Development Observatory 2011.

and Gouandiaka, the focus has been on infrastructure spending (31 percent and 51 percent, respectively). The largest part of Sitakilly's fund was spent on relocating the local population (table 3.1). Because these funds are controlled by mining companies, they have more sway on how the funds are spent. The government considers these funds as de facto transfers to mining communes, because they come as a deduction from equity returns to be paid to the government (Sustainable Development Observatory 2011).[5]

Channel 2: Government Revenue

The main sources of government revenue from gold mining are dividends from state equity participation; property rates, ground rents, and profit taxes; excise and import duties; and royalties. Government revenues increased considerably in each of the three case study countries during 2001–13, although levels reportedly dropped in 2014 following a decline in international gold prices. During 2005–13, gold mining provided Mali's government with $362 million a year (annual average), and, in the same period, Ghana with $300 million and Tanzania with $137 million (figure 3.6). In Mali, primarily customs duties and, later, taxes drove the increase in mining's contribution to government revenue (figure 3.7).

In Tanzania, tax and royalty payments to government were limited in the years following the opening of the first few large-scale mining projects, reportedly averaging only $30 million a year between 1999 and 2006. This led to the claim that incentives offered to mining companies to attract investment gave away too much in tax exemptions and concessions. Despite an increase in the price of gold, tax holidays meant firms were making only partial corporate tax payments; and despite tightening deal terms, most mineral development agreements have stability agreements locking in the original terms.[6] Nevertheless, taxes and royalties improved, to an average of $77 million a year during 2007–09, and to $260 million during 2010–13. But it is still questionable whether Tanzania received a fair amount of tax and royalty payments, given the volume of minerals produced.

Figure 3.6 Government Mining Revenues in Ghana, Mali, and Tanzania, 2001–13

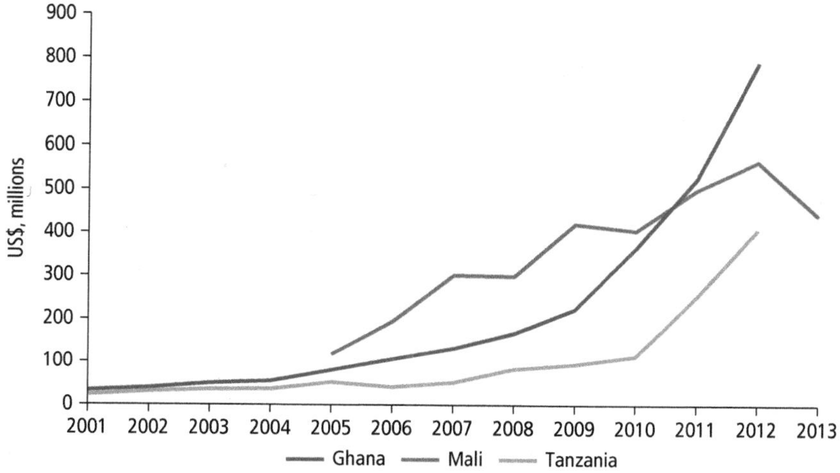

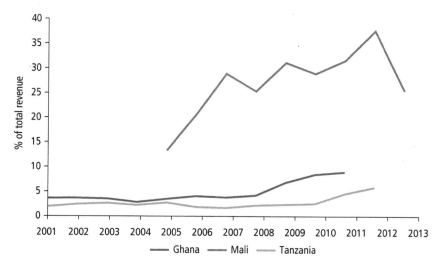

Source: Authors' estimates from administrative data.

Figure 3.7 Government Mining Revenues as a Percentage of Total Revenue in Ghana, Mali, and Tanzania

Source: Authors' estimates from administrative data.

In Mali, tax revenues from mining increased steadily as a proportion of total government resources, from 10 percent in 2005 to 25 percent in 2013, having peaked at 33 percent in 2012, a year that was particularly difficult for the mobilization of resources because of the war in the north. The strong growth of mining's contribution to the national budget was due primarily to revenues from customs duties and, second, from domestic taxes.

All three case study countries are concerned about whether gold mining is adequately taxed. Sanoh and Coulibaly (2015) report that in Mali, the tax burden on mining (the ratio of the tax revenues of mining companies to the value added of mining activity) is more significant than the tax burden on the whole economy (the ratio of total tax revenues to the country's GDP); that is, an average of 57 percent compared to 14 percent (figure 3.8). In 2012, Mali's seven mining companies and their subcontractors represented 45 percent of all corporate taxes in the country. However, the average tax burden on Mali's mining sector is similar to those in other mining countries, including Canada (60 percent), Papua New Guinea (55 percent), and South Africa (45 percent) (Bhushan and Juneja 2012). In developed countries the tax burden is a reflection of the high environmental costs of mining, but this is not the case in Mali.

Fiscal Sharing
Because the central governments of all three case study countries own the natural resources and therefore the revenues, the benefits from natural resources depend largely on whether revenues are put to good use. If history is a guide,

Figure 3.8 Fiscal Burden in Mali

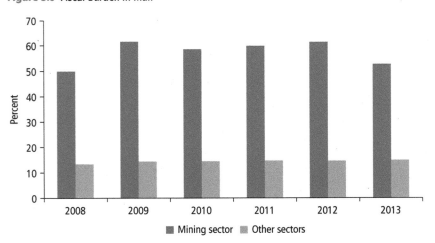

Sources: Mining and Energy Sector Planning and Statistics Unit 2013.

there is ample reason to be cautious. In the mining sector, the areas where mines are located have no property rights to the minerals, and mining firms may feel deprived of the revenue benefits while bearing the bulk of the costs for developing the mine. The fiscal arrangements between central and local governments at various levels will therefore determine how much of the benefits from mining find their way back to the mining areas. In addition, the competency, honesty, and implementation capacity of local government are key to enhancing welfare and development in mining areas.

The country case studies show that Mali has the highest degree of fiscal decentralization and, as such, local authorities receive a larger proportion of the revenues compared to the other two countries. Ghana is in the middle, and its decentralization efforts are fairly new. Tanzania has a more centralized mechanism, whereby all revenues are collected and allocated by the central government. Transfers from Tanzania's central budget fund 90 percent of local government budgets, and the funds are allocated according to criteria and priorities unrelated to the location of mines or the source of the funds.

Ghana

Ghana is an administratively centralized country with three local levels— districts, municipalities, and traditional "stools" presided over by chiefs. Mineral resources in Ghana are owned by the people and their management (according to the Constitution) is vested in the hands of the government. The government is the caretaker of the minerals, but corporations can apply for reconnaissance and prospecting licenses to search for specific minerals. The 1992 Constitution recognizes a decentralized local government system as a way to achieve this objective. Since 2007, the government has mandated that 7.5 percent of total government revenues be transferred to metropolitan, municipal, and district assemblies by a district transfer system. To supplement transfers, these assemblies collect internally generated funds from various sources, including rates, license fees, and fines that constitute 1–20 percent of all revenues from the assemblies for the payment of mining royalties. The government takes the biggest share, 90 percent. Of the rest, 4.95 percent is allocated to the assembly, 2.25 percent to the traditional stool where the mine is located, 1.0 percent to the Office of the Administrator of Stool Lands, and 1.80 percent to the traditional council (Ayee and Dumisa 2014).

Mali

The local authorities in Mali are recognized as autonomous, with specific responsibilities for the provision of public services. Despite some progress in the administrative and financial empowerment of these local entities, they are still largely under the authority of the central government with regard to resources, and even decisions related to local matters. The government seems to be more concerned about national unity and territorial integrity than the enhancement of transfers and public resources to communities.

The local authorities in communes where gold production takes place are supposed to receive 60 percent of the local taxes paid by commercial mining firms and 80 percent of the license fees paid by small-scale miners. Producing *cercles*—the second level administrative subdivision, after the regions—are meant to receive 25 percent and 15 percent of these taxes, respectively, while producing regions retain 15 percent and 5 percent, respectively. Commercial mining companies are exempted from these taxes during the first three years of operation. Local authorities do not have the means to determine the actual level of the license fees that are supposed to be distributed among them—and, in fact, license fees from mining companies are not distributed, as required by law. The share allocated to communes represents 73 percent of the total amounts collected instead of the 60 percent required by law. As a result, all other levels of local authorities receive less than the required percentages: 17 percent at the *cercle* level (the law requires 25 percent), and 1 percent at the regional level (15 percent required).

In general, Mali's local authorities have a low rate of revenue collection and therefore weak self-financing capacity. As a result, government transfers and subsidies are the main source of revenue to support investment expenditures. Indeed, analyses of the budgetary accounts from five mining and 24 neighboring communes reveal a low level of tax collection.[7] Because of the licensing fees paid by mining companies to local authorities, mining communes generate more of their own revenues compared to nonmining ones. These license fees represented more than 50 percent of mining commune revenues from 2011 to 2013, compared to just 2 percent for neighboring communes (figures 3.9)

Although mining communes are less dependent on the transfers from the government, they still remain exposed to the risks related to the closing of mines or the drop of production in this sector because license fee payments are a function of turnover.

Tanzania

All gold mining revenues in Tanzania go to the central government, except for recent annual fees of $200,000 per mine. Revenues are not earmarked, and so there is little point in tracking how much of the gold mining taxes and royalties make it back to the districts. Tanzania's gold belongs to the country and not the local population, and the allocation of funds by the central government to local government authorities in gold mining areas is largely unrelated to the mining revenues sourced in that area. In theory, expenditures are linked to a needs-based formula; in practice, substantial inequities exist in the allocation across local government authorities (ODI 2014). The formula is based on various measures of need, but because employment costs dominate transfers, financial flows

Figure 3.9 Source of Budget Revenues for Mining Communes and Neighboring Communes in Mali, 2011–13

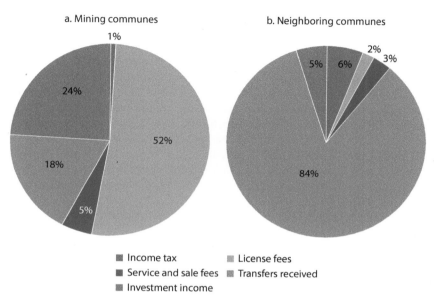

a. Mining communes

b. Neighboring communes

- ■ Income tax
- ■ License fees
- ■ Service and sale fees
- ■ Transfers received
- ■ Investment income

Source: National Directorate of Treasury and Public Sector Accounting.

for the most part follow the number of public servants (mainly teachers and health workers), and this depends in turn on where public servants can be encouraged to locate. Five of Tanzania's six local government authorities hosting large-scale gold mining receive fewer transfers in per capita terms than the national average, except for Tarime District Council.

Negative Externalities: The Costs Borne by Mining Areas

All types of mining can pollute and cause environmental damage unless carefully managed. But even when mining is carefully managed, local communities still face substantial environmental risks. Mercury is typically used in artisanal and small-scale mining; large-scale gold mining uses cyanide and, although highly toxic, is typically better controlled. Nonetheless, large-scale mines do produce toxic tailings, which can be spread by wind—and when tailings dams rupture, the results can be catastrophic.[8] People are often forced to relocate for environmental and other reasons when a mine opens. If the costs of environmental damage and resettlement were treated with the same multipliers and subtracted from the overall impact, the declared benefits would be smaller. These external costs are an obvious source of tension between communities and local authorities, and also between local and national governments.

Arguments asserting the existence of a resource curse often point to the potential for natural resource windfalls to exacerbate rent seeking, corruption, and conflict in society. Mining firms face challenges of securing their investments from theft and violence, some of which are fueled by communities perceptions that they are not benefiting from the mine. In April 2009, armed thieves stole about 100 kilograms of gold worth $4.2 million from the Golden Pride Mine in Tanzania; the North Mara Mine has experienced regular raids. More commonplace is the intrusion of small-scale miners onto mine sites to access tailings and other mining opportunities. Despite theft and violence, Tanzania's mines have continued to produce at a high level (Holeterman 2014).

In Tanzania, large-scale gold mining has been at the center of cases of grand corruption. Take the case of Alex Stewart Assayers. In 2003, the government hired the U.S.-based company to audit gold production following concerns that mining firms were evading taxes and engaging in fraud. The company's hiring terms were contentious; it received tax-free status, was contracted without a formal tender process, had no experience in auditing mining companies, and received a fee equivalent to 1.9 percent of the market value of the country's audited gold exports, leaving only 1.1 percentage points of the 3 percent royalty for the government. The audit by Alex Stewart Assayers eventually cost the government $70 million, without revealing any tax evasion or fraud by the large mining companies (Cooksey 2011).

Outcomes

The country case studies found only marginal improvements in welfare indicators in mining areas, though a lack of data prevents us from drawing definitive conclusions. The study of Mali was, however, able to exploit a relatively rich data source on socioeconomic indicators, which was unfortunately not available for Ghana and Tanzania.

In Mali, for example, enrollment rates in primary schools clearly increase with proximity to a mine, and are higher in neighboring areas than in more distant ones. Not only are the rates higher, but they also increased faster from 1998 to 2009. Outcomes for poverty reduction are inconclusive, however. Although poverty has declined across Mali, the pace of poverty reduction in mining communes has not been faster compared to nonmining communes (figure 3.10).

Figure 3.10 Poverty Headcount in Mining and Other Areas in Mali

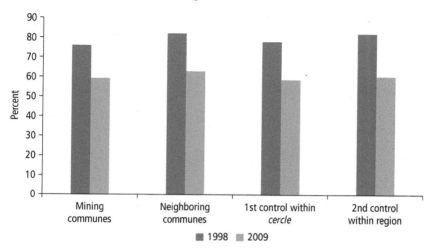

Source: Authors' estimates from census data.
Note: 1998 and 2009 are the years when the two most recent censuses were conducted.

Another interesting outcome in Mali is the differential population growth in mining compared with nonmining areas. The national population growth rate averaged 3 percent annually between 1998 and 2009, but the population growth rate in mining communes was almost double the national rate.[9] Mining communes grew on average 5.7 percent annually, compared with 3.5 percent for neighboring communes and other communes within the same *cercle* (figure 3.11). The population growth rate is above 6 percent in all mining communes, except in Gouandiaka, where, at 2.9 percent, it equals the national rate (figure 3.11, panel b). Because populations migrate from lower- to higher-income areas, the higher population growth in mining is itself indicative of an economic stimulus. However, other things being equal, inward migration tends to slow the rise of wages in mining areas, and it raises average wages in the "donor" ones. This may explain why, despite increased economic activity from mining, the reduction in poverty in mining areas has not significantly outstripped that of other areas. In other words, migration tends to be an equalizer.

Overall social outcomes in Mali are mixed. For access to basic social services, mining communes had low levels of access to electricity and improved cooking fuels before the mining boom started in 1998. For example, fewer than 2 percent of the population used electricity for lighting or improved cooking fuels. However, 30 percent had access to an improved water source, and 50 percent to an improved sanitation facility (table 3.2). In terms of progress, mining

Figure 3.11 Population Growth Rate by Group of Communes and Mining Communes in Mali, 1998–2009

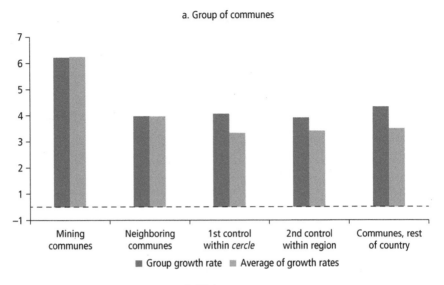

a. Group of communes

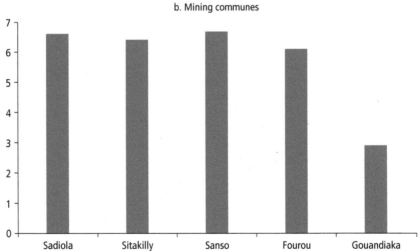

b. Mining communes

Source: Authors' estimate using General Population and Housing Census, 1998 and 2009.

communes saw a significant improvement in these services between 1998 and 2009, when they started from a lower base. However, in 2009, only the share of the population using an improved water source was far greater in mining areas. This may explain the better health outcomes for children in the vicinity of mines (Polat et al. 2014; also see chapter 4 below). Beyond indicators of access, infrastructure outcomes in 2013 were not better in mining areas. For example, while paved roads per capita is slightly higher in mining areas, irrigation per capita is lower than in other areas, though this may reflect differences in rainfall or farming intensity. Mining areas also have fewer nurses and midwives per capita than other types of communes (table 3.3).

Table 3.2 Use of Infrastructure Services, by Group of Communes in Mali, 1998 and 2009
(% of population)

Type of commune and proximity	1998				2009			
	Electric-ity for lighting	Improved water source	Improved cooking fuel	Improved sanita-tion	Electric-ity for lighting	Improved water source	Improved cooking fuel	Improved sanita-tion
Mining communes	1.88	30.31	1.73	50.62	12.97	67.16	2.10	89.25
Neighboring communes	2.73	17.37	1.81	47.94	11.88	42.87	0.65	84.03
1st control within *cercle*	7.71	23.45	2.48	48.97	13.31	42.08	0.61	83.20
2nd control within region	2.62	19.38	2.11	52.35	10.54	29.06	0.47	82.08

Source: Authors' estimate using General Population and Housing Census, 1998 and 2009.

Table 3.3 Infrastructure Outcomes, by Group of Communes in Mali, 2013

Type of commune and proximity	Paved road per 1,000 inh.	Irrigated area per 1,000 inh.	Local health centers per 10,000 inh.	Doctors per 10,000 inh.	Midwives per 5,000 inh.	Nurses per 5,000 inh.	Primary schools per 1,000 inh.	Net primary enrollment (%)
Mining communes	6.80	0.73	0.74	0.52	0.06	0.38	0.88	73.00
Neighbor communes	6.56	4.84	1.17	0.41	0.14	0.82	0.90	63.75
1st control within *cercle*	6.16	5.19	1.03	0.42	0.18	0.58	1.02	61.59
2nd control within region	10.37	6.21	1.07	0.32	0.12	0.72	0.82	55.87

Source: Sustainable Development Observatory database, 2013.
Note: inh = inhabitants.

Figure 3.12 Registered Firms by Employment in Four Tanzanian Towns, 2001 and 2011

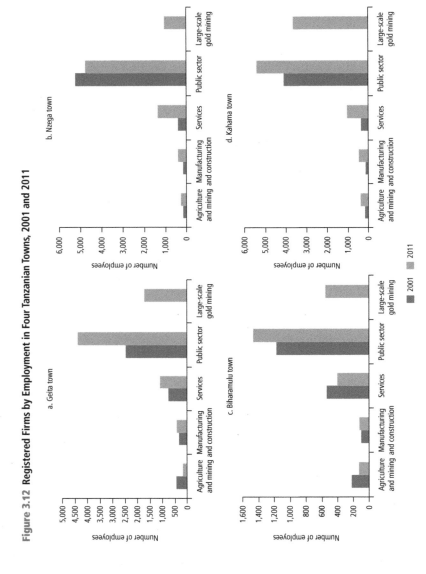

Sources: Central Registry of Establishments Surveys, 2001 and 2011; National Bureau of Statistics.

The case study of Tanzania uses survey data from 2001 and 2011 to track changes in formal employment opportunities in areas around large gold mines. The results from the surveys suggest a considerable increase in employment opportunities, with additional jobs in 2011 relative to 2001 in mining towns. However, as figure 3.12 shows, most additional jobs were in the public sector.[10] Interestingly, only a small increase in employment opportunities occurred in manufacturing, suggesting that linkages have been fairly limited, although this increase does not support the argument of local Dutch-disease-type effects from gold mining.

Conclusions

All changes in an economy bring costs and benefits, and gainers and losers—and so it is with gold mining. From the case studies reviewed here, there is little evidence of economic decline at the national or local level in the three case study countries. But there is evidence that negative externalities have had an impact on communities close to gold mines. The national benefits most likely outweigh these costs, but it is doubtful that compensation is being made or is effective.

Mining is not a major employment generator. Studies of economic growth emphasize that higher productivity in general, and for extractive industries in particular, is a major source of growth and development. However, if the capital is mostly foreign owned and the industry is capital intensive, then the main domestic recipient of the value generated by the gold mines is the government. Thus, in the final analysis, the welfare effects of gold mining—and mineral extraction in general in developing countries—depend on whether government collects its due and puts it to good use.

The conclusions from the case studies are suggestive, but need to be subjected to rigorous statistical analysis to yield more robust results. This is the subject of chapter 4.

Notes

1. This chapter draws on three background papers: Sanoh and Coulibaly (2015) on Mali, Smith and Kinyondo (2015) on Tanzania, and Ayee and Dumisa (2014) on Ghana.
2. As discussed in chapter 2, costs may also arise in the form of Dutch disease and other elements of the resource curse.
3. GDP records the domestic value added of gold exports—that is, the total value of exports minus the associated imports (though these will sometimes be recorded separately.) Disposable income, however, is the important variable for national welfare. Thus, gross national income, which accounts for factor payments to and

from abroad, will deduct the repatriation of profits by gold-mining companies. Other things being equal, the contribution of mining to national income will be less than its contribution to GDP. The repatriation of revenue will be reduced by the royalties and taxes paid by gold-mining companies. Hence, government revenue represents the domestic capture of the rents from mining.

4. The amounts contributed are not based on any standard formula but are decided by the mine or specified in the mining convention. These funds should be seen as another direct form of compensation for some of the costs imposed by mining activities.

5. The state of Mali owns 20 percent equity in all mines.

6. This delayed the start of the payment of a large-scale gold-mining company corporation tax. Added to this was the concession that mining firms could offset all equipment and machinery costs against revenues, and were exempt from the value added tax on goods and services.

7. These budgetary accounts do not include expenditures by the state on behalf of the communes.

8. For example, when the tailings dam at the Baia Mare gold mine in Romania failed in 2000, cyanide leaked into the Somes River, killing 1,400 tons of fish and contaminating the water supply of 2.5 million people.

9. There are many reasons why mining areas may experience higher population growth; among them are simple migration, better health infrastructure, and higher fertility rates.

10. In an export mineral boom, the booming sector is often the public sector. In this case, however, the increase in public sector employment may be due to population growth, which in part could be because of the mining boom and the inward migration that it attracts.

References

Ayee, J., and A. Dumisa. 2014. "The Socio-Economic Impacts of Mining on Local Communities in Ghana." Unpublished, World Bank, Washington, DC.

Bermudez-Lugo, O. 2012. "The Mineral Industry of Ghana." In *Minerals Yearbook: Area Reports International Review of 2011 Africa and the Middle East.* Reston, VA: United States Geological Survey.

Bhushan, Chandra, and Sugandh Juneja. 2012. "Mining, Populations and Environment."

Campbell, B. 2012. "Corporate Social Responsibility and Development in Africa: Redefining the Roles and Responsibilities of Public and Private Actors in the Mining Sector." *Resources Policy* 37 (2): 138–43.

Cooksey, B. 2011. "The Investment and Business Environment for Gold Exploration and Mining in Tanzania.t and Business Environment for Gold Exploration Programme." Overseas Development Institute, London.

ESRF (Economic and Social Research Foundation). 2009. *Governance in Mining Areas in Tanzania with Special References to Land Issues.* Dar es Salaam: ESRF.

Government of Ghana. 2014. *Final Report-Production of Mining Sector GHEITI Report for 2012 and 2013*. Accra: Ministry of Finance.

Holeterman, D. 2014. "Slow Violence, Extraction and Human Rights Defense in Tanzania: Notes from the Field." *Resources Policy* 40: 59–63.

McMahon, G., and S. Moreira. 2014. "The Contribution of the Mining Sector to Socioeconomic and Human Development Extractive." Extractive Industries for Development Series 30, World Bank, Washington, DC.

ODI (Overseas Development Institute). 2014. "Local Government Authority (LGA) Fiscal Inequities and the Challenges of 'Disadvantaged' LGAs in Tanzania." https://www.odi.org/publications/8481-local-government-authority-lga-fiscal-inequities-challenges-disadvantaged-lgas-tanzania#downloads.

Polat, Beyza, Nazli Aktakke, Meltem A. Aran, Andrew L. Dabalen, Punam Chuhan-Pole, and Aly Sanoh. 2014. "Socioeconomic Impact of Mining Activity: Effects of Gold Mining on Local Communities in Tanzania and Mali." Background Paper, World Bank, Washington, DC.

Sanoh, A., and M. Coulibaly. 2015. "The Socioeconomic Impact of Large-Scale Gold Mining in Mali." Unpublished, World Bank, Washington, DC.

Smith, G., and G. Kinyondo. 2015. "The Socioeconomic Impact of Large-Scale Gold Mining in Tanzania." Unpublished, World Bank, Washington, DC.

Sustainable Development Observatory. 2011. "Mines and Socioeconomic Development in Mali: Challenges and Prospects." Unpublished, Sustainable Development Observatory, Brussels.

World Bank. 2002. *Large Mines and Local Communities: Forging Partnerships, Building Sustainability*. World Bank and International Finance Corporation, Washington, DC. http://siteresources.worldbank.org/INTOGMC/Resources/largemineslocalcommunities.pdf.

Chapter 4

Socioeconomic Effects of Large-Scale Gold Mining: Evidence from Ghana, Mali, and Tanzania

Introduction

For more than a decade, starting in about 2000, the minerals sector in Sub-Saharan Africa witnessed a boom. This chapter provides an approach for understanding how the benefits from the minerals sector are captured by local communities, and measures the size of the impact of mining on local welfare. Because the minerals sector in Sub-Saharan Africa is large and diverse, this chapter applies the framework developed in chapter 2 to gold. Gold mining is now an important industry in several countries in Africa (see map 4.1 for the continent's large-scale gold mines). In 2013, four of the world's top 20 gold-producing countries were in Sub-Saharan Africa—Ghana, Mali, South Africa, and Tanzania. This chapter draws from studies trying to identify the local and district-level effects of large-scale gold mining in Ghana, Mali, and Tanzania.[1] Together, these countries accounted for about 35 percent of gold production in Sub-Saharan Africa in 2013.

Our focus on local impacts is motivated by the observation that, in general, the socioeconomic effects of large-scale mining are not well understood. To the extent there is public opinion on the impacts of gold mining on local communities, it is likely to be unfavorable. This is partly because, despite making an important contribution to a country's gross domestic product and export revenue, total employment numbers generated country-wide by mines are generally modest (see chapter 3). Adding to the negative perceptions of the sector is the view that the industry does not contribute enough to fiscal revenue because of low royalty rates and tax holidays.

This study contributes to recent attempts to analyze the welfare impacts of mining. Evidence from Peru shows that mining districts have lower poverty rates

Map 4.1 Large-Scale Gold Mines and Other Mines in Africa

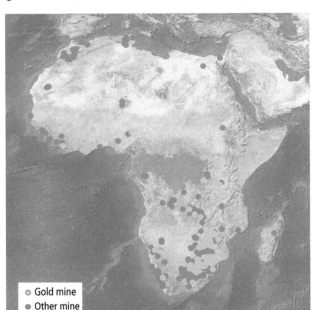

Source: IntierraRMG.
Note: The map shows all large-scale mines in production at any point between 1975 and 2012.

but also higher inequality (Loayza, Teran, and Rigolini 2013). An important finding of the Peruvian studies is that impacts are found both near a mine (local impacts) and in mining districts. More generally, the results show that benefits decline with distance from a mine. The largest positive impacts are found close to a mine, defined as areas within 20 kilometers of a mine, but the impacts disappear altogether at distances that are more than 100 kilometers away (Aragón and Rud 2013a). The effects can be different in the vicinity of a mine and at district levels. Locally, a mine can have a footprint by generating direct employment, while at the district level, welfare can additionally change because of the fiscal revenues mining can bring. The fiscal revenue channel will of course depend on the national fiscal-sharing policies, which for Ghana is 10 percent of royalties. Mining royalties in Mali and Tanzania are not redistributed, although their governments redistribute pooled funds according to criteria that have nothing to do with mining. In Mali, in addition to pooled funds, municipalities with mining production also receive 60 percent of local taxes paid by commercial mining firms.

Despite long-standing interest in the local impacts of mining in Sub-Saharan Africa, studies have been slow in coming. One recent study, however, looked at all large-scale mines across Africa and, using household data from 29 countries, found that mining leads to a structural shift whereby agricultural labor participation decreases, which is partly offset by increases in other sectors such as services (Kotsadam and Tolonen 2015). For gold mining, the decrease in agricultural participation can in part be caused by declining productivity within the sector because of mine pollution. This has been seen near Ghana's gold mines (Aragón and Rud 2013b). Two recent studies explore the effects of gold mining on urbanization rates in Ghana (Fafchamps, Koelle, and Shilpi 2015), and on women's empowerment and infant health in nine African countries (Tolonen 2015).

Using a similar approach, the studies underlying this publication use variation-in-activity status and production volumes across gold mines to identify changes in welfare caused by mining activities. The studies exploit the geographic identification of observations from existing household surveys, such as living standard measurements and demographic and health surveys, to link mines to a household in order to analyze how local- and district-level mining affects livelihoods. In this chapter, we present evidence on the power of a mine to generate structural transformation by exploring effects on occupation, household expenditures, and asset accumulation. We then turn to health indicators and explore child health and access to health care services, and examine access to infrastructure such as electricity and water. To complement the local-level analysis, we explore changes at the administrative-district level. Overall, we try to determine whether both migrants and those permanently settled in mining communities can benefit from the mining activities.

Gold Mining in Ghana, Mali, and Tanzania

Gold mining in Ghana and Mali has a rich historical tradition. Both the ancient kingdoms of Mali and the Gold Coast (Ghana) were renowned for their gold production, and were major sources of gold trade between Europe and Africa in precolonial times. For this study, it may seem that this historical tradition poses a major problem for our empirical strategy, which relies on variation-in-activity status and intensity of production to identify the causal impacts at the local level. However, large-scale modern gold mining in Ghana and Mali began during the colonial era, and only in the 1990s in Tanzania.

To see why historical production is less of a concern, it is worth noting that gold production in Ghana, which started earlier than production in Mali and Tanzania, went into a prolonged and severe slump until the 1990s. But since then, several new large mines have started extracting gold in all three countries. In 2000, three mines opened in Mali, followed by five more over the next

10 years. Tanzania's production in the 1990s was negligible. Its earliest mine during the recent surge in production, Golden Pride, opened in 1999, while the last one to open—Buzwagi, which started extracting in 2009—was within the 1990–2012 study period. During this time, 31 mines were in production in the three countries at one time or another. Table 4.1 shows the first and last

Table 4.1 Mines in Ghana, Mali, and Tanzania, 1990–2011

Name of mine	Opening year	Closing year	Country
Ahafo	2006	Active	Ghana
Bibiani	1998	Active	Ghana
Bogoso Prestea	1990	Active	Ghana
Chirano	2005	Active	Ghana
Damang	1997	Active	Ghana
Edikan (Ayanfuri)	1994	Active	Ghana
Iduapriem	1992	Active	Ghana
Jeni (Bonte)	1998	2003	Ghana
Konongo	1990	Active	Ghana
Kwabeng	1990	1993	Ghana
Nzema	2011	Active	Ghana
Obotan	1997	2001	Ghana
Obuasi	1990	Active	Ghana
Prestea Sankofa	1990	2001	Ghana
Tarkwa	1990	Active	Ghana
Teberebie	1990	2005	Ghana
Wassa	1999	Active	Ghana
Gounkoto (Loulo Permit)	2011	Active	Mali
Loulo (Gara Mine)	2005	Active	Mali
Tabakoto/Segala	2006	Active	Mali
Sadiola Mine	2000	Active	Mali
Yatela	2001	Active	Mali
Morila	2000	Active	Mali
Syama	2000	Active	Mali
Kalana	2004	Active	Mali
Bulyanhulu	2001	Active	Tanzania
Buzwagi	2009	Active	Tanzania
Geita Gold Mine	2000	Active	Tanzania
North Mara	2002	Active	Tanzania
Golden Pride	1999	Active	Tanzania
Tulawaka	2005	Active	Tanzania

Source: Authors' compilation from MineAtlas and IntierraRMG.

years of activity of gold mines in the three countries, and maps 4.2, 4.3, and 4.4 show the the locations of the gold mines.

Annual gold production has risen in the three countries since 1990. Not surprisingly, Ghana has the largest annual production, but the trend has been similar in Mali and Tanzania since the late 1990s (figure 4.1).

Map 4.2 Gold Mines and Gold Districts in Ghana

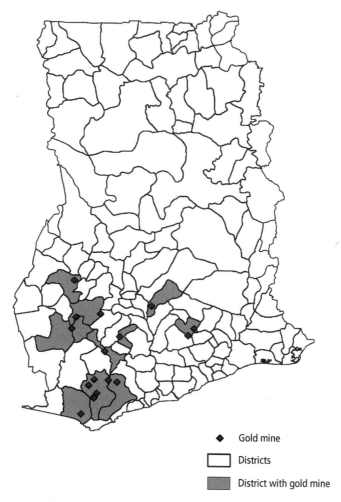

◆   Gold mine

▢   Districts

▨   District with gold mine

Source: Authors' compilation from MineAtlas and IntierraRMG.

Map 4.3 **Gold Mines and Gold Districts in Mali**

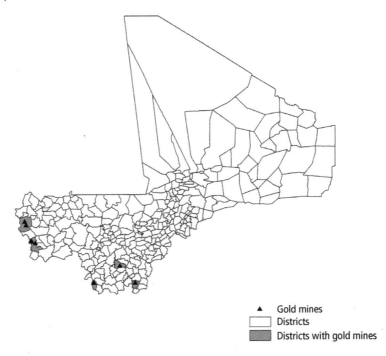

▲   Gold mines
☐   Districts
■   Districts with gold mines

Source: Authors' compilation from MineAtlas and IntierraRMG.

Empirical Methodology

Assessing the Socioeconomic Impact of Gold Mining

The discovery and exploitation of gold can introduce durable changes into an economy. The macroeconomic consequences of the revenue windfalls from such mineral wealth are the subject of a large literature in economics. In this study, we abstain from wading into that debate and focus on local impacts, as discussed in chapter 2. At the local level, the opening of a mine or cluster of mines influences outcomes in desired ways through two channels. In the first, it can draw in resources to the local community and create a virtuous circle; for instance, by increasing the share of workers with higher wages. To meet the inevitable increase in the demand for goods and services by the pool of higher income earners, new local businesses might emerge or existing ones expand, leading to more demand for workers and goods and services. This process could eventually lead to a concentration of economic activity in the local area—sometimes referred to as agglomeration—that could become self-sustaining.

Map 4.4 Gold Mines and Gold Districts in Tanzania

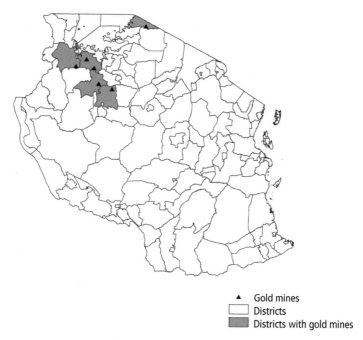

▲   Gold mines
☐   Districts
▓   Districts with gold mines

Source: Authors' compilation from MineAtlas and IntierraRMG.

The second channel is through local or central government action through mine-generated revenues. Imagine that the government sets aside a share of the mining revenues to be spent on local development, which could be implemented by the central or local government. And suppose the local government spends the money on productive public goods—roads, water, electricity, schools, clinics, and so on. Once again, these public investments and services can attract more people into mining areas, create new businesses, and eventually lead to local economic development. These are the possible ways in which positive socioeconomic benefits can emerge. But gold mining can also bring no benefits and even negative impacts by poisoning the water, worsening health outcomes, and rendering agriculture unproductive from pollutants entering the soil. Government revenues may be spent on salaries and not on public goods. And even with no public goods, a boom in gold mining in the government sector represents a rise in income. Therefore, the question of what impacts gold mining has on local socioeconomic development is, importantly, an empirical question.

Figure 4.1 Gold Production in Ghana, Mali, and Tanzania, 1980–2011

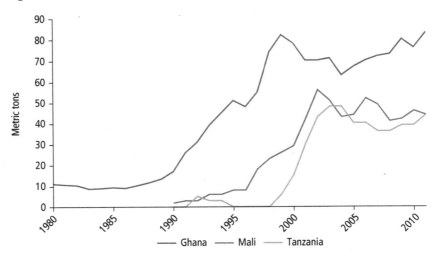

Source: Authors' compilation from MineAtlas and IntierraRMG.

The research that informs this study looks at two definitions of local devel-opment. The first defines it as the district where the mine is located. District refers to political or administrative units that have spending authority. For some of the countries, the latter may be due to a subnational fiscal arrangement in which the district has authority to raise revenue and spend it. In other coun-tries, these units have no taxing authority but instead implement projects on behalf of the central government as part of devolved functions. What they have in common is that one or more mines are available in the unit as described.[2] The second defines it as an area within the vicinity of a mine. We now describe what this analysis looks like.

Measuring Local Effects of Mining: District Level
We begin with how to capture local impacts at the district level, because conceptually it is perhaps the simplest since we identify the effects using an indicator variable capturing whether there are any active large gold mines at the district level. Thus the outcome for individual i in district d in time period t (Y_{idt}) is regressed on an indicator of whether the individual lives in a district with an active mine (ActiveDistrict) at the time of the survey. The regression model also includes district (y) and year fixed effects (g), which will control for cultural differences across districts, and

contemporaneous changes that happen across the country. X_{idt} are characteristics for individuals in district d in time period t. The estimated equation looks like this:

$$Y_{idt} = \beta_0 + \beta_1 ActiveDistrict_{dt} + \gamma_d + g_t + \lambda X_{idt} + \varepsilon_{idt}. \tag{1}$$

This model is a difference-in-differences specification using a district panel. It compares districts with and without gold mines, before and after the mines started producing. The method allows for initial differences across districts; however, it makes a crucial assumption—called the parallel trends assumption. This is the idea that initial differences will not affect estimates of outcomes that will be due to the presence of a mine, as long as the socioeconomic development trends in the districts were similar before mining extraction began. Under this assumption, one can deduce that the change that happened in mining districts at the same time as the mine opening is a result of the mine itself, assuming that no other confounding changes happened at the same time (see box 4.1).

BOX 4.1

Small-Scale Mining Poses Challenges for Identifying Impacts of Large-Scale Mines

The analytic intent of this study is to explore the impact of the large-scale, capital-intensive mining industry in Sub-Saharan Africa on the welfare of local communities. However, not all mining in Sub-Saharan Africa is large scale. Many Sub-Saharan African countries with substantial mining industries, including our three case study countries (Ghana, Mali, Tanzania), have an artisanal and small-scale mining sector, which provides employment (ILO 1999) and livelihood support for many families. It is estimated that about 1 million people in Ghana, 200,000 in Mali, and 550,000 in Tanzania support themselves with revenues from artisanal and small-scale mining. See box 3.1 in chapter 3 for more details.

Unlike large-scale mining, workers in this sector have low skills and capital per worker. Moreover, the sector is associated with hazardous labor conditions, including child labor, mercury exposure, and mine collapses.

Despite huge organizational and operational differences, both sectors often exist side by side. In some instances, competing interests lead to conflict, such as near the Prestea mine in Ghana, where domestic informal small-scale miners have come into conflict with multinational concession owners (Hilson and Yakovleva 2007). This presents challenges for the exact identification of the impact of large-scale mining. Because the data do not always identify individuals working in artisanal and small-scale mining, it is not possible to account for their contribution to these impacts, or for how the opening of a large-scale mine affects participants in this sector.

We can run this equation either using individuals as the level of observation and thus control for their characteristics captured by (X_i), or we could estimate a similar model after collapsing the data to the district level and then control for the average population characteristics captured by means of (X_i). The standard errors are clustered at the level of treatment, the district level. Since the treatment variable is at the same level as our district fixed effects, it is interpretable as the treatment effect. We refer to a year-fixed effect here, because the data structure is not always so simple as to allow the temporal variation to be defined as before and after the mine started producing.

Measuring Spillover Effects at the District Level

Looking for impacts only in districts that have a mine, as equation 1 implies, could miss potential spillovers resulting from mining. There are two main reasons to consider spillover effects across districts. First, the natural economic impact area of a mine can be larger than a district in instances where its administratively or politically determined geographic boundaries are too small for the mine's overall economic and social influence. Second, some mines will be on a district border, and the decision to consider such mines as belonging to one district or another can seem arbitrary. A further reason for considering spillover effects is that mining districts can receive additional fiscal revenue if the mine is within its administrative borders and the country has fiscal-sharing rules. This is an important reason to explore district-level effects. Mining-district spending can also spill over to a neighboring district; for instance, if the mine builds a road to the border of that district. To compare outcomes in mining, neighboring, and nonmining districts, the following estimation is used:

$$Y_{idt} = \beta_0 + \beta_1 ActiveDistrict_{dt} + \beta_2 NeighborDistrict_{dt} + \gamma_d + g_t + \lambda X_{idt} + \varepsilon_{idt}. \quad (2)$$

The interpretation of this model will be similar to the interpretation given for equation 1. However, we are now interested in both models, which allows for a comparison of the difference in districts with mines and districts that border them. Both of the methods outlined in equations 1 and 2 can be further nuanced by allowing for differential effects with intensity of mining, captured by the number of active mines or the annual and aggregated production volumes. In addition, data permitting, a synthetic control method can be used, which compares mining districts to a specially created group (following Abadie, Diamond, and Hainmueller 2010) instead of comparing mining districts to all other districts. The control group is created to be as similar as possible to the treatment group. This method is beneficial when there are few treatment observations (that is, few mining districts), but it puts high demands on pretreatment data. For Tanzania and Mali, this strategy is tried, but for Ghana, it is not possible because its mines opened earlier, and there are too few observations to ensure that we will find the right control group.

Measuring Local Effects of Mining: Vicinity of Mines

Beyond district-level effects (or in addition to them), one can look even more closely at the impact of mining within the vicinity of a mine or mines by measuring its local effects. Here, it is important to determine how large the local area is. As noted above, how broadly a mine's influence extends is an empirical exercise. Along with looking at the vicinity of a mine, where up to 20 kilometers (km) is identified as being close (baseline treatment area), the focus is also on distance bins—concentric circles of varying distances from the mine. These bins can be within a district or span several districts, depending on the mine's location. The spatial lag model divides the plane into small concentric distances, such as 0–10 km, 10–20 km, 20–30 km, and so on up to 100 km from a mine. In the regression specification, each bin can have its own coefficient, and the model thus allows for nonlinear effects with distance. Moreover, it allows us to understand whether there are spillovers from large-scale gold mining farther than our baseline treatment distance. Map 4.5 presents the

Map 4.5 Gold Mines in Ghana and Spatial Buffers

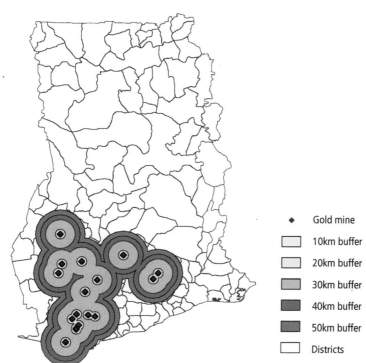

◆	Gold mine
▢	10km buffer
▢	20km buffer
▢	30km buffer
▢	40km buffer
▢	50km buffer
▢	Districts

Source: Authors' compilation from MineAtlas and IntierraRMG.

distribution of mines in Ghana and illustrates how the area these mines affect is captured in the estimation.

For the distance-level analysis, what matters is estimating the outcomes of individuals who live close to the mine, regardless of their administrative jurisdiction. The difference-in-differences model that is applied is as follows:

$$Y_{ivt} = \beta_0 + \beta_1 MineXkm_v * After_t + \beta_3 MineXkm_v + \beta_2 After_t + \gamma_d + g_t + \lambda X_{idt} + \varepsilon_{ivt}, \quad (3a)$$

$$Y_{ivt} = \beta_0 + \beta_1 Mine_v * Active_t + \beta_3 Mine_v + \beta_2 Active_t + \gamma_d + g_t + \lambda X_{idt} + \varepsilon_{ivt}, \quad (3b)$$

where the outcome Y of an individual i who lives in village or neighborhood v in year t is a function of living close to a mine—say, X km from a mine ($MineXkm$)— after the mine has started producing ($After$) or within 20 km of a mine ($Mine$) active at the time of the survey ($Active$). The estimate of interest is the magnitude and direction of the coefficient obtained from the interaction of the two, which captures the average gain for the individuals who live in the vicinity of a mine that is currently extracting gold compared to the average gain of those who do not live in the vicinity. We can still control for individual characteristics and the cross-sectional variation across districts, as well as the broad changes that happen over time. A similar method was used by Aragón and Rud (2013b), Kotsadam and Tolonen (2015), and Tolonen (2015).

It is possible that local procurement, to the extent it might not be captured by the businesses in the vicinity of the mine, will contaminate the control groups, and therefore bias the impact downward—toward zero. In addition, some mines have special programs to increase the amount of domestic procurement from suppliers that are not necessarily in the vicinity of mines. Lack of time series data on the level and composition of goods and services procured by each of the mines studied means this factor cannot be fully controlled for in the estimation. One way to capture these spillover effects in district-level regressions is by adding specific dummies for neighboring districts.

Combining Mining and Household Data

To estimate the models in equations 1–3, this study combines data on mines and household surveys. The mining data are from several sources. The locations of mines, using GPS coordinates for all three case study countries, are from online sources, such as MineAtlas, Google Maps, and the Raw Materials Database of IntierraRMG for Ghana. The mine information on the first year of production and volume of production is from IntierraRMG.

Data on households and individuals come from four main sources: demographic and health surveys, household budget surveys, living standard surveys, and population censuses. The demographic and health surveys are nationally representative household surveys that collect data on marriage, fertility, family

Table 4.2 Household Survey Data for Ghana, Mali, and Tanzania

Country/purpose	Demographic and health surveys	Living standard surveys	Censuses
Ghana	1993, 1998, 2003, 2008	1999, 2004, 2012	—
Mali	1995, 2006, (2001)	1989, 2001, 2010	1987, 1998, 2009
Tanzania	1999, 2010, (2007, 2012)	1992, 2001	1988, 2002
Used for	Individual analysis and district analysis	Individual analysis and district analysis	Synthetic control analysis

Sources: National surveys of the represented countries.
Note: Survey years in parentheses are used in some parts of the analysis; — = not available.

planning, reproductive health, child health, and HIV/AIDS. The household budget surveys are also nationally representative, and are used to track changes in consumption levels; they include information on household characteristics and yearly and monthly household expenditures, as well as income levels in some cases. The living standard surveys also collect demographic and consumption data, as well as detailed information on access to services (education, health, water and sanitation), household enterprises and agricultural production, and labor market activity.

Censuses collect information on a range of household and individual characteristics but cover the whole population. Household characteristics include household size and access to electricity, water, and toilets. Individual characteristics such as occupation, education, age, and marital status are also included. Most of the censuses used for this analysis do not contain information about individuals' income or consumption levels.

Some of the surveys, especially the demographic and health and living standard surveys, are geocoded. Because the mines are also georeferenced, it is easy to determine how far a household observed in such surveys is from the mine. The estimation strategy that uses individuals and households makes use of this information to identify the impacts of mines. Table 4.2 shows the survey years used; annex table 4A.1 lists the outcome variables.

Evolution of Trends in Mining and Nonmining Areas

The assumption of parallel trends is crucial for the difference-in-difference methodology. In the context of this study, the assumption can be interpreted as demanding that the socioeconomic outcomes of interest in mining areas and areas farther away follow the same trend in the absence of the mine becoming active. One way of asserting the validity of this assumption is to analyze pretrends. The balancing table of outcome and control variables was one first attempt to understand pretrends. However, the assumption allows for differences in levels between the control and treatment groups, as long as the variables are evolving on similar paths. We explore this using lights at night and infant mortality as variables. They were chosen because they provide annual variation—in contrast to, say, labor data, which is only available for the survey years. Night lights and infant mortality are also important welfare and development indicators.

Figure 4.2 indicates that night lights in mining areas (defined to within 10 km) are similar to areas further away (30–50 km or 50–100 km) five to 10 years before a mine opens. A small divergence in night lights is already apparent from five years before. In the investment phase, commonly two years before production begins, mining areas are already clearly benefiting from a higher level of night lights. If we do not exclude this preinvestment period from the control group, it will exert a downward bias on our results (this is discussed in the results section, where we try to exclude this phase). The night light estimates are smoothed local polynomials, whereas the infant mortality estimates are linear predictions. In figure 4.2 we allow for a trend break around the preinvestment phase. To the left of the opening year—that is, before the mine started producing—the trends in infant mortality are negative and similar in mining areas and farther away. However, infant mortality rates are higher closer to mines. After mine opening—to the right on the red vertical line—the opposite is true: mine areas have lower infant mortality rates. These results for Ghana, Mali, and Tanzania are confirmed by Tolonen (2015), who found the same patterns, and for other mining countries, including Burkina Faso and Senegal.

Figure 4.2 Parallel Trends in Night Lights and Infant Mortality

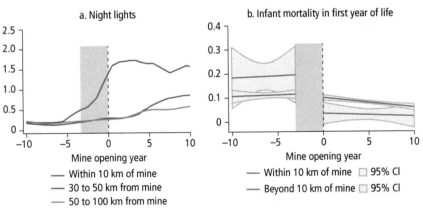

Source: Authors' estimates from survey data.
Note: Horizontal axis in both graphs is years to and after opening of mine. Mine opening is zero, so "years to" are on the left and "years after" are on the right of zero. Vertical axis in panel b is infant mortality in the first year of a child's life. The yellow shaded areas around year 0 show the 2 years leading to opening of mine when some activity already starts. CI = confidence interval.

Livelihoods and Occupations

Using the methods already outlined, we analyze how gold mining has changed livelihoods in Ghana, Mali, and Tanzania. Selected summary statistics from demographic and health surveys in the three countries show that mine areas have developed differently from nonmining ones in terms of occupation (table 4.3). Mining communities, defined as villages and towns within 20 km of a mine, are on average more focused on agricultural production, with a larger share of men working in agriculture than farther away. This is especially true before a mine starts operations.

Mines are land intensive and not surprisingly opened mostly in rural areas, where land is cheaper and where agricultural participation would be expected to be higher before a mine opens. This is certainly true for Mali, but not for Ghana and Tanzania. A notable feature of these surveys is that the participation of women in the services sector is quite low overall, but the summary statistics show the sector has grown, suggesting that the growth rate in services employment might be higher in mining communities.

Table 4.3 Summary Statistics from Demographic and Health Surveys in Ghana, Mali, and Tanzania

	Ghana		Mali		Tanzania	
	(1)	(2)	(3)	(4)	(5)	(6)
	Before	During	Before	During	Before	During
Woman's characteristics						
Age	30.15	30.01	28.59	30.68	29.24	27.68
Wealth	3.01	3.26	—	3.19	3.12	2.80
Nonmigrant	0.36	0.31	0.38	0.49	0.33	0.33
Urban	0.23	0.33	0.25	0.00	0.00	17.8
Woman's occupation						
Not working	0.22	0.21	0.16	0.22	0.14	0.11
Service and sales	0.19	0.25	0.11	0.23	0.01	0.5
Professional	0.06	0.07	0.01	0.00	0.06	0.02
Agriculture	0.41	0.32	0.33	0.06	0.69	0.71
Manual labor	0.12	0.15	0.39	0.06	0.10	0.11
Earning cash	0.88	0.90	0.45	0.60	0.59	0.36
Works all year	0.88	0.88	0.33	0.34	0.17	0.24
Woman's education						
Three years' education	0.78	0.82	0.09	0.07	0.74	0.25
No education	0.17	0.13	0.88	0.88	0.22	0.73

(continued next page)

Table 4.3 (continued)

	Ghana		Mali		Tanzania	
	(1)	(2)	(3)	(4)	(5)	(6)
	Before	During	Before	During	Before	During
Partner's occupation						
Service and sales	0.09	0.12	0.06	0.09	—	0.07
Professional	0.12	0.15	0.04	0.10	—	0.05
Agriculture	0.57	0.42	0.70	0.10	—	0.74
Manual labor	0.21	0.28	0.15	0.15	—	0.13
Child health						
Diarrhea	0.13	0.17	0.22	0.19	0.10	0.12
Cough	0.22	0.18	0.30	0.21	0.29	0.21
Fever	0.24	0.20	0.33	0.22	0.38	0.29

Source: Authors' estimates from demographic and health surveys of the three countries.
Note: Columns 1, 3, and 5 show summary statistics for a sample within 20 km of a nonactive mine. Columns 2, 4, and 6 show summary statistics for a sample within 20 km of an active mine. The demographic and health surveys focus primarily on women. — = not available.

Table 4.4 shows the econometric results for all three case study countries, across different occupations and for men and women. Among women, the likelihood of being a manual worker declined in populations living near mines. This is stronger for Mali and Tanzania and less so for Ghana, where this is observed more for men than for women. For Ghana, there is a shift from agriculture to services for women, but it is not statistically significant. In Mali, in addition to a large decrease in manual work, there is also a large (insignificant) increase—of about 16 percentage points—in services sector employment for women. For Tanzania, agricultural participation rose for women, and there was also a small increase in professional work.

The data used for this estimation come from demographic and health surveys, which primarily focus on women's welfare. This means that fewer men were sampled. This can cause problems in our statistical model for men, since a small number of observations means that we have a problem estimating effects precisely. Not surprisingly, for men, few statistically significant effects are observed, with only a marginally significant drop in manual worker occupation of 6.9 percentage points in Ghana.

Furthermore, these results were obtained by using a 20-km cutoff distance for the treatment area; that is, it is assumed the mine influences outcomes within this distance. But, in fact, there is no strong reason to assume that 20 km is the true radius of the catchment area of a mine. This cutoff was selected based on guidance from studies using similar methodologies; Aragón and Rud (2013b) and Kotsadam and Tolonen (2015) use this distance for exploring the

Table 4.4 Occupations of Men and Women in Proximity to Mines in Ghana, Mali, and Tanzania

	Ghana	Mali	Tanzania	Ghana	Mali	Tanzania
Sample	Men	Men	Men	Women	Women	Women
Treatment distance	20 km	20 km	20 km	20 km	20 km	20 km
Worked last 12 months	0.006	−0.023	0.049	0.006	−0.141	0.124**
	(0.023)	(0.069)	(0.063)	(0.023)	(0.113)	(0.053)
Agriculture	0.05	−0.125	0.103	−0.025	−0.137	0.172***
	(0.051)	(0.164)	(0.117)	(0.039)	(0.232)	(0.062)
Services sector	0.02	0.111	−0.015	0.024	0.160	−0.017
	(0.02)	(0.074)	(0.021)	(0.031)	(0.127)	(0.013)
Professional	0.027	−0.004	−0.011	−0.017*	−0.010	0.023***
	(0.026)	(0.011)	(0.01)	(0.009)	(0.007)	(0.008)
Manual worker	−0.069*	−0.117	−0.029	0.012	−0.227***	−0.071**
	(0.036)	(0.091)	(0.061)	(0.021)	(0.086)	(0.03)

Source: Authors' estimates from survey data.
Note: Each line is a new regression estimated using the baseline model. Reported coefficients are for active*mine in equation 3. All regressions control for year and district fixed effects, urban dummy, age, and years of education. Standard errors are in parentheses.
***$p<0.01$, **$p<0.05$, *$p<0.1$.

effects of mining on local agricultural and labor markets in Ghana and Africa. However, Tolonen (2015) shows that most health and labor effects are concentrated within 10–15 km in Africa's gold-producing countries. By contrast, Aragón and Rud's (2013a) study of one large gold mine in Peru showed effects can be found as far as 100 km.

The Geography of Mining

Instead of using a binary variable—comparing people within 20 km of a mine with everyone else outside that distance—to capture the impacts, a spatial lag model is used, which allows for nonlinear effects with distance. The results from this model are presented in figure 4.3. The focus is on women's access to occupations, since the demographic and health survey data that these results are based on are more suitable for women subsamples.

Figure 4.3 shows that services sector employment for women is significantly higher close to active mines. In fact, the effects are stronger within 0–10 km of a mine than within 10–20 km. In Mali, the probability that a woman works in services and sales increases by 30 percentage points, and in Ghana by 17 percentage points, in the closest distance to a mine. For Ghana and Mali, agricultural participation drops close to mines, by roughly 10 to 20 percentage points. In Tanzania, no clear change is noticed, either in services, sales, or agricultural employment. The occupation pattern is similar across the three countries between women migrants and never-movers (that is, those who have never moved) (figure 4.4).

Figure 4.3 Spatial Lag Model Illustrating Geographic Distribution of Effects on Services Sector and Agricultural Employment for Women in Ghana, Mali, and Tanzania

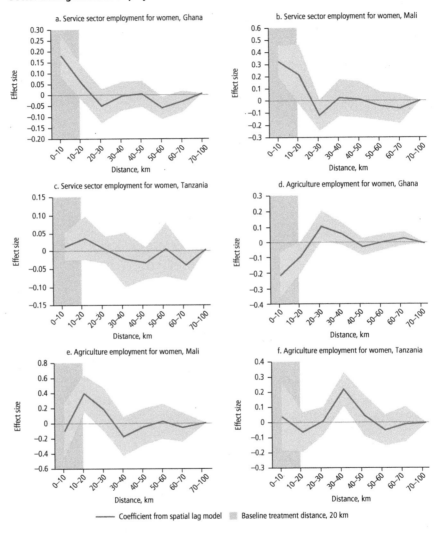

Source: Authors' estimates from survey data.
Note: Shaded area along lines represents 95 percent confidence interval.

Figure 4.4 Spatial Lag Model Illustrating Migrants and Never-Movers, by Occupation in Services and Agriculture in Ghana, Mali, and Tanzania

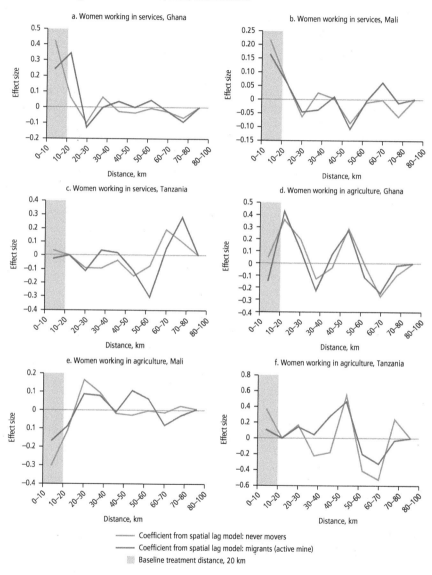

Source: Authors' estimates from survey data.

A similar analysis using demographic and health survey data can be done for men, since women give their partner's occupation in answering the survey questions. Figure 4.5 shows that men are less likely to work in agriculture if they live within 10 km of a mine (statistically significant in Mali). A pattern in the data indicates the possibility of a geographic displacement of farming activities from very close to a mine to slightly further away (20–30 km), especially in Ghana. Men are not more likely to do manual labor in Ghana or in Mali. For Ghana, data on mining employment from the Ghana Living Standards Survey data set confirm a 10-percentage-points increase in the likelihood that a man living close to a mine works in mining.

Taking a closer look—as we have done—at the impacts of mines on employment prospects and wages is one way of looking at the local impacts of mining. But the costs and benefits within the neighborhood of a mine discussed so far are not exhaustive. As we argued at the beginning of this chapter, mining can have additional impacts beyond the neighborhood of the mine if mining royalties and revenues are spent on populations living in districts where a mine is located. The injection of additional expenditures into a district could increase spending on welfare-enhancing services, such as schooling or health care. But the likelihood of identifying these channels depends on a host of factors, including whether a rules-based formula for sharing mining revenues actually exists, and the quality and performance of local politicians and the bureaucracy.

Unfortunately, although information is available on whether or not the three case study countries have a revenue-sharing rule, time series data on the actual revenue flows or a measure of bureaucratic performance are lacking. The availability of such data would have allowed us to estimate impacts by looking at within-district variation over time. Instead, we present a first approximation of additional impacts by simply comparing outcomes between mining and non-mining districts. This district-level analysis makes use of data from demographic and health surveys, household budget surveys, and censuses. In Mali and Tanzania, we mapped (using well-known imputation methods) the outcome variables that do not exist in the censuses;[3] namely, malnutrition outcomes of children and expenditures per capita. The averages of all the outcome variables for each district were calculated. Then, a simple difference-in-differences analysis and a synthetic control group analysis using district-level averages were undertaken. For Tanzania, the analysis includes only the districts that are on the mainland; it excludes the districts of Pemba and Zanzibar.

In the synthetic control analysis, an average of the outcomes of the mining and neighboring districts was used to compute one representative mining district and one representative neighboring district. The synthetic control method gives weights to the remaining districts to come up with the most representative control district.[4] Following Abadie, Diamond, and Hainmueller (2010), placebo tests are used to find out whether the significance of the results can be found by chance.

Figure 4.5 **Spatial Lag Model Illustrating Agriculture, Manual Labor, Mining, and Wage Earnings for Men in Ghana and Mali**

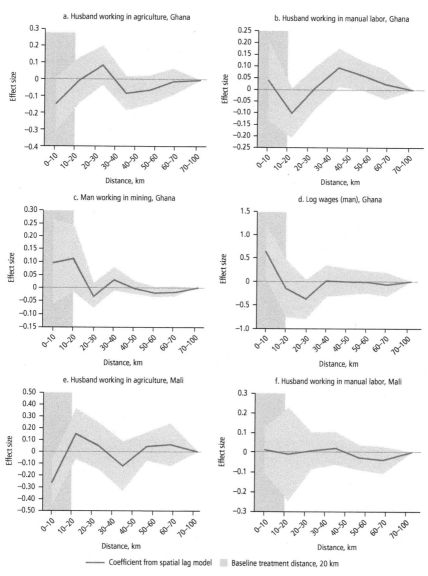

a. Husband working in agriculture, Ghana

b. Husband working in manual labor, Ghana

c. Man working in mining, Ghana

d. Log wages (man), Ghana

e. Husband working in agriculture, Mali

f. Husband working in manual labor, Mali

——— Coefficient from spatial lag model   ▒ Baseline treatment distance, 20 km

Source: Authors' estimates from survey data.
Note: Shaded area along lines represents 95 percent confidence interval.

That is, we try to determine whether a district that is randomly assigned to be the treatment district differs significantly from its synthetic control district in the posttreatment period. This will show us how often the difference between the outcomes of the real treatment district and its synthetic control counterpart stands out. Ideally, the outcome of the real treatment district should be significantly different from its synthetic control district, while for other districts that are randomly assigned as treatment districts, the difference should not be as high.

Overall, the district-level analysis of changes in employment for men and women confirms the findings of the distance-level analysis. Table 4.5 reports the simple difference-in-differences at the district level for Ghana. The results indicate that agricultural employment decreases in mining districts by 8.5 percentage points relative to nonmining districts for women (panel a). Moreover, there is a negative relationship between tons of gold produced and agricultural employment (panel b). In addition, the probability of a woman working all year increases by 5.4 percentage points, as does the probability of doing manual work (panel a). The same is not observed in adjacent districts (panel b). For men, there is a decrease of 5.2 percentage points in agricultural participation, but no significant increases in other sectors. However, the insignificant point estimates indicate that men might be shifting toward services

Table 4.5 District-Level Effects on Occupation in Ghana's Gold and Neighboring Districts[a]

Occupation status	(1) Not working	(2) Agriculture	(3) Service or sales	(4) Professional	(5) Manual work	(6) Earns cash	(7) Works all year
Panel A. Mine districts: women							
Active district	0.019	−0.085**	0.034	−0.018**	0.050**	−0.021	0.054*
	(0.027)[b]	(0.042)	(0.030)	(0.008)	(0.020)	(0.049)	(0.032)
Panel B. Spillovers: women							
Gold period district[c]	0.004	−0.009**	0.003*	0.004***	−0.002	0.001	0.006
	(0.004)	(0.004)	(0.002)	(0.002)	(0.004)	(0.003)	(0.004)
Neighboring gold production	−0.004	0.005	−0.001	−0.002***	0.001	0.008*	−0.002
	(0.004)	(0.004)	(0.004)	(0.001)	(0.003)	(0.004)	(0.004)
Panel C. Mine district: men							
Active district	0.008	−0.052**	0.020	−0.009	0.024		
	(0.009)	(0.023)	(0.030)	(0.026)	(0.027)		

Source: Authors' estimates from survey data.
a. Labor market opportunities for women and men according to demographic and health surveys.
b. Robust standard errors clustered at the district level are in parentheses. All regressions control for year and district fixed effects, urban dummy, age, and years of education. Active is active status of mine in the survey year.
c. Gold period district is equal to total production for the years before the survey.
***$p<0.01$, **$p<0.05$, *$p<0.1$.

sector employment and manual work. Previously, results from the Ghana Living Standards Survey showed that men might shift into mining employment. This information is not available in the demographic and health surveys, so the finding cannot be confirmed here.

Table 4.6 shows the results from a district analysis for Tanzania and Mali. Tanzania's data come from household budget surveys and compare across districts; of the 103 districts in the analysis, four are mining districts (Geita, Kahama, Nzega, and Tarime). Mali has 257 districts, five of them are mining districts (Fourou, Kalana, Kenieba Central, Sadiola, and Sanso). The difference-in-differences district analysis shows significant increases in the likelihood of mining employment. In Mali, men and women are almost 10.0 and 2.3 percentage points more likely to work as miners, respectively, after the mine opens. Note, however, that these changes can also be due to increases in small-scale mining over the same period. Overall, agricultural employment decreases for men and women, but these results are not statistically significant. Tanzania (table 4.6, panel b), has no recorded information on mining employment. And similar to Mali, there is an economically significant decrease in agricultural employment (8 percentage points for men, 11 percentage points for women), but these estimates are not statistically significant.

A district-level analysis that compares mining districts to control districts using the synthetic control method was done for Mali and Tanzania.

Table 4.6 District-Level Effects on Employment in Gold Districts in Mali and Tanzania

	(1)	(2)	(3)	(4)	(5)	(6)
Employment area	Agriculture (men)	Agriculture (women)	Service empl. (men)	Service empl. (women)	Mining empl. (men)	Mining empl. (women)
Panel A. Mine districts: Mali						
Active district	−0.12	−0.35	0.02	−0.01	0.097***	0.023**
	(0.342)	(0.035)	(0.454)	(0.552)	(0.000)	(0.002)
R-squared	0.10	0.02	0.12	0.01	0.14	0.05
Observations	514	514	514	514	514	514
Panel B. Mine districts: Tanzania						
Active district	−0.08	−0.11	−0.0003	−0.006		
	(0.5456)	(0.4428)	(0.9875)	(0.7083)		
R-squared	0.02	0.133	0.01	0.012		
Observations	206	206	206	206		

Source: Authors' estimates from survey data.
Note: Standard errors in parentheses. Unit of observation is district level. Mining districts have at least one active gold mine. The regressions control for year fixed effects and initial conditions in mining districts. No information is available on mining employment for Tanzania.
***$p<0.01$, **$p<0.05$.

Although the findings do not indicate large positive impacts of mines on the overall employment rates of men or women in mining districts compared to non-mining districts, there is some evidence of significant changes in the composition of employment. For example, in Mali, employment rates of men and women working in manufacturing increased, while agricultural employment for women decreased considerably (annex table 4A.2). In Tanzania, by contrast, there were no significant differences between mining and nonmining districts in overall employment changes, or in the composition of employment for both men and women (annex table 4A.3). Overall, these district-level results are consistent with the finding using individual-level estimates that were reported in the previous section.

Is Local Structural Transformation Occurring?

Recall that one mechanism through which mining can have large impacts is agglomeration economies; that is, gains in productivity unleashed with clustering of economic activities around a mine. The first sign of such a change would be the movement of labor and other factors away from traditional sectors to new sectors. In the three country case studies, this would mean a change in the structure of the local economy from being dominated by traditional farming—defined by low inputs and low capital per worker—to a more balanced local economy. Therefore, an important question is whether the results on employment and occupations lead us to believe that gold extraction in these countries helped shift workers from agriculture to other sectors with higher productivity, higher wages, and greater opportunities for economic growth. Thus, raising the question: were there signs of local structural transformation?

The empirical results so far show that in some of the three countries women shift from agriculture to service sector employment in the close vicinity of mines, and that employment in mining increased for men. The shift into mining or into services is away from subsistence farming, the dominant occupation before a mine begins operations. Summary statistics show that participation in the agricultural sector is between 33 and 70 percent in mining communities at the start of our period (table 4.3) for men and women. After mining begins, participation rates for both drop sharply in Ghana and Mali. This is possibly caused by pull factors, whereby higher productivity and wages in mines encourage community members to change occupations. A competing hypothesis is considered by Aragón and Rud (2013b), who show that mine pollution decreased agricultural productivity around Ghana's gold mines. This effect could be reinforced by the land-intensive nature of mining, which increases competition over limited land resources, and leads to a decrease in available arable land if mines are located in agricultural hinterlands.

The increases in employment in the services and other sectors can be understood as "local multipliers" (Moretti 2010). Here, for each job created directly in mining, additional jobs are created in the tradable or nontradable sector. The size of the multiplier depends on total mine employment, miners' wages and spending habits, and how mining companies source inputs such as food, electricity, and housing for their workers. Mining companies can try to boost the multiplier by, for example, ensuring that they source inputs from local suppliers. There are also local fiscal multipliers: a mine may result in local tax contributions that, when spent by the local government, can help stimulate the local economy. Unfortunately, the data are insufficient to calculate these multipliers, but the results support this hypothesis.

Findings from the Ghana Living Standards Survey show women are not benefiting as much from direct employment in mining as men, which highlights the structural change that happens when mining is gender specific. Gender segregation in labor markets has been found to be important in determining how extractive industries generate employment for men and women. This argument was first made by Ross (2008) for oil industries, and the hypothesis later tested for African mining using microdata (Kotsadam and Tolonen 2015).

Income, Wages, and Expenditures in Mining Communities in Ghana

One sign of structural transformation is the shift toward wage and nonfarm activities. The findings so far show there are signs that the latter is happening in local communities around mines in the three countries. Is similar evidence available for wages? The available household surveys have two drawbacks for understanding wages and mining: they are not geocoded, so the workers cannot be linked to a mine, and most workers have no wage data. The exception is Ghana, where geocoordinates for households are available for those surveyed in the Ghana Living Standards Survey. This allows mapping of wages, income, and expenditure changes in mining communities. The analysis shows that in mining communities, household total wages increase, as do women's wages (table 4.7). Men's wages increase too, but the increase is not precisely estimated. In general, men's wages are higher, so despite a larger increase in women's wages, these estimates do not indicate that women's wages are higher than men's. Although household total wages increase, household expenditures decrease (table 4.7, column 4). Note that wage earnings are only recorded for those who are engaging in wage labor; in fact, only 13.3 percent of people in the Ghana Living Standards Survey sample have recorded wage earnings. So although the wage rate increases for those who earn wages, what happens to total earnings in households without any wage labor is not clear.

Findings on changes in expenditures in Ghana are presented in table 4.8. The evidence shows that regional food prices are higher in mining areas

Table 4.7 Changes in Income, Wages, and Expenditures in Ghana

	(1) Natural logarithm wages, all	(2) Natural logarithm wages, men	(3) Natural logarithm wages, women	(4) Natural logarithm per capita exp.	(5) Total household exp.
Active*mine	0.520** (0.226)	0.391 (0.238)	0.694*** (0.241)	−0.178* (0.093)	−0.126 (0.089)
Controls					
Individual	Yes	Yes	Yes	No	No
Household head	No	No	No	Yes	Yes
Household size	No	No	No	No	Yes
District dummies	Yes	Yes	Yes	Yes	Yes
Year dummies	Yes	Yes	Yes	Yes	Yes
Deflated	No	No	No	Yes	Yes
Mean (in logs)	15.30	15.31	15.29	13.04	14.19

Source: Authors' estimates from Ghana Living Standards Survey data.
Note: (1) annual wages and salaries for individuals in all ages (nondeflated), (2) annual wages and salaries for women in all ages (nondeflated), (3) annual wages and salaries for men in all ages (nondeflated), (4) real per capita annual food and nonfood expenditures (regionally deflated), (5) total annual regionally adjusted household expenditures (local currency). All regressions control for year and district fixed effects, urban dummy, age, and years of education. Active*mine defines proximity to an active mine. Standard errors in parentheses.
***$p<0.01$, **$p<0.05$, *$p<0.1$.

Table 4.8 Mapping Changes in Expenditure Composition in Ghana, Using the Living Standards Survey

	(1) Food price index	(2) Food expenditures	(3) Education health	(4) Housing	(5) Electricity and gas
Panel A: Household Expenditures					
Active*mine	0.035*** (0.012)	−0.069 (0.095)	−0.168 (0.199)	0.316** (0.139)	0.297** (0.119)
Mean (in logs)	—	13.42	10.88	10.74	9.52
Observations	7,557	7,396	6,541	7,420	4,752
R-squared	0.582	0.963	0.837	0.933	0.950
Deflated	—	Yes	No	No	No

	(6) Food share	(7) Food share	(8) Education and health share	(9) Housing share	(10) Electricity and gas share
Active*mine	−0.017 (0.054)	−0.022 (0.053)	−0.097 (0.186)	0.404*** (0.121)	0.267** (0.129)
Observations	7,396	7,396	6,541	7,420	4,752
R-squared	0.196	0.245	0.145	0.225	0.171
Expenditures per capita	No	Yes	No	No	No
Deflated	Yes	Yes	No	No	No

Source: Authors' estimates from survey data.
Note: All expenditure and food share variables are used in natural logarithms. All regressions control for household head, household size, district fixed effects, and year fixed effects. Numbers in parentheses are estimated standard errors. Active*mine defines proximity to an active mine. — = not available.
***$p<0.01$, **$p<0.05$.

(column 1), which is similar to the findings in Peru (Aragón and Rud 2013a). But unlike the Peru study, regionally deflated food expenditures do not increase (column 2), nor does the share of food in total deflated household expenditures (columns 6 or 7) rise. However, total household expenditures on housing increase by 31.6 percent with the mining onset, all else being equal (column 4, not regionally deflated prices), along with the share of this component in total expenditures. The same is true for energy costs, such as electricity and natural gas, which rise 29.7 percent with the onset of mining, all else being equal. This might be due to a rise in electrification that is observed in the demographic and health survey data (results are presented later in the chapter).

Similar analyses for Mali and Tanzania, using the district-level analysis comparing mining districts to control districts using the synthetic control method, show an increase in income inequality in mining and neighboring districts compared to control districts in Mali, while the opposite happens in Tanzania (tables 4.9 and 4.10). In Tanzania, average real per capita expenditures decrease when mining and neighboring districts are taken together as treated units in the difference-in-differences analysis; however, the decrease was significant for mining districts only in the synthetic control analysis.

Table 4.9 Wealth Outcomes for Variables from Synthetic Control Analysis in Tanzania

Type of district	Mining districts	Synthetic control group: mining districts	Neighboring districts	Synthetic control group: neighboring districts	Control group
Real expenditures per capita					
1988	4,867.5	4,868.3	5,062.9	5,052.7	4,747.1
2002	2,231.4	3,058.6	2,201.6	3,172.2	2,982.7
Gini					
1988	0.329	0.328	0.332	0.331	0.344
2002	0.371	0.362	0.323	0.362	0.364
Income share of bottom 40%					
1988	0.189	0.188	0.198	0.198	0.184
2002	0.154	0.161	0.153	0.161	0.162
Income share of upper 5%					
1988	0.178	0.178	0.184	0.182	0.182
2002	0.202	0.199	0.186	0.198	0.199

Source: Authors' estimates from survey data.
Note: Reported outcomes for a mining district are the average outcome of mining districts. For a neighboring district, it is the average outcome of these districts. Control group is the average outcome of the districts, except neighboring districts and mining districts.

Table 4.10 Wealth Outcomes for Variables from Synthetic Control Analysis in Mali

Type of district	Mining districts	Synthetic control group: mining districts	Neighboring districts	Synthetic control group: neighboring districts	Control group
Real expenditures per capita					
1987	174,626	165,184	154,242	151,096	137,099
1998	133,798	137,750	121,767	125,681	122,919
2009	142,779	115,028	120,288	117,702	115,153
Gini					
1987	0.319	0.327	0.276	0.277	0.288
1998	0.382	0.371	0.333	0.333	0.348
2009	0.366	0.313	0.300	0.287	0.285
Income share of bottom 40%					
1987	0.218	0.208	0.231	0.229	0.205
1998	0.184	0.195	0.205	0.208	0.185
2009	0.194	0.223	0.219	0.233	0.229
Income share of upper 5%					
1987	0.182	0.173	0.147	0.150	0.149
1998	0.207	0.208	0.175	0.172	0.176
2009	0.201	0.176	0.164	0.161	0.156

Source: Authors' estimates from survey data.
Note: Reported outcomes for a mining district are the average outcome of the mining districts. For a neighboring district, it is the average outcome of these districts. Control group is the average outcome of the districts, except neighboring districts and mining districts.

Household Accumulation of Assets

How does the opening of a mine close to a community affect a household's probability of ownership of assets, such as cement flooring, radios, and cars? The regression results using the baseline specification in table 4.11 show that households (close to a mine) in Mali are 30 percentage points more likely to have floors made of cement, tile, wood, or materials other than earth, sand, or dung. Households in Mali are also 5 percentage points more likely to own a car (but are 11 percentage points less likely to own a bicycle, at a 90 percent confidence level). Households in Ghana are 14 percentage points more likely to own a radio. Table 4.12 decomposes the effects by the migration status of the surveyed women. Radio ownership increases for both migrant women and nonmigrant women in Ghana, but for Mali the positive effects on household assets seem to be driven by migrant households. In Tanzania, no significant changes in assets were found, according to table 4.11, but the decomposition shows that radio ownership increased among nonmigrant households. These effects are also illustrated in figures 4.6 and 4.7.

Table 4.11 Household Asset Accumulation in Ghana, Mali, and Tanzania

	(1)	(2)	(3)	(4)
	Floor (cement)	Bicycle	Car	Radio
Ghana				
Active*mine	−0.000	0.036	0.010	0.137***
	(0.044)	(0.026)	(0.011)	(0.038)
Observations	14,099	14,114	14,112	14,102
R-squared	0.235	0.280	0.093	0.146
Mali				
Active*mine	0.299***	−0.113*	0.049**	0.003
	(0.091)	(0.068)	(0.023)	(0.081)
Observations	6,861	6,884	6,847	6,881
R-squared	0.311	0.204	0.087	0.049
Tanzania				
Active*mine	0.048	0.011	−0.003	0.024
	(0.054)	(0.107)	(0.007)	(0.049)
Observations	6,942	6,945	6,938	6,942
R-squared	0.363	0.175	0.082	0.054

Source: Authors' estimates from survey data.
Note: Reported coefficients are the coefficients of the interaction variable for being close to a mine that was active in the survey year. Unreported coefficients include coefficients of the treatment dummy, year dummy, and the control variables. Standard errors are in parentheses. Error terms are clustered at the sample cluster level. See annex table 4A.1 for variable definitions. All outcome variables are indicator variables that take the value 1 or 0. Floor (cement) captures whether flooring is made of cement, tile, wood, or materials other than earth, sand, or dung. Bicycle, car, and radio captures whether the household has these assets. Active*mine defines proximity to an active mine.
***p<0.01; **p<0.05; *p<0.1.

Table 4.12 Household Asset Accumulation by Migration Status in Ghana, Mali, and Tanzania

	(1)	(2)	(3)	(4)
	Floor (cement)	Bicycle	Car	Radio
Ghana migrants				
Active*mine	−0.045	0.067**	0.010	0.113***
	(0.046)	(0.029)	(0.013)	(0.042)
Ghana nonmigrants				
Active*mine	0.055	0.001	0.022	0.212***
	(0.058)	(0.035)	(0.015)	(0.057)
Mali migrants				
Active*mine	0.449***	−0.147*	0.062**	0.132***
	(0.107)	(0.087)	(0.026)	(0.050)
Mali nonmigrants				
Active*mine	0.116	−0.053	0.038	−0.141
	(0.075)	(0.101)	(0.030)	(0.121)

(continued next page)

Table 4.12 (continued)

	(1)	(2)	(3)	(4)
	Floor (cement)	Bicycle	Car	Radio
Tanzania migrants				
Active*mine	−0.099	0.076	0.001	−0.082
	(0.088)	(0.193)	(0.012)	(0.083)
Tanzania nonmigrants				
Active*mine	−0.184	−0.191*	0.005	0.248**
	(0.111)	(0.103)	(0.008)	(0.095)

Source: Authors' estimates from survey data.
Note: Reported coefficients are the coefficients of the interaction variable for being close to a mine that was active in the survey year. Unreported coefficients include coefficients of the treatment dummy, year dummy, and the control variables. Standard errors are in parentheses. Error terms are clustered at the sample cluster level. See annex table 4A.1 for variable definitions. All outcome variables are indicator variables that take the value 1 or 0. Floor (cement) captures whether flooring is made of cement, tile, wood, or materials other than earth, sand, or dung. Bicycle, car, and radio captures whether the household has these assets. Migrants are women who have moved in their life, and nonmigrants are women who have never moved. Active*mine defines proximity to an active mine.
***p<0.01, **p<0.05, *p<0.1.

Figure 4.6 Spatial Lag Model Illustrating Geographic Distribution of Effects on Household Radio Ownership in Ghana, Mali, and Tanzania

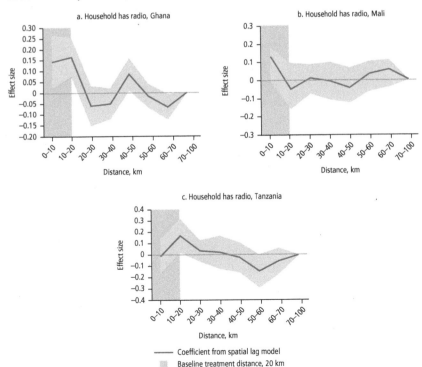

Source: Authors' estimates from survey data.
Note: Shaded area along lines represents 95 percent confidence interval.

Figure 4.7 Spatial Lag Model Illustrating Geographic Distribution of Effects on Radio Ownership for Migrants and Nonmigrants in Ghana, Mali, and Tanzania

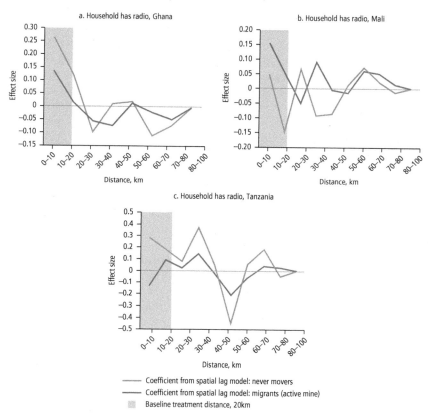

a. Household has radio, Ghana

b. Household has radio, Mali

c. Household has radio, Tanzania

—— Coefficient from spatial lag model: never movers
—— Coefficient from spatial lag model: migrants (active mine)
▨ Baseline treatment distance, 20km

Source: Authors' estimates from survey data.
Note: Shaded area along lines represents 95 percent confidence interval.

Child Health

Large-scale gold mining affects children's health in different ways. It can change household income, with higher income of course enabling a household to buy better and more nutritious food. It can affect child health by changing the environment in which children live, and it can reduce the disease-environment by making it possible for households to buy better-quality housing with proper sanitation and clean water. Higher incomes can also directly buy better health care. However, if large-scale gold mining causes local agriculture production to decline, it can increase food insecurity among households in the vicinity; and if it leads to environmental degradation and pollution that is harmful for humans, the effects on child health could be negative. Thus, how a mine affects child health remains theoretically ambiguous.

The literature, however, does provide some clues. Using a data set from nine African countries and more than 60 gold mines, Tolonen (2015) shows that infant mortality decreases sharply in gold mining communities with the onset of large-scale mining. She argues for an income story to explain this. In another econometric study, von der Goltz and Barnwal (2014), focusing on different types of mineral mines across developing countries, find that mines associated with lead pollution cause increased rates of anemia in women and stunting in children in very close proximity—less than 5 km—to large mines.

Summary statistics show mixed trends across a range of child (under five years) health outcomes across countries and between mining and nonmining areas (figure 4.8). With a few exceptions, the broad trend is lower incidence of diseases (declines in prevalence of cough and fever), but mixed trends in prevalence of diarrhea.

The empirical analysis finds positive effects on access to health care and health outcomes in Mali (table 4.13). Pregnant mothers receive many more prenatal health visits. Infant mortality decreases by 5.3 percentage points (although it is not significantly estimated), and stunting decreases by 27 percentage points, which is equivalent to a 45 percent decrease in the prevalence from the pre-mine average rate of stunting. Stunting is an indicator of chronic malnutrition, which affects children's growth patterns and thus makes them short for their age. By contrast, wasting measures acute malnutrition. Wasting is life-threatening if a child rapidly loses weight and becomes severely malnourished. For Mali, the estimated effect is negative but insignificant for wasting, but negative and significant for being underweight, which is a composite measure of acute and chronic malnourishment.

The results for Mali also show the prevalence of a decrease in cough, fever, and diarrhea, although all but fever are only marginally statistically significant. The significant drop in diarrheal incidence of children in mining communities in Mali is a welcome development, since diarrhea remains a serious threat to children in developing countries, even though it is a disease that is easy to cure and prevent. Access to safe water and sanitation are important in fighting diarrheal diseases, and this could be a way in which a mine affects diarrheal incidence in Mali. Table 4.13 shows that households in Mali are 6.5 percentage points less likely to spend more than 10 minutes fetching water (insignificant), although this suggests little about the quality of that water. Some evidence (box 4.2) shows that access to a private toilet, which might be important to stop the spread of diarrheal diseases,

Figure 4.8 Child Health Statistics in Mining and Nonmining Areas in Ghana, Mali, and Tanzania

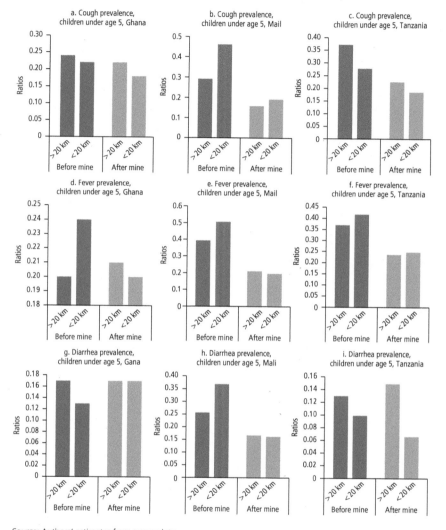

Source: Authors' estimates from survey data.

and access to flush toilets, increase in mining communities (although this is insignificant).

In contrast with Mali, the evidence on child health effects of the onset of mining in Ghana and Tanzania is ambiguous. The likelihood that a child is stunted increases 12.3 percentage points in Tanzania, and being underweight

Table 4.13 Health Outcomes in Infancy and Children under Age 5 in Treatment Distance

	(1)	(2)	(3)
Country	**Ghana**	**Mali**	**Tanzania**
Treatment distance	**20 km**	**20 km**	**20 km**
Outcomes in infancy			
Prenatal care	−0.151	0.398***	0.007
	(0.331)	(0.086)	(0.018)
Infant mortality	−0.041*	−0.053	0.027
	(0.022)	(0.035)	(0.017)
Anthropometrics (child under age 5)			
Stunted	0.148	−0.274***	0.123*
	(0.120)	(0.066)	(0.067)
Wasted	0.095	−0.063	0.004
	(0.119)	(0.056)	(0.022)
Underweight	0.065*	−0.160***	0.113***
	(0.037)	(0.06)	(0.032)
Health outcomes last 2 weeks (child under age 5)			
Cough (last 2 weeks)	−0.061*	−0.195*	0.103
	(0.033)	(0.104)	(0.075)
Fever (last 2 weeks)	−0.035	−0.154	0.074
	(0.037)	(0.102)	(0.074)
Diarrhea (last 2 weeks)	0.042	−0.164**	−0.002
	(0.027)	(0.065)	(0.023)
Household access to sanitation			
Flush toilet	−0.008	−0.001	−0.014
	(0.022)	(0.012)	(0.035)
Pit toilet	0.046	0.177	−0.170
	(0.038)	(0.187)	(0.107)
No toilet	−0.038	−0.176	0.184*
	(0.033)	(0.186)	(0.111)

Source: Authors' estimates from survey data.
Note: Reported coefficients are the coefficients of the interaction variable for being close to a mine that was active in the survey year. Unreported coefficients include coefficients of the treatment dummy, year dummy, and the control variables. Standard errors are in parentheses. Error terms are clustered at the sample cluster level. See annex table 4A.1 for variable definitions.
***$p<0.01$, **$p<0.05$, *$p<0.1$.

BOX 4.2

Effect of a Mine Opening on Household Access to Sanitation in Mali

The opening of a mine does not significantly change access to sanitation, and there are no significant shifts between having no toilet and having a pit latrine or a flush toilet (see table 4.13).[a] For Tanzania, a marginally significant increase is observed in the likelihood that a household does not have a toilet in the mine compound. In Mali, the results indicate a shift in the likelihood of having no toilet (a decrease of 17.6 percentage points) to having access to a pit toilet (an increase of 17.7 percentage points), although they are not statistically significant.

To understand the effect of a mine opening on household access to sanitation, we explore whether households are more likely to not share their toilet and whether they are more likely to have access to a flush toilet the closer the household is to an open mine. Figure B4.2.1, panel a, shows the likelihood of a household sharing its toilet with another household decreases close to active mines, and that the likelihood of a household having a flush toilet increases (panel b), although these results are not significant, as indicated by the 95 percent confidence intervals, in gray. Figure B4.2.2. shows no clear change in access to any type of toilet or pit toilet is

Figure B4.2.1 Spatial Lag Model Illustrating Household Access to Toilets in Mali

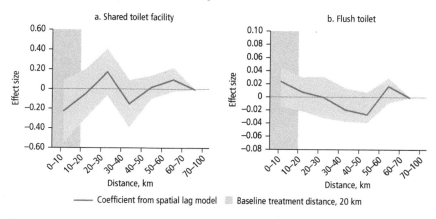

Source: Authors' estimates from survey data.
Note: Shaded area along the lines represents 95 percent confidence interval.

(continued next page)

Box 4.2 (continued)

Figure B4.2.2 Spatial Lag Model Illustrating No Toilet or Pit Toilet among Migrants and Never-Movers in Mali

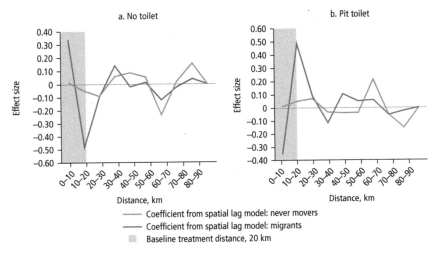

Source: Authors' estimates from survey data.
Note: Shaded area along the lines represents 95 percent confidence interval.

found in households in which the woman is a never-mover. However, for the migrant population, it seems that migrants living very close to the mine (within 10 km) have better sanitation facilities than migrants living a little farther away. Note that no confidence intervals are presented here, and that these effects are not significantly estimated.

a. Decomposing these effects by migration status shows no significant differences across migrants and never-movers.

increases in mining communities in both Ghana and Tanzania. However, mines have some positive effects. Importantly, infant mortality decreases in Ghana, and there is also a marginally significant decrease in cough prevalence. The effect of a mine on diarrheal incidence in Ghana is positive but insignificant. Disaggregating this effect by groups shows that in Ghana migrants experience higher rates of diarrhea and never-movers lower rates.

The district-level analysis confirms some of the child health findings. Table 4.14, looking at Ghana's gold-mining districts, uses five measures of child

Table 4.14 District-Level Effects on Access to Health Services for Children in Ghana's Gold Districts

	(1)	(2)	(3)	(4)	(5)
	Prenatal Visits	Prenatal: physician	Prenatal: midwife	Has health card	Infant mortality
Active district	0.759***	0.055	0.125***	0.039	−0.085***
	(0.244)	(0.115)	(0.033)	(0.059)	(0.031)
Observations	9,245	9,462	9,462	11,047	9,270
R-squared	0.242	0.160	0.154	1.161	0.138

Source: Authors' estimates from survey data.
Note: Robust standard errors clustered at the district level in parentheses. All regressions control for year and district fixed effects, urban dummy, mother's age, and mother's years of education. Active is active status of mine in the birth year, except has health card, which is a measure of contemporary health care access.
***$p<0.01$.

health care access. Mothers have 0.759 more prenatal visits per child, and are 12.5 percentage points more likely to be attended to by a trained midwife. Moreover, infant mortality is 8.5 percentage points lower in active mining communities. No changes are noticed for district-level access to water (measured in time) and household electrification.

Findings from the district-level analysis (which compares mining districts to control districts using the synthetic control method) for Mali and Tanzania indicate some positive outcomes (tables 4.15 and 4.16). For example, the results show improvements in children's nutrition status in mining and neighboring districts compared to control districts.

Diarrheal diseases are major killers of young children in developing countries, despite the existence of simple and inexpensive remedies, such as oral rehydration solutions. The main result in figure 4.9 indicates that diarrheal incidence among children ages under five increased in mining communities in Ghana. This is surprising given expectations that local industrial developments such as mines can increase infrastructure investment in access to sanitation and water systems (including electricity and road networks) in mining communities, and that this improved access is important in preventing diarrheal disease. Perhaps, the result stems from the possibility that the same industrial developments can also increase competition over available resources, such as clean water, or can increase the population pressure on limited resources through inward migration.

Migrants may be a particularly vulnerable group if they are less settled in the community and live in more informal dwellings. If so, diarrheal diseases could increase particularly in this group (figure 4.9). Diarrheal disease increases significantly up to 30 km from a mine among children born to women who have migrated compared to children born to women who have migrated but live

Table 4.15 Health Outcomes for Variables from Synthetic Control Analysis in Tanzania

	Mining districts	Synthetic control group: mining districts	Neighboring districts	Synthetic control group: neighboring districts	Control group
Stunted					
1988	0.415	0.417	0.405	0.406	0.397
2002	0.465	0.512	0.428	0.51	0.509
Severely stunted					
1988	0.316	0.316	0.305	0.305	0.279
2002	0.112	0.26	0.093	0.267	0.272
Wasted					
1988	0.231	0.229	0.21	0.208	0.209
2002	0.016	0.141	0.019	0.144	0.145
Underweight					
1988	0.328	0.326	0.315	0.315	0.292
2002	0.101	0.273	0.067	0.277	0.283

Source: Authors' estimates from survey data.
Note: Reported outcomes for a mining district are the average outcome of mining districts. For a neighboring district, it is the average outcome of these districts. Control group is the average outcome of the districts, except neighboring districts and mining districts.

Table 4.16 Health Outcomes for Variables from Synthetic Control Analysis in Mali

	Mining districts	Synthetic control group: mining districts	Neighboring districts	Synthetic control group: neighboring districts	Control group
Stunted					
1987	0.222	0.234	0.199	0.204	0.180
1998	0.396	0.385	0.390	0.384	0.328
2009	0.296	0.319	0.297	0.297	0.352
Severely stunted					
1987	0.156	0.123	0.116	0.119	0.042
1998	0.229	0.258	0.234	0.231	0.209
2009	0.028	0.068	0.035	0.038	0.060
Wasted					
1987	0.166	0.083	0.115	0.120	0.051
1998	0.165	0.248	0.166	0.162	0.192
2009	0.002	0.021	0.002	0.003	0.010

(continued next page)

Table 4.16 (continued)

	Mining districts	Synthetic control group: mining districts	Neighboring districts	Synthetic control group: neighboring districts	Control group
Underweight					
1987	0.209	0.169	0.177	0.177	0.142
1998	0.303	0.332	0.303	0.302	0.278
2009	0.056	0.114	0.065	0.072	0.110

Source: Authors' estimates from survey data.
Note: Reported outcomes for a mining district are the average outcome of the mining districts. For a neighboring district, it is the average outcome of these districts. Control group is the average outcome of the districts, except neighboring districts and mining districts.

Figure 4.9 Diarrhea Incidence in Ghana for Children under Age 5, by Migration Status

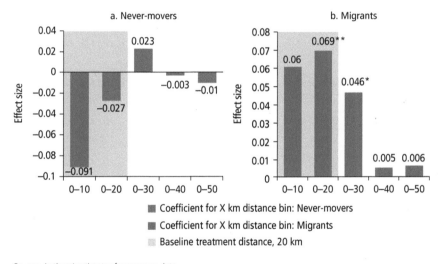

■ Coefficient for X km distance bin: Never-movers
■ Coefficient for X km distance bin: Migrants
▨ Baseline treatment distance, 20 km

Source: Authors' estimates from survey data.
**p<0.05, *p<0.1.

farther away. The largest treatment coefficient is for the baseline distance, within 20 km of a mine, where the mine is associated with an increase of 6.9 percentage points in diarrheal incidence.

Interestingly, children who never moved have (insignificantly) less diarrheal disease. Within the first 10 km, the effect is a decrease of

9.1 percentage points. This shows that in Ghana, child health—measured by diarrheal incidence—is very different among migrants compared with those who have been settled for longer. Migrants living in mining areas seem particularly vulnerable. The reasons for migration to these areas are not known; it could, for example be relocation or displacement because of the mine, or that a household took up a job or income opportunity offered by the mine, or for reasons irrespective of the mine. Thus, it is difficult to draw strong conclusions on why this population is doing less well. Migration is discussed in more detail later in this chapter.

Table 4.17 shows that the strongest differences in child health across migrants and never-movers are in Ghana. In Mali, no significant effects of mining across the two groups are apparent. In Ghana, a decrease in the prevalence of cough in the last two weeks among children born to migrants and children born to never-movers is noticeable. However, as noted, children born to migrants in Ghana see an increase in diarrheal incidence. The results for Tanzania are not presented because the sample sizes are too small once controlled for migration status.

Table 4.17 Child Health among Migrants and Never-Movers in Ghana and Mali

	(1)	(2)	(3)	(4)	(5)	(6)
	Fever (last 2 weeks)		Cough (last 2 weeks)		Diarrhea (last 2 weeks)	
Country	Ghana	Mali	Ghana	Mali	Ghana	Mali
Migrants						
Active*mine	0.034	−0.033	−0.081**	0.027	0.068*	−0.046
	(0.043)	(0.084)	(0.031)	(0.079)	(0.040)	(0.063)
Observations	4,723	3,075	4,633	3,076	4,672	3,077
R-squared	0.043	0.064	0.066	0.061	0.043	0.050
Never-movers						
Active*mine	−0.006	0.114	−0.118*	−0.083	−0.063	0.083
	(0.066)	(0.119)	(0.060)	(0.112)	(0.048)	(0.074)
Observations	2,451	2,547	2,405	2,545	2,420	2,546
R-squared	0.073	0.075	0.093	0.082	0.059	0.065

Source: Authors' estimates from survey data.
Note: Reported coefficients are the coefficients of the interaction variable for being close to a mine that was active in the survey year. Unreported coefficients include coefficients of the treatment dummy, year dummy, and the control variables, including child's age, mother's age and education, survey month, and urban area dummy. No results are presented for Tanzania because the sample size is too small when controlling for migration status. Error terms are clustered at the sample cluster level. Numbers in parentheses are estimated standard errors. Active*mine defines proximity to an active mine.
**p<0.05, *p<0.1.

Access to Infrastructure for Welfare Benefits

Access to adequate infrastructure contributes to improvements in welfare. How is this access affected by the opening of a mine? Table 4.18 shows how the opening of a mine close to a community affects the probability of a household having access to infrastructure, such as electricity and a private toilet. The regression results using the baseline specification in table 4.18 show that households close to a mine are generally more likely to have access to a private toilet facility. The results are especially strong for Tanzania, where households in mining communities are 24 percentage points less likely to share a toilet with other households. Figure 4.10 shows that access to electricity increases in Mali, but with no discernible effect for either Ghana or Tanzania, using a spatial lag model.

Table 4.18 Household Access to Infrastructure in Ghana, Mali, and Tanzania

	(1)	(2)	(3)
	Electricity	**Shared toilet**	**Water >10 min**
Ghana			
Active*mine	−0.046	−0.050	−0.001
	(0.052)	(0.044)	(0.054)
Observations	14,112	6,059	11,552
R-squared	0.494	0.127	0.162
Mali			
Active*mine	0.134	−0.046	−0.065
	(0.086)	(0.110)	(0.094)
Observations	6,876	4,230	6,009
R-squared	0.169	0.064	0.173
Tanzania			
Active*mine	0.007	−0.235***	0.048
	(0.033)	(0.070)	(0.070)
Observations	6,941	4,681	6,862
R-squared	0.415	0.113	0.192

Source: Authors' estimates from survey data.
Note: Reported estimates are the coefficients of the interaction variable for being close to a mine that was active in the survey year. Unreported coefficients include coefficients of the treatment dummy, year dummy, and the control variables. Standard errors are in parentheses. Error terms are clustered at the sample cluster level. See annex table 4A.1 for variable definitions. All outcome variables are indicator variables that take the value 1 or 0. Shared toilet is whether the household shares toilet facilities with other households rather than having a private toilet facility. Water > 10 min, indicates whether it takes more than 10 minutes to fetch drinking water from the home. Active*mine defines proximity to an active mine.
***$p < 0.01$.

Figure 4.10 Spatial Lag Model Illustrating Geographic Distribution of Effects on Electricity in Ghana, Mali, and Tanzania

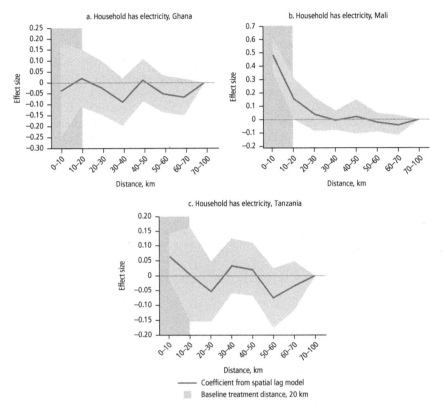

Source: Authors' estimates from survey data.
Note: Shaded area along lines represents 95 percent confidence interval.

This analysis is complementary to figure 4.11, which shows differences for migrants and never-movers in the same communities for access to electricity. The migration analysis shows differences in access across the three case study countries. Migrants in Ghana have seemingly less access to electricity than never-movers. In Mali, the relationship is reversed, with migrants having better access. In Tanzania, no difference in access rates is apparent between the two groups.

Figure 4.11 Spatial Lag Model Illustrating Access to Electricity for Migrants and Never-Movers in Ghana, Mali, and Tanzania

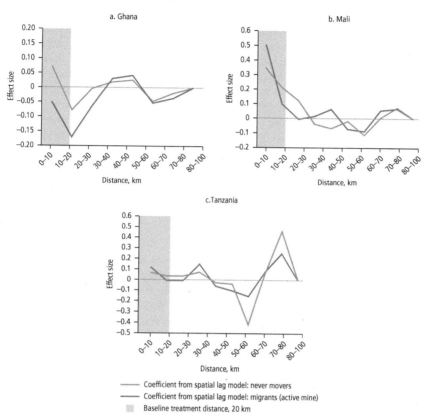

Source: Authors' estimates from survey data.
Note: shaded area along lines represents 95 percent confidence interval.

Controlling for Mine-Induced Migration

The discussion so far has been on how mining affects the composition of local employment, women's economic opportunities, accumulation of assets, and children's health outcomes. The underlying assumption is that these impacts apply to people who lived in the vicinity of a mine before it opened. However, such a result rests on the assumption that either there is no migration or, if there is, it had no influence on the estimated impacts. But as we go on to show, the first assumption does not hold. The opening of a mine is a magnet for workers from both near and far as they seek opportunities to improve their incomes and employment status.

What about the second assumption? If migrants and local populations have exactly the same characteristics—that is, identical in all dimensions that matter for being successful at taking advantage of the opportunities offered by a mine— then the estimated impacts remain valid. However, if people who move to a mining area from afar are different—say, in skills, ability, motivation, health status, and so on—from the people who lived in the mining area before the mine opened, then there would be selection bias. Imagine if men who are more interested in and trained for mining jobs move into these communities, and women who have a particular interest or aptitude for work in the services sector do the same. Then the results on the composition of occupations and changing employment opportunities for women are picking up the change in composition of the labor force in the mining communities that is due to migration and not due to the mine alone.

It should be noted that the study is interested in identifying the impact of a mine or cluster of mines on local populations who lived there before the mine opened, as well as exploring how the local economy is changing, even if the population changes with it. This is why isolating the role of migration in the estimated effects is important and not trivial. Because the data are repeated cross-sections, the analysis cannot follow an individual over time. Thus, the analysis of migrants compares people who have moved to their current place of residence (migrants) with never-movers. In this sense, the analysis compares migrants in mining communities with migrants who live elsewhere. Any difference noted between these groups could stem from selection into migration to mining communities, and so the results should not be interpreted causally. For example, if only poorer households with children in poor health move to mining communities, the results indicate that migrants in mining communities are worse off. But this is not because of the mine. With this important caveat in mind, the analysis is conducted to shed light on the welfare of migrants in mining communities.

Most of the data available for the three case study countries track migratory history in detail. For most individuals, it is known whether they have ever moved and in what year they moved to their current location. In the following discussion, migration rates in mining communities are presented, and the outcomes between migrants and never-movers are compared.

Figure 4.12 shows the share of the population of these countries that moved in a given year and was living within 100 km of a mine. The figure does not use a calendar year but rather a "mine year," defined as counting down to a mine's opening, with the mine opening year indicated as time zero. Thus, the figure

Figure 4.12 Migration to Mining Areas in Ghana, Mali, and Tanzania

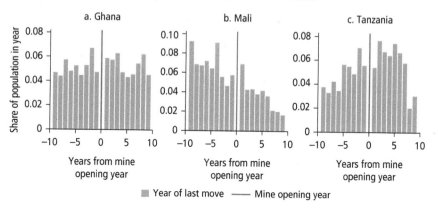

Source: Authors' estimates from survey data.
Note: Mining areas are defined as population living within 100 km of a mine.

presents the fraction of the population that migrated prior to the opening of a mine over 20 years—10 years prior to the opening of the mine and 10 years after the mine opens. As expected, there is plenty of in-migration, but the migratory patterns are different across all three countries.

In Ghana, 4 to 6 percent of the population can be considered migrants, but no clear evidence shows that the opening of a mine affected migration patterns in any particular way. Migration before and after a mine opened remained relatively stable. In Mali, migration rates appear to have been decreasing. Migration to mining areas was quite high four to 10 years prior to the opening of a mine; then it slowed and stabilized for the three years prior to the opening. Migration surged a year after the mine opened, but the trend reversed, so that less than 2 percent of the population living within 100 km of a mine was considered migrants 10 years after the mine opened. The opposite seemed to have happened in Tanzania. Migration rates increased leading up to the opening of a mine. Migration rates peaked two years after a mine opened, and remained fairly stable and high for the following four years, after which they declined.

Two points need to be kept in mind about these migration patterns. First, the higher rates in Mali and Tanzania could be explained by the relatively young nature of the sector in these countries relative to Ghana. Second, although mines are major magnets for people seeking employment, not all this migration is due to a mine opening. For our estimation of impacts, however, knowing whether people moved because of a mine or not is not going to help identify the impact of mines on the local community. Instead, what matters is the knowledge of whether or not migrants differ substantively from the local population living in that locality before the mine opened. The differences between migrants and never-movers are now explored through women's occupation and household access to electricity and radio ownership.

Occupations of Migrant and Nonmigrant Women

Empirical analysis finds no difference in the labor market outcomes between migrant and nonmigrant women. Figure 4.4 shows the increase in the likelihood of a woman working in nonfarm employment, in this case proxied by services sector employment. In Ghana and Mali, the chances of working in this sector are substantially higher for women living near a mine compared with those living further away, although the effect size is larger in Ghana. However, women born in local communities and who did not move away, and those who plausibly moved to mining areas because of the mine, have equal chances of working in the services sector. In other words, migrants do not seem to have major advantages or disadvantages when it comes to success in finding new employment.

In Tanzania, women living closer to mines do not enjoy better chances of working in nonfarm jobs than women living farther away. It seems the pull of the nontraded sector is no greater closer to a mine than farther away. It is also the case that nonmigrant women do not enjoy any advantages living closer to a mine (20 km) compared to migrant women. The pattern for working in agriculture (figure 4.4, second-row panels) is less clear. In Mali, women are less likely to work in agriculture than those farther away, a finding that in some ways reinforces the results for services sector jobs. The effect size is larger for women who never moved. But in Ghana and Tanzania, the prospect of working in agriculture for women closer to mines is not that different from women living farther away. And closer to mines, the change in probability of working in agriculture between migrant and nonmigrant women is the same.

Access to Electricity and Radio Ownership

Figure 4.11 shows whether migrants, in general, have access to better infrastructure (in this case, electricity) or lower assets. There are several hypotheses for why access to infrastructure could be different between migrants and never-movers. It could come from income differences: those with higher incomes can afford to pay for electricity and other services. It could also come from service delivery failures by local governments, which may not reach places where migrants settle. And if migrants have lower assets to begin with, then these impacts would be underestimating the effect of mines on asset ownership.

There are three points to note for variation in access to electricity between migrants and never-movers from figure 4.11. First, the difference in access to infrastructure between migrants and never-movers is largest in Ghana, where the effect of a mine on local electrification for the nonmigrant population is positive at the closest distance (within 20 km of the mine). Second, access to electricity for both migrants and never-movers near a mine is highest in Mali, where household access to electricity increases sharply—by 30 to 50 percentage points—within the first 20 km.

And third, these differences in access to electricity for migrants and never-movers can be partially explained by looking at the differences in the migration patterns in some of the case study countries. For example, access to electricity might not be readily available to community members and, if it entails a household investment, one could expect people settled in communities for a longer time to do better. With that in mind, recall that in Mali most migration movements happened a few years before a mine opened, so it can be assumed that many migrants may have already settled in the local community by the time the mine opened. By contrast, in Ghana, migration patterns continued to flow at the same pace from year to year. Given this migration pattern, lower access to electricity for migrants in Ghana and equal access in Mali would be expected, which is observed in figure 4.11.

Summary of Results

Although the mining industry is generally associated with weak direct employment generation compared with its contributions to gross domestic product and export revenue at the national level, it nonetheless has the potential to have large local impacts through the clustering of economic activities. This chapter looked at these local impacts for individuals living in the neighborhood of gold mines and districts with a gold-mining sector. The results led to four major conclusions.

First, there appear to be signs of structural transformation associated with the mining sector. Both the individual and district results find that employment in agriculture is declining, while employment in nonfarm occupations such as services, manufacturing, and mining is rising. Where wage data are available, such as Ghana, there is evidence that mine-worker wages are higher. These results are robust, especially for countries where gold mining started earlier, such as Ghana and Mali.

Second, mining is associated with improvements in women's nonfarm employment opportunities. Employment in sales and services for women is substantially higher for women living closer to mining sites than for those living farther away. In the same vein, their employment in agriculture declines.

The probability of working throughout the year also rises for women living closer to mines and those in mining districts.

The finding of structural transformation in large-scale gold-mining communities is further supported by changes in expenditures. Overall, despite increasing food prices, neither total deflated food expenditures nor the food share of total household expenditures increases. Instead, the results show that expenditures on housing and energy increase, which is in line with the higher electrification rates found in mining communities.

Third, results are mixed for child health outcomes between mining and non-mining areas. In Ghana, infant mortality decreases faster and is statistically significant in mining communities and districts. In Mali, stunting decreases for children who live close to mines, and the estimated effect is negative but insignificant for wasting. In Ghana and Tanzania, these outcomes appear worse for mining areas, although the results are not always statistically significant. The incidence of cough declines in both Ghana and Mali, but not in Tanzania. Similarly, the incidence of diarrheal disease decreases in Mali but is positive and insignificant in Ghana, although in Ghana this appears to be driven by poor health outcomes among migrants living near mines, where the incidence among children born to migrants is much higher than children born to nonmigrants living near a mine and to migrants living farther away. In addition, women of migrant households have less access to important infrastructure, such as electricity.

It is not clear why these child health outcomes differ across the three case study countries at the local level. Stunting, which is a measure of long-term nutritional deficiency, may reflect a significant income effect. In other words, those living closer to mines may have a higher income and use it to buy more nutritious food for their children. By contrast, wasting is a short-term measure of nutritional deficiency and can be explained in large part by access to health services.

And fourth, migration patterns may explain some of the differences in child health outcomes across the three case study countries. For instance, Mali, which shows the most positive changes, also has the lowest level of migration around the time of mine opening, and migrants in mining areas in Mali seem less vulnerable than in Ghana or Tanzania. Tanzania, which shows little evidence of structural transformation and few gains in child health, seems to have the largest increase in migration flows after a mine opens.

Annex 4A: Variable Definitions for Demographic and Health Surveys and Outcomes for Variables from Synthetic Control Analysis in Mali and Tanzania

Table 4A.1 Variable Definitions for Demographic and Health Surveys

Women and household characteristics	
Age	Age of respondent
Wealth	Household wealth index score
Nonmigrant	Respondent born in the location and never moved
Migrant	Any respondent who has moved
Urban	Household in urban area
Household characteristics	
Electricity	Household has access to electricity
Shared toilet	Toilet facilities shared
Flush toilet	Household has a flush toilet
Pit toilet	Household has pit toilet
No toilet	Household has no toilet facility
Water < 10 min	Less than 10 minutes to drinking water sources
Floor (cement)	House has cement, tile, or wood floor
Bicycle	Household has bicycle
Car	Household has car
Radio	Household has radio
Woman's occupation and education	
Not working	Not working in last 12 months
Service and sales	Works in services or sales
Professional	Works as a professional
Agriculture	Works in agriculture
Manual labor	Does manual labor
Earning cash	Earns cash for work (0 = not paid in kind)
Works all year	Works all year (0 = seasonally, occasionally)
Three years of education	At least three years of education
No education	No education
Partner's occupation	
Service and sales	Partner of woman works in services or sales
Professional	Partner of woman works as a professional
Agriculture	Partner of woman works in agriculture
Manual labor	Partner of woman does manual labor

(continued next page)

Table 4A.1 (continued)

Child health

Diarrhea	Diarrhea in last 2 weeks
Cough	Cough in last 2 weeks
Fever	Fever in last 2 weeks
Infant mortality	Died within first 12 months of birth
Prenatal care	Mother had at least one prenatal care visit
Stunted	Child age under 5 is stunted (below 2 standard deviations of height/age)
Wasted	Child age under 5 is wasted (below 2 standard deviations of weight/age)
Underweight	Child is underweight (below 2 standard deviations of weight/height)
Prenatal visits	Number of visits per child
Health card	Child has a health card

Table 4A.2 Outcomes for Variables from Synthetic Control Analysis, Mali

	Mining districts	Synthetic control group: mining districts	Neighboring districts	Synthetic control group: neighboring districts	Control group
Employment rate (men)					
1987	0.902	0.904	0.904	0.912	0.904
1998	0.888	0.886	0.877	0.871	0.887
2009	0.833	0.826	0.822	0.827	0.824
Employment rate (women)					
1987	0.721	0.666	0.672	0.703	0.491
1998	0.422	0.480	0.515	0.484	0.409
2009	0.325	0.389	0.413	0.504	0.424
Working as a professional (men)					
1987	0.019	0.019	0.016	0.014	0.016
1998	0.022	0.022	0.016	0.019	0.018
2009	0.041	0.039	0.027	0.027	0.031
Working as a professional (women)					
1987	0.007	0.004	0.003	0.004	0.004
1998	0.001	0.005	0.003	0.002	0.004
2009	0.009	0.012	0.008	0.007	0.009
Working as a services worker (men)					
1987	0.015	0.021	0.014	0.015	0.018
1998	0.033	0.027	0.026	0.025	0.031
2009	0.066	0.049	0.053	0.047	0.048
Working as a services worker (women)					
1987	0.018	0.021	0.026	0.018	0.021
1998	0.008	0.014	0.017	0.024	0.034
2009	0.013	0.028	0.020	0.017	0.030

(continued next page)

Table 4A.2 (continued)

Working as skilled agriculture or fishery worker (men)					
1987	0.779	0.772	0.812	0.818	0.801
1998	0.755	0.762	0.790	0.780	0.783
2009	0.524	0.664	0.635	0.673	0.673
Working as skilled agriculture or fishery worker (women)					
1987	0.659	0.585	0.616	0.647	0.377
1998	0.391	0.464	0.487	0.456	0.339
2009	0.246	0.419	0.340	0.463	0.338
Working as a craftsman (men)					
1987	0.083	0.088	0.050	0.051	0.056
1998	0.036	0.029	0.027	0.025	0.030
2009	0.183	0.051	0.085	0.049	0.051
Working as a craftsman (women)					
1987	0.013	0.016	0.011	0.010	0.066
1998	0.004	0.005	0.002	0.003	0.014
2009	0.030	0.004	0.017	0.004	0.016
Working in elementary jobs (men)					
1987	0.002	0.005	0.003	0.003	0.006
1998	0.010	0.008	0.008	0.008	0.012
2009	0.009	0.006	0.006	0.015	0.008
Working in elementary jobs (women)					
1987	0.019	0.014	0.013	0.012	0.020
1998	0.000	0.005	0.000	0.002	0.004
2009	0.009	0.006	0.004	0.003	0.006
Working as an employer (men)					
1987	0.001	0.001	0.003	0.002	0.002
1998	0.003	0.004	0.005	0.006	0.005
2009	0.007	0.006	0.005	0.006	0.006
Working as an employer (women)					
1987	0.002	0.001	0.000	0.001	0.001
1998	0.001	0.002	0.001	0.001	0.001
2009	0.002	0.002	0.002	0.002	0.002
Working as own-account worker (men)					
1987	0.491	0.542	0.483	0.513	0.541
1998	0.606	0.550	0.566	0.540	0.572
2009	0.568	0.592	0.599	0.574	0.594
Working as own-account worker (women)					
1987	0.074	0.073	0.063	0.075	0.083
1998	0.150	0.160	0.198	0.187	0.153
2009	0.061	0.142	0.066	0.075	0.080

(continued next page)

Table 4A.2 (continued)

Working as wage worker (men)					
1987	0.071	0.075	0.041	0.040	0.043
1998	0.053	0.045	0.027	0.029	0.031
2009	0.083	0.026	0.021	0.018	0.018
Working as wage worker (women)					
1987	0.007	0.007	0.005	0.005	0.008
1998	0.003	0.005	0.005	0.004	0.007
2009	0.010	0.003	0.003	0.004	0.006
Working as unpaid worker (men)					
1987	0.332	0.282	0.357	0.339	0.312
1998	0.219	0.275	0.272	0.291	0.271
2009	0.133	0.176	0.171	0.177	0.183
Working as unpaid worker (women)					
1987	0.636	0.512	0.596	0.639	0.397
1998	0.262	0.386	0.305	0.263	0.243
2009	0.237	0.300	0.324	0.479	0.314
Working in agriculture (men)					
1987	0.775	0.773	0.813	0.816	0.800
1998	0.754	0.755	0.784	0.781	0.779
2009	0.525	0.658	0.636	0.688	0.674
Working in agriculture (women)					
1987	0.658	0.594	0.617	0.647	0.378
1998	0.388	0.452	0.484	0.453	0.339
2009	0.246	0.392	0.340	0.460	0.339
Working in manufacturing (men)					
1987	0.041	0.050	0.019	0.019	0.027
1998	0.053	0.031	0.016	0.016	0.021
2009	0.145	0.037	0.057	0.028	0.026
Working in manufacturing (women)					
1987	0.010	0.016	0.007	0.006	0.066
1998	0.013	0.008	0.003	0.004	0.023
2009	0.030	0.003	0.016	0.004	0.016
Working in mining (men)					
1987	0.015	0.031	0.000	0.001	0.001
1998	0.037	0.020	0.001	0.001	0.001
2009	0.117	0.007	0.034	0.004	0.002
Working in mining (women)					
1987	0.004	0.007	0.000	0.000	0.000
1998	0.007	0.004	0.000	0.000	0.000
2009	0.028	0.001	0.014	0.001	0.001

(continued next page)

Table 4A.2 (continued)

Working in construction (men)				
1987	0.016	0.016	0.005	0.007	0.004
1998	0.006	0.007	0.010	0.008	0.006
2009	0.015	0.016	0.017	0.015	0.015
Working in construction (women)				
1987	0.000	0.000	0.000	0.000	0.000
1998	0.000	0.000	0.000	0.000	0.000
2009	0.000	0.000	0.000	0.000	0.000
Working in services (men)				
1987	0.067	0.077	0.060	0.064	0.069
1998	0.067	0.059	0.063	0.060	0.075
2009	0.159	0.134	0.123	0.108	0.123
Working in services (women)				
1987	0.048	0.040	0.045	0.038	0.045
1998	0.015	0.023	0.024	0.031	0.041
2009	0.044	0.061	0.046	0.039	0.058

Note: Reported outcomes for a mining district are the average outcome of the mining districts. For neighboring district, it is the average outcome of neighboring districts. Control group is the average outcome of the districts, except neighboring districts and mining districts.

Table 4A.3 Outcomes for Variables from Synthetic Control Analysis, Tanzania

	Mining districts	Synthetic control group: mining districts	Neighboring districts	Synthetic control group: neighboring districts	Control group
Employment rate (men)					
1988	0.881	0.878	0.877	0.874	0.866
2002	0.758	0.827	0.810	0.821	0.816
Employment rate (women)					
1988	0.833	0.831	0.864	0.862	0.817
2002	0.612	0.734	0.721	0.768	0.719
Working as a professional (men)					
1988	0.050	0.050	0.062	0.063	0.073
2002	0.053	0.043	0.044	0.052	0.060
Working as a professional (women)					
1988	0.022	0.022	0.025	0.025	0.030
2002	0.028	0.028	0.022	0.031	0.035
Working as a services worker (men)					
1988	0.023	0.023	0.030	0.030	0.034
2002	0.024	0.026	0.024	0.032	0.035

(continued next page)

Table 4A.3 (continued)

Working as a services worker (women)					
1988	0.019	0.020	0.015	0.015	0.021
2002	0.015	0.021	0.015	0.017	0.023
Working as agricultural worker (men)					
1988	0.691	0.688	0.691	0.689	0.636
2002	0.544	0.624	0.621	0.625	0.571
Working as agricultural worker (women)					
1988	0.751	0.749	0.799	0.800	0.728
2002	0.494	0.606	0.614	0.666	0.581
Working in crafts (men)					
1988	0.004	0.004	0.007	0.007	0.007
2002	0.051	0.041	0.036	0.056	0.056
Working in crafts (women)					
1988	0.001	0.001	0.001	0.001	0.002
2002	0.012	0.010	0.009	0.010	0.012
Working in elementary jobs (men)					
1988	0.097	0.097	0.072	0.072	0.102
2002	0.076	0.080	0.075	0.066	0.083
Working in elementary jobs (women)					
1988	0.030	0.030	0.016	0.016	0.026
2002	0.057	0.067	0.054	0.049	0.063
Working as an employer (men)					
1988	0.007	0.006	0.005	0.005	0.007
2002	0.001	0.001	0.001	0.001	0.001
Working as an employer (women)					
1988	0.003	0.003	0.001	0.001	0.003
2002	0.001	0	0	0	0.000
Working as own-account worker (men)					
1988	0.733	0.736	0.705	0.704	0.680
2002	0.628	0.729	0.697	0.699	0.679
Working as own-account worker (women)					
1988	0.730	0.725	0.781	0.781	0.732
2002	0.536	0.645	0.656	0.699	0.651
Working as wage worker (men)					
1988	0.092	0.092	0.131	0.131	0.156
2002	0.076	0.070	0.075	0.094	0.112
Working as wage worker (women)					
1988	0.035	0.034	0.038	0.038	0.051
2002	0.023	0.034	0.027	0.036	0.047

(continued next page)

Table 4A.3 (continued)

Working as unpaid worker (men)					
1988	0.035	0.035	0.022	0.022	0.012
2002	0.048	0.028	0.032	0.022	0.017
Working as unpaid worker (women)					
1988	0.057	0.057	0.036	0.036	0.024
2002	0.05	0.031	0.036	0.022	0.017

Note: Reported outcomes for a mining district are the average outcome of the mining districts. For neighboring districts, it is the average outcome of these districts. Control group is the average outcome of the districts, except neighboring districts and mining districts.

Notes

1. This chapter is based on two papers that are also part of this study: Chuhan-Pole et al. (2015) and Polat et al. (2014).
2. For details of how districts are defined for the purposes of econometric estimation, see Chuhan-Pole et al. (2015) and Polat et al. (2014).
3. See table 2 of Polat et al. (2014) for the list of variables used in mapping.
4. See Polat et al. (2014) for details of how this was constructed.

References

Abadie, Alberto, Alexis Diamond, and Jens Hainmueller. 2010. "Synthetic Control Methods for Comparative Case Studies: Estimating the Effect of California's Tobacco Control Program." *Journal of the American Statistical Association* 105 (490): 493–505.

Aragón, Fernando M., and Juan Pablo Rud. 2013a. "Natural Resources and Local Communities: Evidence from a Peruvian Gold Mine." *American Economic Journal: Economic Policy* 5 (2): 1–25.

———. 2013b. " Modern Industries, Pollution and Agricultural Productivity: Evidence from Mining in Ghana." Working Paper, International Growth Centre, London.

Chuhan-Pole, P., A. Dabalen, A. Kotsadam, A. Sanoh, and A. Tolonen. 2015. "The Local Socioeconomic Effects of Gold Mining: Evidence from Ghana." Policy Research Working Paper 7250, World Bank, Washington, DC.

Fafchamps, Marcel, Michael Koelle, and Forhad Shilpi. 2015. "Gold Mining and Proto-Urbanization: Recent Evidence from Ghana." Policy Research Working Paper 7347, World Bank, Washington, DC.

Hilson, G., and N. Yakovleva. 2007. "Strained Relations: A Critical Analysis of the Mining Conflict in Prestea, Ghana." *Political Geography* 26 (1): 98–119.

ILO (International Labour Organization). 1999. *Social and Labour Issues in Small-Scale Mines: Report for Discussion at the Tripartite Meeting on Social and Labour Issues in Small-Scale Mines.* Geneva: ILO.

Kotsadam, A., and A. Tolonen. 2015. "Mining, Gender and Local Employment." Policy Research Working Paper 7251, World Bank, Washington, DC.

Loayza, N., A. M. Teran, and J. Rigolini. 2013. "Poverty, Inequality, and the Local Natural Resource Curse." Discussion Paper Series 7225, Forschungsinstitut zur Zukunft der Arbeit, Bonn.

Moretti, E. 2010. "Local Multipliers." *American Economic Review* 100 (2): 373–77.

Polat, Beyza, Nazli Aktakke, Meltem A. Aran, Andrew L. Dabalen, Punam Chuhan-Pole, and Aly Sanoh. 2014. "Socioeconomic Impact of Mining Activity: Effects of Gold Mining on Local Communities in Tanzania and Mali." Development Analytics Research Paper Series 1402, Development Analytics, Sariyer, Turkey.

Ross, M. 2008. "Oil, Islam and Women." *American Political Science Review* 102 (1): 107–23.

Tolonen, A. 2015. "Local Industrial Shocks, Female Empowerment and Infant Health: Evidence from Africa's Gold Mining Industry." Dissertation, University of Gothenburg.

von der Goltz, J., and P. Barnwal. 2014. "Mines: The Local Welfare Effects of Mineral Mining in Developing Countries." Working Paper, Columbia University, New York.

Chapter 5

Does Mining Reduce Agricultural Growth? Evidence from Large-Scale Gold Mining in Burkina Faso, Ghana, Mali, and Tanzania

Introduction

This chapter provides another perspective on the impact of resource extraction on local economic growth by focusing on agricultural growth.[1] The issue of interest is whether opening gold mines has spillover effects on the local economy, especially on agriculture. Agricultural production could be affected by mining in several ways, including a rise in local wages, reduced profit margins, and the exit of families from farming—something akin to a localized Dutch disease. Negative environmental spillovers, such as pollution or local health problems, could also dampen productivity of the land and of farmers, thereby reducing the viability of farming. Alternatively, mining could create a miniboom in the local economy through higher employment and wages that can lead to an increase in local-area aggregate demand, including for regional food crops.

In this chapter, remote sensing data are used to estimate levels and changes in agricultural and nonagricultural production in gold mining and nonmining localities in Burkina Faso, Ghana, Mali, and Tanzania. The study investigates the spatial relationship between mining and local agricultural development by using a vegetation index as a proxy for agricultural production. To estimate the level and composition of production—agricultural and nonagricultural—at the local level, the study selects a specified distance circle around mining areas. For all four countries, 32 large-scale gold mines were identified (see table 4.1 and box 4.1 in chapter 4).

Satellite remote sensing missions are generally designed for specific applications, often earth-sciences-related, such as vegetation classification and weather forecasting. Very few, if any, sensors are designed for social science applications (Hall 2010). The Defense Meteorological Satellite Program Operational Linescan System (DMSP-OLS) sensor, also known as night lights, has attracted recent attention due to its capability to depict human settlement and development. The sensor is sensitive enough to detect streetlights (Sei-Ichi et al. 2010). The light detected by the DMSP-OLS is largely the result of human activity, emitted from settlements, shipping fleets, gas flaring, and fires from slash-and-burn agriculture. As such, night light imagery is a unique view of the Earth's surface to highlight human activity. One of the central uses of the night lights data set is as a measure of and proxy for economic activity.

The relationship between economic activity and light has been explored by several authors, and all conclude there is indeed a positive relationship between the light emitted and level of economic development within a region. This understanding has been used to estimate both levels of income as measured by gross domestic product (GDP) and its growth. This chapter aims to contribute to the literature on the connection between extractive industries and local clustering of economic activity using remote sensing data.

We start with a literature review of remote sensing and economic activity, with a particular focus on agriculture. This is followed by a description of the data used, and then a description of the various methodologies and their results, including the econometric results using a difference-in-differences estimation framework. This framework was previously used to understand the economic effects of gold mining in Africa by Aragón and Rud (2015), Kotsadam et al. (2015), and Tolonen (2015). The chapter closes by offering conclusions on using remote sensing data to estimate the level and growth of gold mining on local economic activity such as agriculture.

Remote Sensing and Economic Activity

Several recent economic studies have exploited human-generated night lights data to understand the structure, growth, and spatial distribution of economic activity in countries or localized areas (Chen and Nordhaus 2011; Doll, Muller, and Morley 2006; Ebener et al. 2005; Elvidge et al. 1997; Ghosh et al. 2010; Henderson, Storeygard, and Weil 2012; Sutton and Costanza 2002).

An early identification of the strength of the relationship between night lights and economic development was made by Elvidge et al. (1997), who explored the relationship between lighted areas and GDP, as well as population and electrical power consumption in Madagascar, South American countries, the United States, and several island nations of the Caribbean and the Indian Ocean. Using simple linear regression over a six-month period (October 1994 to March 1995), they found that GDP exhibits a strong linear relationship with lighted areas. Their study is unique in that it associated the relationship between economic activity and lighted areas; most other studies using such data relate economic activity to light intensity. Doll, Muller, and Morley (2006) were one of the first to apply Elvidge et al.'s (1997) relationship to estimating economic activity on a national and subnational basis. These authors identified a unique linear relationship between gross regional product and lighting for the European Union and the United States using a six-month period (October 1996 to March 1997); they found that one linear relationship was not appropriate because some cities were outliers. However, once the outliers were removed, they were able to generate simple linear regressions—which showed strong links between gross regional product and light intensity—for each country. They used this to generate a gridded map of gross regional product at the 5-kilometer level.

Building on this approach, Ghosh et al. (2010) used gross state product, GDP, and light intensity in 2006 for various administrative units in China, India, Mexico, and the United States to obtain an estimate of total economic activity for each administrative unit. These values were then spatially distributed within a global grid using the percent contribution of agriculture toward GDP, a population grid, and the night lights image. This is an improvement over Doll, Muller, and Morley (2006), in the sense that it was able to assign economic activity to agricultural areas, which are not usually picked up by the night lights data set since these areas are not often lit. This is an important observation about night lights data that will inform our study.

Chen and Nordhaus (2011) was one of the first studies to exploit time-series variation in GDP and night lights. To show the strength of the correlation between economic activity and night lights, their method assigns weights to light intensity to reduce the difference between the true GDP values and the estimated GDP (that is, they minimize the mean squared error) for all countries of the world for 1992 to 2008. They show that light intensity data do not add much value to data-rich countries; in other words, the night lights data do not provide additional information from what has already been obtained from the actual data. The opposite is true for data-poor countries. The authors show that GDP estimation using night lights in data-poor countries, both at the national and subnational level, improves substantially with night lights data.

One of the most recent applications of the night lights data set to economic activity is by Henderson, Storeygard, and Weil (2012). Rather than exploring the relationship of lights with GDP levels, they look at the relationship between real GDP growth and GDP growth estimated using night lights. Like Chen and Nordhaus (2011), they use a time series of growth and night lights data for 1992 to 2008. Their statistical model correlates GDP growth using country-specific economic data with light-intensity values. Similar to Chen and Nordhaus, they construct different weights for the night lights data and existing economic data based on the quality of the economic data. They find large differences (both positive and negative) between the recorded economic growth and the estimated growth for countries with "bad" data.

In general, this short review of the literature using remote sensing data leads to two conclusions. First, it demonstrates that these data provide a strong and accurate prediction of economic activity. Second, although various types of remote sensing data are available, the one that is most widely used tends to be night lights data. To date, most studies have used light intensity rather than lighted area to explain either GDP or growth within and across countries in a given year, and, on a few occasions, over time. However, night lights, while certainly informative of human activity, do not exhaust economic activity in all places. In particular, in countries where electricity is unreliable and there is significant reliance on generators for production activity, night lights could be underestimating economic activity. This would be true especially if generators are not turned on at night for cost reasons. In addition, in mostly rural countries where the mainstay of the economy is agriculture, an overreliance on night lights might miss a big fraction of economic activity, even if electricity is reliable. Fortunately, remote sensing data can be used for capturing agricultural activity as well. We now discuss one such datum.

Numerous methods exist for estimating the production of agricultural commodities in a specified geographic area using remote sensing technology. But most approaches rely on the idea that vegetation, including crops, is very reflective in the red and near-infrared wavelengths. Combinations of these two wavelengths (that is, vegetation indexes) are good measures of plant vigor and are the mainstay of nearly all approaches to crop yield estimation (Lobell 2013). Yields are then estimated by establishing the empirical relationship between ground-based yield measures and some vegetation indexes, typically the Normalized Difference Vegetation Index (NDVI), which is a measure of greenness.

Errors in remote-sensing crop-yield estimates vary, mainly as a function of sensor properties (spatial-, temporal-, and spectral-resolution) and landscape complexity. The classification of crop types is more problematic in regions characterized by multiple crops with similar life cycles (that is, phonologies), or in regions with intercropped fields (Lobell 2013). Additional complexity is added with cassava, a major crop for which even farmers have difficulty estimating yields, basically because it is a root crop with staggered harvesting but also with widely differing above-ground architecture. Sometimes overlooked is the problem of cloud cover in satellite-based remote sensing, which could severely limit the number of available observations for a particular geographic region. Nevertheless, yield estimation in mixed cropping systems, which are characteristic of African smallholder agriculture, should be possible using a remote sensor platform with the correct properties.

Long-term analysis of the NDVI can reveal important information on vegetation anomalies caused by variations in rainfall, temperature, and sunlight (irradiance), as well as the trend for a certain location. Phenological metrics—such as the start and end of growing seasons, length of season, midseason time, seasonal amplitude in the NDVI, and the rate of increase and decrease at the beginning and end of a season—can be related to management and crop yields for individual years and for longer periods. Medium-resolution remote-sensing data from the moderate resolution imaging spectroradiometer, known as MODIS, are available from 2000, aggregated into 16-day averages (for every 16 days, observations are available on how the vegetation changes at each pixel level).[2] Phenological metrics are extracted using Timesat software, which gives information in graphs showing how the vegetation changes at every pixel (Eklundh and Jönsson 2012).

For mapping the output of agricultural products using remote sensing that can be compared to other data that are thought to control crop yields, we use explanatory variables—such as greenness, temperature, moisture levels, and management variables—which are then statistically analyzed to derive the relative importance of each variable in driving crop yields. The literature contains several examples of this approach (for example, Lobell et al. 2005), but few that account for spatial autocorrelation and other peculiarities associated with spatial data analysis. Thriving on the possibilities of remote sensing data (large sample size compared with others), we attempt to identify interactions, nonlinearities, or thresholds that are not evident in small samples and from using ordinary statistical tools.

A second method to study causes of yield gap is to examine the spatial distribution of average yields, with the average calculated over varying lengths of time. The basic idea is that longer periods will show less spatial variation than averages for shorter periods, since factors that are less persistent tend to cancel out across years. This approach has been used extensively by David Lobell in various study sites (Lobell 2013). Among other things, the steepness of these curves can provide insights into the persistence of spatial yield differences throughout the study period. This can then be related to other persistent factors (soil quality, hydrology, and so on). Lack of persistence of yield patterns does not suggest that, for example, farmer skills or socioeconomic factors are not important, but rather that variations in these factors are not sufficient to explain yield differences.

Data

Three sources of remote sensing data are used to estimate the effects of gold mining on local economic activity: night lights, the NDVI, and forest loss. Night lights data are from the National Oceanic and Atmospheric Administration's National Geophysical Data Center, which produces three annual night light products: cloud-free composite, average visible lights composite, and stable lights composite.[3] For this study, these data were processed in two steps. First, gas flares were removed using a set of shapefiles from the Environmental Systems Research Institute, which contain polygons outlining the location of gas flares for each country.[4] Second, the data were intercalibrated to allow cross-year analysis. The intercalibration procedure developed by Elvidge et al. (2009) was aimed at overcoming the limited comparability of the DMSP-OLS data by calibrating each composite against one base composite. It is a regression-based technique that works under the assumption that the lighting levels in a reference area remain relatively constant and can therefore be used as the dependent variable.

Table 5.1 shows the satellite-year pairs used for the intercalibration. As indicated in the table, satellite F18 and year 2010 (denoted as F182010) were chosen as the base composite because, overall, its pixels contained the highest intensity, measured by digital numbers.[5] Next, for each composite the following quadratic regression equation was estimated:

$$y = C_0 + C_1 x + C_2 x^2. \tag{1}$$

Table 5.1 shows the resulting calibration coefficients (C), which were applied to each composite so that a new value (y) was calculated based on the original value (x). Any values over 63 were truncated so that the range of the values remained between 0 and 63. In principle, we can obtain light-intensity data for very small areas, up to a cell size of 1 square kilometer. Alternatively, one can take the average over small areas and create 21 composites, each representing one year of night lights between 1992 and 2012.

Since the focus of the analysis is on assessing the impact of mining on local economic activity, a measure of the total intensity of lighting is created—a sum of light—for all the cells around the mining areas, and for each unit of the lowest administrative level possible in each country. The latter helps us link the intensity of light to local economic activity, where, unlike the areas around a mine, the locality here is defined as a district.

The NDVI data are provided as a global data set, with a 16-day temporal resolution and a spatial resolution of 250 × 250 meters.[6] The NDVI is a dimensionless spectral index that relates to the photosynthetic uptake by vegetation (Myneni and Williams 1994; Sellers 1985). It is calculated from the near infrared and red wavelength bands by using the following relationship:

$$NDVI = (NIR - Red) / (NIR + Red). \tag{2}$$

It has been shown that the NDVI is related to vegetation greenness, the leaf area index, and the primary productivity of vegetation (Johnson 2003;

Table 5.1 Satellite-Year Pairs Used for Intercalibration Coefficients

Satellite	Year	C_0	C_1	C_2
F10	1992	0.0577	1.8322	−0.0140
	1993	−0.1031	1.9334	−0.0156
	1994	0.0711	1.9056	−0.0155
F12	1994	0.0996	1.5284	−0.0086
	1995	−0.0196	1.6398	−0.0108
	1996	0.0850	1.7066	−0.0119
	1997	−0.0270	1.5579	−0.0092
	1998	−0.0345	1.4509	−0.0078
	1999	0.0394	1.3969	−0.0070
F14	1997	−0.0204	2.1047	−0.0186
	1998	0.1002	2.0889	−0.0188
	1999	−0.0281	1.9474	−0.0161
	2000	0.0920	1.8814	−0.0153
	2001	−0.0131	1.7926	−0.0135
	2002	0.0784	1.7011	−0.0122
	2003	−0.0185	1.7744	−0.0133
F15	2000	−0.1015	1.4326	−0.0073
	2001	−0.0916	1.4454	−0.0071
	2002	−0.0326	1.3646	−0.0060
	2003	−0.0387	2.0021	−0.0168
	2004	0.0820	1.8514	−0.0144
	2005	−0.0311	1.7861	−0.0130
	2006	−0.0035	1.8146	−0.0135
	2007	0.1053	1.8927	−0.0151
F16	2004	0.0017	1.6334	−0.0107
	2005	−0.0734	1.8601	−0.0143
	2006	−0.0087	1.5660	−0.0091
	2007	−0.0205	1.3583	−0.0060
	2008	−0.0179	1.4378	−0.0073
	2009	0.1349	1.5622	−0.0095
F18	2010	0.0000	1.0000	0.0000
	2011	0.0938	1.2698	−0.0055
	2012	0.0122	1.1210	−0.0024

Source: Authors' compilation using remote sensing data.
Note: The column values are the estimated coefficients from equation 1.

Paruelo et al. 1997). Furthermore, Hill and Donald (2003) documented that a time series of the NDVI can be used to assess changes in vegetation cover and responses over time. It can also be used to estimate agricultural yields (Labus et al. 2010; Ren et al. 2008). This makes it possible to evaluate vegetation status and agricultural productivity on a large scale by using remotely sensed NDVI in regions where field data are sparse.

To decrease the NDVI data's processing time, a mask was constructed to exclude areas not associated with the agricultural economy, which was produced by combining land covers from the MODIS Land Cover Type product.[7] The MODIS land cover scheme identifies 17 land cover classes, which include 11 natural vegetation classes, three developed and mosaic land classes, and three nonvegetated land classes.[8] Here, desired classes were croplands (number 12) and the cropland/natural vegetation mosaic (number 14). For areas within these two classes, yearly amplitude in the NDVI was calculated.

The global data set of Hansen et al. (2013) was used to quantify forest loss annually.[9] This is a map of the extent, loss, and gain of global tree cover from 2000 to 2012 at a spatial resolution of 30 meters. The data set improves on existing knowledge of global forest extent and change by being spatially explicit, quantifying gross forest loss and gain, providing annual loss information, and quantifying trends in forest loss. Forest loss is defined as a stand-replacement disturbance or the complete removal of tree cover canopy at the Landsat pixel scale. Tiles were merged into larger composites and reclassified into 12 layers, one for each year, thus separating each individual forest-loss year. The sum of forest loss was calculated in the same way as night lights.

Agricultural production data were obtained from the statistics offices in Ghana, Mali, and Tanzania to analyze the relationship between the NDVI and agricultural production. The data were compiled at the district level and represent all agricultural products produced during one year. Ghana had data for 2001 to 2012, Tanzania for 2007 and 2008, and Mali for 2002 to 2007. Official GDP data from 1992 to 2012 for each country were obtained from the World Bank's World Development Indicators Database. All GDP data are expressed in constant 2005 U.S. dollars.

Growth Model and Results

To use remote sensing data, it has to be demonstrated that they can indeed predict or track the pattern of data collected through statistics offices. In other words, it is important to demonstrate the strength of the correlation between the remote sensing data and the actual data collected by national administrative agencies. Especially for the NDVI, some knowledge of the agricultural production at the district level, and preferably for local administrative units, is needed.

Our analysis of the growth model and the results has three parts. First, we establish the correlation between the NDVI and actual agricultural production. Second, we estimate the national and local growth model based on time series analysis covering 2001 to 2012 at the district level in the case study countries, and combine night lights, NDVI, and forest-loss data to estimate the size of a local economy. Third, we apply a difference-in-differences framework to estimate the effect of mining on local economic activity, focusing on local agricultural production.

NDVI and Agricultural Production

The remote sensing data allow the computation of the NDVI for areas of any size, but actual agricultural production data are only available at the district level for this study. Therefore, the first task is to show a spatial correlation of the NDVI and actual agricultural production at district level. An important difference between spatial and traditional (aspatial) estimations, such as ordinary least squares regression, is that spatial statistics integrate space and spatial relationships directly into their models. Depending on the specific technique, spatial dependency can enter the regression model as relationships between the independent variables and the outcome variable, between the outcome variables and a spatial lag of itself, or in unexplained (that is, error) terms. Geographically weighted regression is a spatial regression, applied to small geographic areas, which generates parameters disaggregated by the spatial units of analysis. This allows for an assessment of the spatial heterogeneity in the estimated relationships between the independent and dependent variables (Fotheringham, Brundsdon, and Charlton 2002).

The analysis shows a strong association between actual (or reported) agricultural production and the NDVI using spatial regression. Map 5.1 illustrates the varying spatial relationship between the two estimates of agricultural production using 2007 data: the NDVI, and official statistics covering agricultural production. Other years show similar results, and the summary of the strength of the association is shown in annex figure 5A.1 and annex table 5A.1. The sum of the NDVI at the district level is used as a predictor for the level of agricultural production. The pattern that emerges is one of a highly to moderately strong correlation between agricultural production and the NDVI in areas with high population densities. In most years and countries—with the exception of Mali—over 60 percent of the variation in district-level agricultural production can be explained by the differences in the average district-level NDVI intensity (see annex table 5A.1). We were not able to determine whether the agricultural data include nonmarketed production, which in all these countries could be substantial. That said, the strong

Map 5.1 Geographically Weighted Regression, by District in Ghana, Mali, and Tanzania, 2007

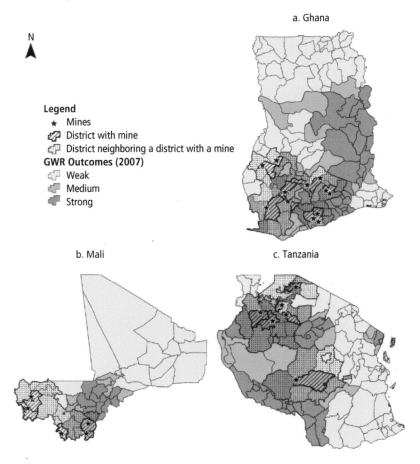

Source: Authors' calculation using remote sensing and agricultural production data.
Note: GWR = geographically weight regression.

correlation between the NDVI and agricultural production gives us confidence to use this index to predict agricultural production for small areas—say, around a mine.

National Growth Model

Whether gold mining has substantial economic benefits—spillover effects—on local economies in addition to its impact on agriculture is of interest. We have shown that the strong association between the NDVI and agricultural production justifies the use of NDVI data for measuring changes to agricultural production around gold mines. Similarly, one could use the night lights data, which have been demonstrated to predict economic activity and capture changes to the local economy around mines. Although district-level agricultural output data are available, district-level GDP information are not. Consequently, a national model is needed to estimate aggregate GDP; parameters from this model can then be used to obtain local economic production.

The basic estimation strategy follows Henderson et al. (2012), whose framework can be shown as:

$$Y_{jt} = \widehat{\psi} X_{jt} + c_j + d_t + e_{jt}, \tag{3}$$

where Y_{jt} is the true GDP of country j in time t. X_{jt} is the level of observed night lights at corresponding country and time, c_j and d_j are country and year fixed effects, and e_{jt} is the error term. This model of an aggregate economy suggests that total production—or total economic activity (or its changes)—is explained by the level of measured night lights (or its percentage growth) observed by satellite adjusted for country- and time-invariant effects and an error term.

Following standard practices, the error term is assumed to be uncorrelated with the GDP measurement. Given that GDP and night lights come from two independent sources, the assumption seems to be appropriate. However, using gridded data of land cover and night lights, we find that it is possible for agriculture's value-added to increase without emitting more observable night lights into space. If this is the case, then the error term is actually dependent on the agricultural share since the higher the share, the higher the measurement error from the night lights.

Given this observation, our estimation follows the framework in equation 1, but takes note of the fact that not all economic growth, especially in heavily agricultural societies, is captured by growth in observed night lights. The working assumption here is that night lights observed in space are the result of growth in only the nonagricultural sector. We therefore split the Henderson et al. (2012) model into separate nonagricultural (equation 4) and agricultural (equation 5) parts. The separate models are expressed as:

$$Y_{jt}^{na} = \widehat{\psi}^{na} X_{jt}^{na} + c_j^{na} + d_t^{na} + e_{jt}^{na} \tag{4}$$

$$Y_t^{a} = \left(\widehat{\psi}^{a1} \ \widehat{\psi}^{a2} \ \ldots \ \widehat{\psi}^{an} \right) \begin{pmatrix} l_{jt}^{a1} \\ l_{jt}^{a2} \\ \vdots \\ l_{jt}^{an} \end{pmatrix} + c_j^{a} + d_t^{a} + e_{jt}^{a} \tag{5}$$

Equation 3 is the familiar model that links GDP level (or growth) to the sum (or growth) of night lights. We argue that this model is mostly predictive of nonagricultural data. In equation 5 we extend this model to the agricultural sector by introducing two variables: MODIS NDVI and forest loss. Finally, a year dummy (2004 as a cutoff year) is added to obtain three models of income (growth) for each country, combining night lights, the NDVI, and forest loss, that is:

$$Log\ GDP \sim Log\ Night\ lights + Year\ dummy. \tag{6}$$

$$Log\ GDP \sim Log\ Night\ lights + NDVI + Year\ dummy. \tag{7}$$

$$Log\ GDP \sim Log\ Night\ lights + NDVI + Forestloss + Year\ dummy. \tag{8}$$

The rationale for using a year dummy—and specifically 2004—is related to Ghana rebasing its GDP around 2006, and commodity prices starting to rise about that time. The model is designed so that the regression line departs from the origin, with the y-intercept being equal to 0. The rationale behind not using the intercept is that in the second step of the model, we are estimating local growth by using the national growth model to fit with local parameters at the district level. The dynamics of the local economy are dependent on the relationship between the variables used in the national growth model. Including a national intercept term would result in a mismatch due to the spatial scale of the local estimations.

Figure 5.1 shows the correspondence between the actual evolution of aggregate production and the pattern of predicted output that can be obtained using the three different models (equations 6–8) for each country. Three observations can be drawn from figure 5.1. First, the remote sensing data are strongly predictive of the actual evolution of GDP in all countries, and with better-predicted levels of GDP when including all three types of remote sensing data. The best fit is the model for Ghana, especially after 2004. In Burkina Faso and Mali, the actual log (GDP) and predicted log (GDP)—using log night lights, forest loss, and the NDVI—are very close for almost every year except for larger spikes in 2001 and 2009. Although the correlations are strong for Tanzania, there are periods when the remote sensing data underestimate and others when they overpredict total production. Similar data spikes, especially for log night lights, can be observed in Tanzania. The odd pattern in the last years of the model for Burkina Faso, Mali, and Tanzania is similar to that observed for night lights data at the global level (annex figure 5A.2). This pattern might be explained by a combination of the following reasons related to night lights: real variation in the night lights data between years, calibration effects, and truncation of values over 63 (light-intensive over 63).

Figure 5.1 Actual and Predicted Log (GDP) Using Three Different Models in Burkina Faso, Ghana, Mali, and Tanzania, 2001–12

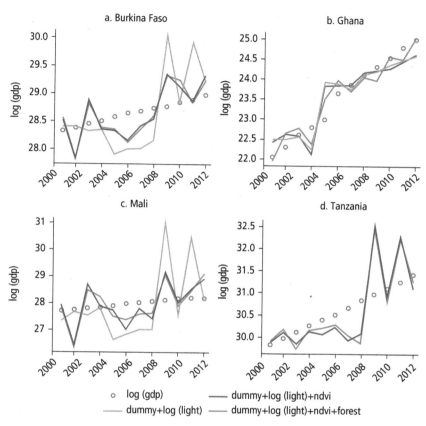

Second, as expected, night lights alone are not sufficient to predict aggregate production. While it is true that night light stand out as strongly correlated with GDP, the NDVI's inclusion improves the fit of the model (table 5.2). In fact, the country models seem to suggest that night lights with the NDVI perform better than any other specification (for example, night lights, the NDVI, and forest loss) in predicting log (GDP). Only in Ghana is the forest loss statistically significant. Results from the other countries do not show any statistical significance by adding forest loss, so this variable is dropped in all the estimation models.

And third, even though agriculture accounts for the largest share of economic activity in all these countries, the NDVI is strongly statistically significant only for the Burkina Faso and Mali models. Adding forest loss to the model does not change the model fit, and the variable is only significant in Ghana.

Table 5.2 Estimated Growth, Using Remote Sensing Data in Burkina Faso, Ghana, Mali, and Tanzania

Country	Model specification	Dummy	Lights	NDVI	Forest	R-squared
Burkina Faso	log(gdp) ~ 0 + log(light) + dummy	−0,6375	2,6873***			0,314
	log(gdp) ~ 0 + log(light) + ndvi + dummy	−0,1954	1,8140***	8,188E-06**		0,434
	log(gdp) ~0 + log(light) + ndvi + forest + dummy	−0,2595	1,8477***	7,821E-06**	5,12E-07	0,433
Ghana	log(gdp) ~ 0 + log(light) + dummy	1,6512***	1,8172***			0,837
	log(gdp) ~ 0 + log(light) + ndvi + dummy	1,6370***	1,7550***	1,713E-06		0,844
	log(gdp) ~ 0 + log(light) + ndvi + forest + dummy	1,7860***	1,7590***	3,644E-06	−2,34E-06*	0,915
Mali	log(gdp) ~ 0 + log(light) + dummy	−1,0713	2,5732***			0,201
	log(gdp) ~ 0 + log(light) + ndvi + dummy	−0,4041	1,3282***	1,064E-05**		0,223
	log(gdp) ~ 0 + log(light) + ndvi + forest + dummy	−0,4554	1,3731**	1,009E-05**	2,62E-06	0,259
Tanzania	log(gdp) ~ 0 + log(light) + dummy	0,3340	2,5921***			0,489
	log(gdp) ~ 0 + log(light) + ndvi + dummy	0,3322	2,5913***	4,347E-08		0,488
	log(gdp) ~ 0 + log(light) + ndvi + forest + dummy	0,5441	2,6175***	7,163E-08	−1,58E-07	0,483

Source: Authors' calculation using remote sensing data.
Note: NDVI = Normalized Difference Vegetation Index.
***$p<0.01$, **$p<0.05$, *$p<0.1$

The year dummy is strongly statistically significant for Ghana, but does not influence the results for the other countries.

Growth Model at the District Level

Ideally, we would like to estimate a model linking GDP at the local level to geo-referenced data. Unfortunately, while the georeferenced data can be compiled for areas smaller than even a district, administrative data for district-level GDP are not available for the case study countries. Therefore, the parameters of the relationship between GDP and georeferenced data at the national level are used to impute district-level production in each country. The models are based on the regression results from equations 6–8 and are presented in table 5.3.

When developing the growth model for districts, several methods were used to provide accurate dimensions for the local economy. Population data and average district-level household expenditures were included as weights in the model estimating local growth patterns. However, population at the district level was highly correlated with night light intensity at the district level, and average household expenditures at the district level were highly correlated with GDP at the local level (see annex figures 5A.3 and 5A.4 for correlation analysis), and therefore were not used in the estimations.

The results of the district-level growth patterns are displayed in a series of maps and graphs in annex 5A. Annex map 5A.1 presents maps of the imputed growth patterns at the district level. The maps tag districts into those that are predicted to have had negative, moderate, or high growth. These maps provide a visual display of the geography of growth in each of the case study countries.

The maps lead to three main conclusions. First, average growth in gold-mining districts appears to be higher than in nonmining districts. In Ghana, average growth rates turn positive if the growth in districts neighboring mining districts are taken into account. Annex map 5A.1 suggests that effects of mining could evolve differently around mining and nonmining areas in different countries. And the differential evolution could have an impact on local economic growth. However, to test whether these spatial patterns of measured local economic growth are due to mining requires a more rigorous test than a mere visual inspection. A suitable test and the results follow.

Table 5.3 Observed and Predicted Gross Domestic Product in Burkina Faso, Ghana, Mali, and Tanzania

	Burkina Faso	Ghana	Mali	Tanzania
Average log (GDP)	28.65	23.59	27.98	30.62
Average log (model GDP)	28.65	23.60	27.96	30.60
Residual standard error	0.67	0.43	1.39	0.72

Night Lights and the NDVI in a Difference-in-Differences Framework

Empirical Framework

To understand whether night lights and the NDVI in mining communities are linked with the onset of mining, a difference-in-differences empirical estimation strategy is used.[10] This strategy allows comparison of outcomes in the geographic proximity of mines with areas farther away, both before and after mines start producing. In effect, this involves making three comparisons: close to and far away, before and after, and both comparisons at the same time. The cross-sectional differences in areas with and without an active mine are modeled as:

$$Y_{jt} = \beta_1 active_{jt} + \varepsilon_j, \tag{9}$$

where Y is the outcome variable (night lights and the NDVI), *active* is a binary variable that takes the value 1 if the mine is active in that year, and subscript j is for the mine and t for the year. The importance of proximity can be modeled as:

$$Y_j = \beta_1 close_j + \varepsilon_j, \tag{10}$$

where *close* captures the cross-sectional difference between areas that are close to mines and those that are further away. The interest is in knowing the relative change that happens in the geographic proximity of mines with the onset of mine production, compared with what happens far away from the mine. This is captured by the difference-in-differences estimation model, which includes an interaction effect of the two binary variables, as follows:

$$Y_{jt} = \beta_1 active_{jt} + \beta_2 close_j + \beta_3 active_{jt} * close_j + \delta_j + \varepsilon_{jt}, \tag{11}$$

where δ_j is a mine fixed effect, which means that any change that is peculiar to a mine is accounted for. Year fixed effects, which will take care of year-specific shocks that happen across all mines, are also captured. To decide the relevant distances for examining the footprint of gold mines, the analysis draws guidance from recent studies in the African context (see chapter 4). These studies find that areas up to a 20-kilometer (km) radius are relevant, and that beyond 50 km mines have little economic footprint. Because we rely on the geographic results found in this study, a distance of 10 km is chosen to understand the footprint close to mines. This is compared with an area 10 km, 20 km, 30 km, and 50 km to 100 km away. The total sample size is 32 large-scale gold mines in Burkina Faso, Ghana, Mali, and Tanzania.

Results

Figure 5.2 explores the change in the different distances from a mine over its lifetime. The figures are based on summary statistics, and do not control for any systematic differences across the mines. Overall, it seems that areas very close

Figure 5.2 Night Lights and Normalized Difference Vegetation Index over a Mine's Lifetime

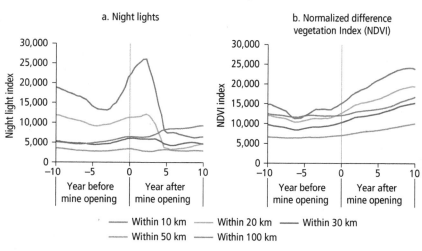

Source: Authors' estimates from survey data.
Note: Nonparametric (local polynomial smooth) measures of night lights and the NDVI close to mines. Night lights and the NDVI are measured as averages across limited geographic areas, varying from within 10 km from the mine center point, to 20 km, 30 km, 50 km, and 100 km.

to mines are on a steeper trend in night lights than those farther away, especially closer to a mine opening year. One interpretation of this pattern is that from a few years before a mine starts extracting gold, economic activity that emits night lights increases in these areas. One reason why this happens before the mine opening year is because mines are capital-intensive and the local economy is stimulated during this investment phase, a pattern confirmed in previously mentioned econometric studies.

For the NDVI, no big difference in patterns is observed across mining and nonmining areas. Although both areas seem to be on an upward-sloping trend, this needs to be interpreted with caution, because it can be driven by the unbalanced sample.[11] If anything, we detect that areas close to mines are getting relatively greener over time compared with areas farther away.

Table 5.4 shows the regression results from the strategies outlined in the empirical framework section. The results indicate there are clear increases in night lights close to mines. The strongest effects are found within 10 km of a mine for log night lights. The measures are simple differences, and compare within a given area before and after a mine opening. The larger the distance used to define the area close to a mine, the smaller the effect sizes. Note that these estimates are simple differences and do not take into account local trends in night lights (for that, see the difference-in-differences analysis that follows and table 5.5).

Table 5.4 Simple Difference Specification: Comparing before and after Mine Opening

	(1)	(2)	(3)	(4)	(5)
Distance	**10 km**	**20 km**	**30 km**	**40 km**	**50 km**
Log night lights					
Active mine	0.704**	0.446***	0.281*	0.235	0.468***
	(0.272)	(0.135)	(0.146)	(0.149)	(0.070)
Observations	620	620	620	620	620
R-squared	0.649	0.728	0.775	0.820	0.896
Log NDVI					
Active mine	0.026***	0.014*	0.014	0.030**	0.049
	(0.009)	(0.007)	(0.024)	(0.012)	(0.061)
Observations	347	347	347	347	347
R-squared	0.601	0.709	0.649	0.635	0.452
Mine FE	Yes	Yes	Yes	Yes	Yes

Note: Clustered standard errors at the mine level are in parentheses. The simple difference is capturing the percentage increase in night lights and the NDVI after mine opening within 10 km, 20 km, 30 km, 40 km, and 50 km. The simple difference is thus a comparison of values before and after mine opening within the same geographic area. FE = fixed effects; NDVI = Normalized Difference Vegetation Index.
$***p<0.01$, $**p<0.05$, $*p<0.1$.

Table 5.5 Difference-in-Differences Specification

	(1)	(2)	(3)	(4)
	Night lights	**Night lights**	**NDVI**	**NDVI**
Active_close	−0.540	−0.545	−0.052	−0.034
	(0.365)	(0.375)	(0.270)	(0.265)
Active	0.692***	0.191	0.316	−0.028
	(0.204)	(0.240)	(0.228)	(0.232)
Close (20 km)	0.209	0.199	−0.144	−0.168
	(0.333)	(0.344)	(0.207)	(0.200)
Mine FE	Yes	Yes	Yes	Yes
Year FE	No	Yes	No	Yes
Observations	1,063	1,063	684	684
R-squared	0.655	0.693	0.691	0.727

Note: Clustered standard errors at the mine level are in parentheses. The difference-in-differences estimate compares outcomes close to mines with far away (20–100 km), and before and after mine opening. The two years preceding the mine opening year are excluded from the analysis. Close is defined as within 20 km of a mine. FE = fixed effect; NDVI = Normalized Difference Vegetation Index.
$***p<0.01$.

The model also possibly overestimates the effect size because it does not capture changes in the composition of local production with just night lights. For instance, if households engaging in subsistence farming do not have electricity, but demand it to change to more modern sectors at the time of a mine opening, then the increased demand for electricity will lead to an increase in night lights. However, the decrease in farming that will result from occupational switching will not be reflected in the changes in night lights if subsistence farming does not use electricity. In such a scenario, the effect of a mine on the local economy would be overestimated.

Findings from the difference-in-differences analysis are presented in table 5.5. The results do not show any robust increases in night lights or the NDVI in mining communities at 20 km, compared with those farther away (20–100 km). The estimated effects are insignificant for the main treatment coefficient *active_close*. The statistically significant coefficient for *active* in the first specification shows more night lights across the whole area after mine opening compared with before. The coefficient is insignificant when controlling for year fixed effects, which indicates trends in night lights. Assessing the visual evidence in figure 5.2 suggests only a modest increase in night lights within 20 km of a gold mine around the time of its opening, but that this is not true in the long run.

If mines increase the urbanization rate or lead to decreased local farming— as found by Aragón and Rud (2015)—greenness in mining areas should decrease. In short, values of the NDVI measure of greenness used in our model should decline. Table 5.4 shows that areas close to mines have higher levels of the NDVI (columns 1, 2, and 4). This could be indicative of mining areas being more rural in general. However, the interaction terms (table 5.5, columns 3 and 4) are statistically insignificant and negative, indicating that the NDVI does not change statistically with the onset of mining.

Conclusions

The objective of this chapter was to use remote sensing data to estimate the level and growth of local economic activity around mining areas in Burkina Faso, Ghana, Mali, and Tanzania. The analysis was divided into two parts.

First, it established the spatial relationship between the NDVI, a greenness indicator, and actual agricultural production at the district level on one hand, and night lights and overall economic output (GDP) on the other. The remote sensing data sets used in the study covered 2001–12, providing not only high spatial resolution but also a time series perspective to account for change over time. The results were encouraging. The analysis found that the NDVI and night lights are good predictors (a relatively high R-squared) of economic activity in these countries. However, forest loss as a predictor of economic growth did not provide increased explanatory power to model economic growth on the national level, so it was dropped when modeling economic growth on local levels.

Second, having shown that remote sensing data provide a useful measure of economic activity, the chapter makes use of these data to compare growth in economic activity around mining areas to those far away using a difference-in-differences framework.

The findings can be summarized in two points. One, the analysis of a selected set of 32 gold mines from four African countries (Burkina Faso, Ghana, Mali, and Tanzania) suggests the onset of mines is associated with increased economic activity—as proxied by night lights—within the vicinity of the mines. Graphical analysis of the night lights data shows strong increases in night lights in mining communities within 10 km of a mine in the years immediately before its opening and the years following. A simple difference-in-differences analysis illustrates that areas very near mines (within 10 km) have significantly higher levels of economic activity after a mine opening.[12] However, the difference-in-differences analysis illustrates that over time, areas near mines are not significantly better off than areas farther away. This may partially indicate that with time, the economic benefits from mining spread over a larger area from a mine's center point. The finding that economic growth increases is in contrast to the common perception that views large-scale mines as economic enclaves separated from the local economies.

Two, despite the risks that mines pose to agricultural productivity (for example, through environmental pollution or structural shifts in the labor market), there is no evidence of a decrease in greenness, which is the measure of agricultural production.[13]

Annex 5A: District-Level Growth Pattern Results

Figure 5A.1 GWR-Local *R*-Squared for Relationship between Dependent Variable Total Agricultural Production, by District and Independent Variable NDVI Intensity Sum, by District

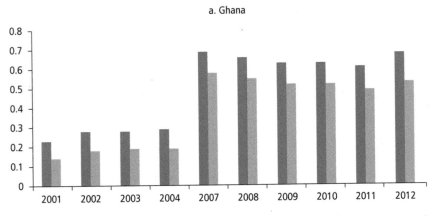

a. Ghana

(continued next page)

Figure 5A.1 (continued)

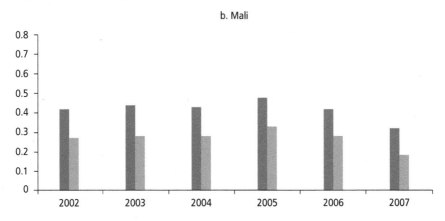

b. Mali

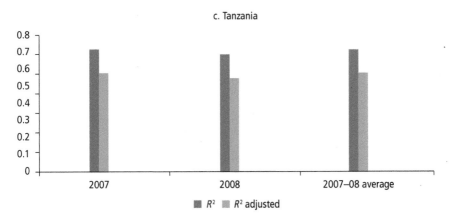

c. Tanzania

■ R^2 ■ R^2 adjusted

Source: NDVI processed by authors and agricultural production data provided by the World Bank.
Note: GWR = geographically weight regression; NDVI = Normalized Difference Vegetation Index.

Table 5A.1 GWR-Local R-Squared for Relationship between Dependent Variable Total Agricultural Production, by District and Independent Variable, Sum of NDVI Intensity by District

Country	Year	R^2	R^2 Adjusted
Ghana	2001	0,23	0,14
Ghana	2002	0,28	0,18
Ghana	2003	0,28	0,19

(continued next page)

Table 5A.1 (continued)

Country	Year	R^2	R^2 Adjusted
Ghana	2004	0,29	0,19
Ghana	2007	0,69	0,58
Ghana	2008	0,66	0,55
Ghana	2009	0,63	0,52
Ghana	2010	0,63	0,52
Ghana	2011	0,61	0,49
Ghana	2012	0,68	0,53
Mali	2002	0,43	0,28
Mali	2003	0,45	0,29
Mali	2004	0,44	0,29
Mali	2005	0,49	0,34
Mali	2006	0,43	0,29
Mali	2007	0,33	0,19
Tanzania	2007	0,72	0,58
Tanzania	2008	0,69	0,55

Source: NDVI processed by authors and agricultural production data provided by the World Bank.
Note: GWR = geographically weight regression; NDVI = Normalized Difference Vegetation Index.

Figure 5A.2 **Log (global light sum), 2008–12**

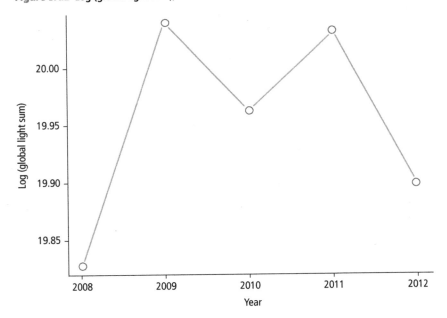

Map 5A.1 Spatial Analysis of Average Growth in Districts, Estimated by Growth Model in Burkina Faso, Ghana, Mali, and Tanzania, 2001–12

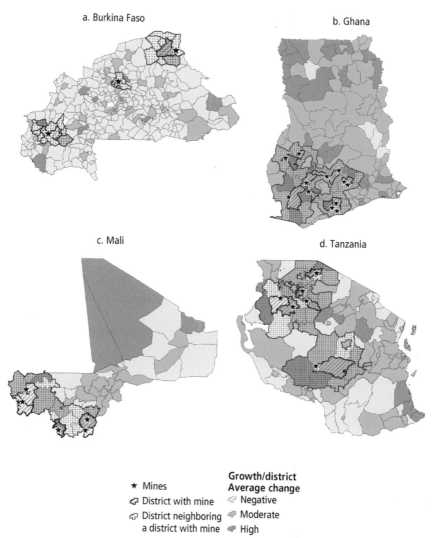

a. Burkina Faso

b. Ghana

c. Mali

d. Tanzania

★ Mines
⊄ District with mine
⊄ District neighboring a district with mine

Growth/district Average change
⊄ Negative
⊄ Moderate
⊄ High

Source: Authors' calculation using remote sensing and agricultural production data.

Figure 5A.3 Correlation between GDP and Household Expenditures per Capita Levels for Ghana, 1991/92 and 2005/06

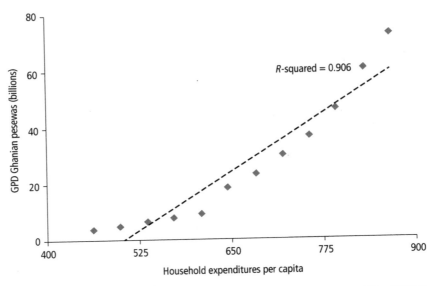

Source: World Bank, World Development Indicators Database; Ghana Living Standards Surveys 1991/92 and 2005/06.

Figure 5A.4 Correlation Between Night Light Intensity and Population at District Levels for Ghana, 2010

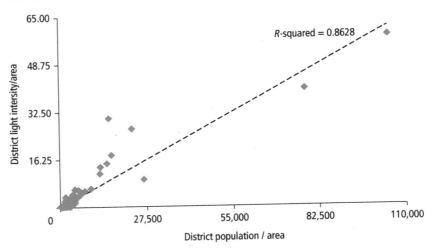

Sources: Defense Meteorological Satellite Program Operational Linescan System data, processed by the authors; population data provided by the World Bank.

Notes

1. This chapter is based on Andersson at al. (2015).
2. MODIS is a key instrument aboard the Terra (EOS AM) and Aqua (EOS PM) satellites launched by the U.S. National Aeronautics and Space Administration.
3. See the National Oceanic and Atmospheric Administration–National Geophysical Data Center website (http://ngdc.noaa.gov/eog/archive.html) for a description of each of these data sets.
4. This is an international supplier of geographic information system software.
5. In their studies, Elvidge et al. (2009, 2013) selected F121999 as the base composite. The difference in the selection is attributed to the fact that the authors were intercalibrating a worldwide data set, while this study examines only the case of Africa.
6. The NDVI from MODIS vegetation indexes product MOD13Q1 were used.
7. For this purpose, the MODIS land cover type product (MCD12Q1) was used (Friedl et al. 2010).
8. These are the land cover classes defined by the International Geosphere Biosphere Programme.
9. Annual forest loss data from http://www.earthenginepartners.appspot.com/science-2013-global-forest/download.html.
10. This strategy is employed to understand the economic effects of gold mining in Africa by Aragón and Rud (2015), Chuhan-Pole et al. (2015), and Tolonen (2015).
11. The sample is unbalanced because the data on night lights start in 2002, but mines may have opened long before then, as well as after 2002. If a mine opened before 2002, night lights data are only available during a mine's active period. Such mines would then add to the estimates of night lights on the right side of the red line in figure 5.2, but not to the left. There are too few mines for which night lights data are available for the whole 20-year period to do these figures on a perfectly balanced subsample.
12. Proximity is defined as an area within 10 km, 20 km, 30 km, or 40 km of the location of the mine, and the control group is drawn from an area 50–100 km away.
13. Note, however, that the effects of small-scale and artisanal mining activity, common in the case study countries, on economic growth and greenness are not addressed in this study. These effects are not estimated separately either (see chapter 4 box 4.1).

References

Andersson, Magnus, Punam Chuhan-Pole, Andrew Dabalaen, Ola Hall, Nicolas Olen, Aly Sanoh, and Anja Tolonen. 2015. "Does Large-Scale Gold Mining Reduce Agricultural Growth? Case Studies from Burkina Faso, Ghana, Mali, and Tanzania." Unpublished.

Aragón, F. M., and J. P. Rud. 2015. "Polluting Industries and Agricultural Productivity: Evidence from Mining in Ghana." *Economic Journal.* doi.10.1111/ecoj.12244.

Chen, Xi, and William D. Nordhaus. 2011. "Using Luminosity Data as a Proxy for Economic Statistics." *Proceedings of the National Academy of Sciences* 108 (21): 8589–94.

Chuhan-Pole, P., A. Dabalen, A. Kotsadam, A. Sanoh, and A. Tolonen. 2015. "The Local Socioeconomic Effects of Gold Mining: Evidence from Ghana." Policy Research Working Paper 7250, World Bank, Washington, DC.

Doll, C. N. H., J.-P. Muller, and J. G. Morley. 2006. "Mapping Regional Economic Activity from Night-Time Light Satellite Imagery." *Ecological Economics* 57 (1): 75–92.

Ebener, S., C. Murray, A. Tandon, and C. D. Elvidge. 2005. "From Wealth to Health: Modelling the Distribution of Income Per Capita at the Sub-National Level Using Night-Time Light Imagery." *International Journal of Health Geographics* 5: 1–17.

Eklundh, L., and P. Jönsson. 2012. "TIMESAT 3.1 Software Manual." Lund University, Lund, Sweden.

Elvidge, C. D., K. E. Baugh, E. A. Kihn, H. W. Kroehl, E. R. David, and C.W. Davis. 1997. "Relation between Satellite Observed Visible-Near Infrared Emissions, Population, Economic Activity and Electric Power Consumption." *International Journal of Remote Sensing* 18 (6): 1373–79.

Elvidge, C. D., F. C. Hsu, K. E. Baugh, and T. Ghosh. 2013. "National Trends in Satellite Observed Lighting: 1992–2012." In *Global Urban Monitoring and Assessment Through Earth Observation*, edited by Q. Weng. Boca Raton, FL: CRC Press.

Elvidge, C. D., D. Ziskin, K. E. Baugh, B. T. Tuttle, T. Ghosh, D. W. Pack, and M. Zhizhin. 2009. "A Fifteen Year Record of Global Natural Gas Flaring Derived from Satellite Data." *Energies* 2 (3): 595–622.

Fotheringham, A. S., C. Brunsdon, and M. E. Charlton. 2002. *Geographically Weighted Regression: The Analysis of Spatially Varying Relationships.* Chichester, UK: Wiley.

Friedl, M. A., D. Sulla-Menashe, B. Tan, A. Schneider, N. Ramankutty, A. Sibley, and X. Huang. 2010. "MODIS Collection 5 Global Land Cover: Algorithm Refinements and Characterization of New Datasets." *Remote Sensing of Environment* 114 (1): 168–82.

Ghosh, T., R. L. Powell, C. D. Elvidge, K. E. Baugh, P. C. Sutton, and S. Anderson. 2010. "Shedding Light on the Global Distribution of Economic Activity." *Open Geography Journal* 3: 148–61.

Hall, Ola. 2010. "Remote Sensing in Social Science Research." *Open Remote Sensing Journal* 3: 1–16.

Hall, Ola, and Andersson Magnus. 2014. "African Economic Growth." Light and Vegetation Database.

Hansen, M.C., P. V. Potapov, R. Moore, M. Hancher, S. A. Turubanova, A. Tyukavina, D. Thau, et al. 2013. "High-Resolution Global Maps of 21st-Century Forest Cover Change." *Science* 342 (6160): 850–53.

Henderson, J. Vernon, Adam Storeygard, and David N. Weil. 2012. "Measuring Economic Growth from Outer Space." *American Economic Review* 102 (2): 994–1028.

Hill, M. J., and G. E. Donald. 2003. "Estimating Spatio-Temporal Patterns of Agricultural Productivity in Fragmented Landscapes Using AVHRR NDVI Time Series." *Remote Sensing of Environment* 84 (3): 367–84.

Johnson, L. F. 2003. "Temporal Stability of an NDVI-LAI Relationship in a Napa Valley Vineyard." *Australian Journal of Grape and Wine Research* 9 (2): 96–101. doi:10.1111/j.1755-0238.2003.tb00258.x.

Keola, S., M. Andersson, and O. Hall. 2015. "Monitoring Economic Development from Space: Using Night-Time Light and Land Cover Data to Measure Economic Growth." *World Development* 66: 322–34.

Labus, M. P., G. A. Nielsen, R. L. Lawrence, R. Engel, and D. S. Long. 2010. "Wheat Yield Estimates Using Multi-Temporal NDVI Satellite Imagery." *International Journal of Remote Sensing* 23 (20): 4169–80. doi:10.1080/01431160110107653.

Lobell, David B. 2013. "The Use of Satellite Data for Crop Yield Gap Analysis." *Field Crops Research* 143 (March): 56–64.

Lobell, David B., J. I. Ortiz-Monasterio, G. P. Asner, P. A. Matson, R. L. Naylor, and W. P. Falcon. 2005. "Analysis of Wheat Yield and Climatic Trends in Mexico." *Field Crops Research* 94: 250–56.

Myneni, R. B., and D. L. Williams. 1994. "On the Relationship between FAPAR and NDVI." *Remote Sensing of Environment* 49 (3): 200–11. doi:10.1016/0034 -4257(94)90016-7.

Paruelo, J. M., H. E. Epstein, W. K. Lauenroth, and I. C. Burke. 1997. "ANPP Estimates from NDVI for the Central Grassland Region of the United States." *Ecology* 78 (3): 953–58. doi:10.1890/0012-9658(1997)078[0953:aefnft]2.0.co;2.

Ren, J., Z. Chen, Q. Zhou, and H. Tang. 2008. "Regional Yield Estimation for Winter Wheat with MODIS-NDVI Data in Shandong, China." *International Journal of Applied Earth Observation and Geoinformation* 10 (4): 403–13.

Sei-Ichi, Saitoh, A. Fukaya, K. Saitoh, B. Semedi, and R. Mugo. 2010. "Estimation of Number of Pacific Saury Fishing Vessels Using Night-Time Visible Images." *International Archives of the Photogrammetry, Remote Sensing and Spatial Information Science* 38 (Part 8): 1013–16.

Sellers, P. J. 1985. "Canopy Reflectance, Photosynthesis and Transpiration." *International Journal of Remote Sensing* 6 (8): 1335–72.

Sutton, Paul C., and Robert Costanza. 2002. "Global Estimates of Market and Non-Market Values Derived from Nighttime Satellite Imagery, Land Cover, and Ecosystem Service Valuation." *Ecological Economics* 41 (3): 509–27.

Tolonen, A. 2015. "Local Industrial Shocks, Female Empowerment and Infant Health: Evidence from Africa's Gold Mining Industry." Dissertation, University of Gothenburg, Sweden.

assessment framework, 10
fiscal revenue windfalls and, 40–41
gold mining's impact on, 5
for migrants, 31*n*1, 133*f*, 136
in mining communities, 14, 23,
    24*f*, 83, 85
socioeconomic effects of large-scale
    gold mining, 131–32, 131*t*,
    132–33*f*
input-output analysis, 54
intergovernmental transfers, 54–55
International Geosphere Biosphere
    Programme, 171*n*8
IntierraRMG, 102
Isham, Jonathan, 37

J
Jia, Ruixue, 56

K
Keniston, Daniel, 59*n*13
Khemani, Stuti, 41
Kinyondo, G., 70*b*
Koelle, Michael, 44
Kotsadam, Andreas, 50, 102, 106, 148

L
Land, Bryan Christopher, 33, 36, 47, 54
Lei, Yu-Hsiang, 38
life expectancy, 3
literacy, 3
living standard surveys, 103, 103*t*.
    See also socioeconomic effects
    of large-scale gold mining
Loayza, Norman, 50
Lobell, David, 151
local demand shock, 42–45, 43*f*
local impact assessment of resource
    abundance, 39–56
    analytical framework, 40–46, 41*f*,
        43*f*, 46*f*
    corruption and conflict, 50–52, 51*t*
    economic growth, 47
    empirical evidence, 47–53, 47–49*t*,
        51*t*, 53*t*

employment, 47, 49–50
fiscal revenue windfall, 40–42, 41*f*
input-output analysis, 54
institutional role, 54–56
lessons learned, 53–54
local demand shock, 42–45, 43*f*
negative externalities, 45–46, 46*f*
pollution, 52–53, 53*t*
resource endowments and
    specialization, 40, 57, 58*f*

M
Makongolosi, Tanzania, 9*b*
Mali
    agricultural impacts of gold mining,
        19–21, 20*f*, 22*f*, 147–71
    data results, 151–54, 153*t*
    difference-in-differences
        framework, 162–65
    district level growth model, 161,
        166–68*f*, 167–68*t*, 169*m*, 170*f*
    economic growth and, 148–51
    growth model for, 154–65, 156*m*,
        159*f*, 160–61*t*, 163*f*, 164*t*
    national growth model, 156–61,
        156*m*, 159*f*, 160*t*
    NDVI as measure for, 155–56,
        162–65, 163*f*, 164*t*
    night lights measure for, 162–65,
        163*f*, 164*t*
    remote sensing for, 148–51
    artisanal and small-scale mining, 70*b*
    asset accumulation, 22, 23*f*, 118,
        119–20*t*, 120–21*f*
    car ownership, 118, 119–20*t*
    case study, 5–6
    child health outcomes, 14–15, 24–27,
        25–26*f*, 121–30, 123*f*, 124*t*,
        125–26*b*, 127–30*t*, 129*f*
    country background, 68, 69*f*, 70*b*
    economic growth attributed to
        extractives, 4, 68
    employment, 14, 15–19, 17–18*f*,
        71–72, 73*f*, 105–17, 105–7*t*,
        108–9*f*, 111*f*, 112–13*t*, 116–18*t*

fiscal sharing, 78f, 79–80, 81f
gold mining, 10, 93–95, 94t,
    96m, 98f
government mining revenues, 27–29,
    28f, 76–81, 77–78f, 81f, 88n5
infrastructure access, 23, 24f, 85–87,
    85t, 86f, 131–32, 131t, 132–33f
mine-induced migration, 133–37, 135f
policy priorities, 29–31
poverty, 82–83, 83f
radio ownership, 118, 119–20t,
    120–21f
sanitation access, 125–26b
structural transformation, 114–15
manufacturing sector, 53–54, 114
Marchand, Joseph, 59n13
market channel
    analytical framework, 6, 7f
    in case studies, 67
    natural resource effects on local
        communities through, 5, 5f
Matundasi, Tanzania, 9b
McKinnish, Terra, 59n13
McMahon, G., 73
Measham, Thomas G., 59n13
Mehlum, Halvor, 38
Mexico, night lights measures for, 149
Michaels, Guy, 38, 49, 50, 59n13
migrants
    asset accumulation, 136
    child health outcomes, 26, 127,
        129–30, 129f, 130t
    employment, 136
    infrastructure access, 31n1,
        133f, 136
    socioeconomic effects of large-scale
        gold mining, 133–37, 135f, 138
MineAtlas, 102
mineral sector. See gold mining
mining communities. See also local
        impact assessment of resource
        abundance
    asset accumulation in, 22, 23f
    child health outcomes in, 24–27,
        25–26f
    defined, 12–13b

infrastructure access in, 23, 24f
welfare gains in, 14–27, 17–18f, 20f,
    22–26f
moderate resolution imaging
    spectroradiometer (MODIS),
    151, 154, 158, 171n2
Moene, Karl, 38
Monteiro, Joana, 51, 60n14
Moreira, S., 73
Moretti, Enrico, 44
Morley, J. G., 149
Muller, J.-P., 149
multiplier effects, 72–73

N

National Geophysical Data Center,
    151–52, 171n3
natural resource curse, 3, 36–38
NDVI. See Normalized Difference
    Vegetation Index
negative externalities
    case studies, 74–76, 75f, 76t, 81–82
    local impact assessment of resource
        abundance, 45–46, 46f
Newmont Ghana Gold, 29, 74
Nie, Huihua, 56
Nigeria
    nonmonetary welfare indicators, 3, 4f
    oil revenues, 34
night lights
    agricultural productivity measured
        by, 21, 22f
    data results, 151–54, 153t, 171n11
    economic activity measured by,
        148–51
    infant mortality trends parallel to,
        104, 104f
nonmonetary welfare indicators, 3, 4f
non-resource-rich countries. See also
        specific countries
    economic growth in, 1, 2f
    nonmonetary welfare indicators
        in, 3, 4f
Nordhaus, William D., 149
Normalized Difference Vegetation
    Index (NDVI)

as measure of agricultural growth, 14,
    21, 21*b*, 22*f*, 150–51, 155–56
night lights and, 162–65, 163*f*, 164*t*
Norway, resource abundance in, 34

O

Obuasi mine (Ghana), 9*b*
occupation. *See* employment
oil exports, 1

P

Pande, Rohini, 42
Papua New Guinea, tax burden on
    mining industry, 78
Peru
    poverty, 91–92
    resource abundance, 56
    revenue-sharing scheme, 50
    socioeconomic effects of large-scale
        gold mining, 107, 117
Pettersson, Jan, 37, 38
policy priorities, 29–31
political capture, 59*n*9
political competition, 42
political economy, 37–38
pollution
    agricultural production and, 45–46, 93
    health and environment effects of, 8,
        9*b*, 29, 45, 46*f*, 52
    local impact assessment of resource
        abundance, 52–53, 53*t*
population growth, 44, 83, 84*f*, 88*n*9
prenatal care, 24, 25*f*, 26, 127, 127*t*
Prestea mine (Ghana), 9*b*

R

radio ownership, 22, 23*f*, 118,
    119–20*t*, 120–21*f*
rapacity effect, 36, 41, 52
Rau, Tomás, 52
Ravallion, Martin, 55
Raw Materials Database, 102
remote sensing, 21*b*. *See also* night
    lights; Normalized Difference
    Vegetation Index
rent seeking, 8, 35–36, 53, 82

Republic of Congo, oil revenues in, 35
resource abundance, 33–58
    assessing local impacts of, 39–56
    literature review, 38–39
    natural resource curse, 36–38
    negative impact of, 34–36
    theory and evidence of impact of,
        34–39
resource-rich countries. *See also specific
    countries*
    economic growth in, 1, 2*f*
    Human Development Index in, 3, 4*f*
    nonmonetary welfare indicators in,
        3, 4*f*
revenue-sharing schemes, 50, 55
Reyes, Loreto, 52
Rigolini, Jamele, 50
Roine, Jesper, 37, 38
Rosen-Roback framework, 42–43
Ross, M., 115
Rud, Juan Pablo, 50, 52, 102, 106–7,
    148, 165, 171*n*10

S

Sala-i-Martin, Xavier, 37
Sanders, Seth, 59*n*13
sanitation access, 125–26*b*
Sanoh, A., 15, 71, 72, 78
Santos, Rafael José, 60*n*16
São Tomé and Príncipe, oil
    discoveries in, 51
Schieffer, Jack, 47
Senegal, socioeconomic effects of
    large-scale gold mining, 104
Shilpi, Forhad, 44
small-scale mining, 70*b*, 99*b*, 171*n*13
Smith, G., 70*b*
social responsibility, 29, 74
socioeconomic effects of large-scale
    gold mining, 91–138
    asset accumulation, 118, 119–20*t*,
        120–21*f*
    child health, 121–30, 123*f*, 124*t*,
        125–26*b*, 127–30*t*, 129*f*
    empirical methodology, 96–103, 99*b*,
        101*m*, 103*t*

employment, 105–17, 105–7t, 108–9f, 111f, 112–13t, 116–18t
infrastructure access, 131–32, 131t, 132–33f
mine-induced migration, 133–37, 135f
overview, 91–95
spillover effects, 100–103
summary of results, 137–38
trends in mining vs. nonmining areas, 103–4, 104f
South Africa
employment, 15
gold mining, 10
tax burden on mining industry, 78
spatial dependency, 155
spatial equilibrium models, 44
spillover effects, 6, 44
Storeygard, Adam, 149
structural transformation, 114–15, 137, 138
stunting, 14, 24–26, 25f, 122–23, 128t
Subramanian, Arvind, 37
Sub-Saharan Africa. *See also specific countries*
agricultural production, 19
gold mining, 10, 11f
sustainable development, 8
Sweden, resource abundance in, 34

T
Tanzania
agricultural impacts of gold mining, 19–21, 20f, 22f, 147–71
data results, 151–54, 153t
difference-in-differences framework, 162–65
district level growth model, 161, 166–68f, 167–68t, 169m, 170f
economic growth and, 148–51
growth model for, 154–65, 156m, 159f, 160–61t, 163f, 164t
national growth model, 156–61, 156m, 159f, 160t
NDVI as measure for, 155–56, 162–65, 163f, 164t

night lights measure for, 162–65, 163f, 164t
remote sensing for, 148–51
artisanal and small-scale mining, 70b
asset accumulation, 22, 23f, 118, 119–20t, 120–21f
car ownership, 118, 119–20t
case study, 5–6
child health outcomes, 14–15, 24–27, 25–26f, 121–30, 123f, 124t, 125–26b, 127–30t, 129f
country background, 68, 69f, 70b
economic growth attributed to extractives, 68
employment, 15–19, 17–18f, 71–72, 72–73f, 105–17, 105–7t, 108–9f, 111f, 112–13t, 116–18t
fiscal sharing, 80–81
gold mining, 10, 93–95, 94t, 97m, 98f
government mining revenues, 27–29, 28f, 76–81, 77f
health risks in mining communities, 9b
infrastructure access, 23, 24f, 131–32, 131t, 132–33f
mine-induced migration, 133–37, 135f
policy priorities, 29–31
radio ownership, 118, 119–20t, 120–21f
structural transformation, 114–15
tax-sharing schemes, 55
Teran, Alfredo Mier y, 50
Tolonen, Anja, 50, 52, 102, 104, 106–7, 122, 148, 171n10
Torvik, Ragnar, 38
Tsui, Kevin K., 38

U
United States
employment, 47
input-output analysis, 54
night lights measures for, 149
resource abundance, 34, 56, 59n13

urbanization, 93, 165
Urzúa, Sergio S., 52

V
value chain of natural resource
    management, 8
Vargas, Juan F., 52
Venezuela, resource abundance in, 34
Vicente, Pedro C., 51
Von der Goltz, Jan, 52, 122

W
wages. *See* employment
Weil, David N., 149

women
    employment in mining communities,
        15–19, 17–18*f*, 31*n*3, 136, 137
    malnutrition among, 3
    migrants, 136
World Development Indicators
        Database, 154
World Health Organization (WHO), 9*b*

Z
Zambia, poverty in, 3, 34
Zhang, Xiaobo, 42
Zoega, Gylfi, 59*n*6
Zuo, Na, 47